WordPerfect® For Dummies®

Cheat Sheet

O9-AIE-950

About the Keyboard Template

The WordPerfect For Dummies keyboard template shows some of the most popular key combinations used in WordPerfect. Place the keyboard template over the top row of function keys on your keyboard and use it as a handy reference.

Note: Only the most common WordPerfect commands are on the template. In fact, the Merge key, F9, isn't on the template at all. After all, if you need help merging, you'll probably look in the book (Chapter 15) anyway.

Oddball - Character Quick Reference

You can insert oddball characters by pressing Ctrl-V, typing the code numbers, and pressing Enter.

Code	Character	Name
4,0	●	Dot
4,1	○	Hollow dot
4,2	□	Square
4,11	£	English Pound symbol
4,12	¥	Japanese Yen symbol
4,17	½	One-half
4,18	¼	One-quarter
4,19	¢	Cents
4,22	®	Registered symbol
4,23	©	Copyright symbol
4,41	™	Trademark symbol
5,7	☺	Hollow happy face
5,8	☻	Happy face
5,26	☹	Mr. Grumpy
6,21	→	Right arrow
6,22	←	Left arrow
6,23	↑	Up arrow
6,24	↓	Down arrow

Getting Around in a Document

↑	Moves the cursor up one line of text
↓	Moves the cursor down to the next line of text
→	Moves the cursor right to the next character
←	Moves the cursor left to the preceding character
Ctrl-↑	Moves the cursor up one paragraph
Ctrl-↓	Moves the cursor down to the next paragraph
Ctrl-→	Moves the cursor right one word
Ctrl-←	Moves the cursor left one word
-	Moves the cursor to the top of the screen. If the cursor is already at the top of the screen, pressing the minus key moves you up to the preceding screen (the preceding 24 lines of test).
+	Moves the cursor to the bottom of the screen. If the cursor is already on the last line of the screen, pressing the plus key shows you the next screen (the next 24 lines in the document).
PgUp	Moves the cursor to the top of the preceding page. If you're on page 1, this command moves you to the top of that page.
PgDn	Moves the cursor to the top of the next page. If you're on the last page in the document, PgDn moves you to the last line on that page.
Home,↑	Moves the cursor to the top of the screen
Home,↓	Moves the cursor to the end of the screen
Home,→	Moves the cursor to the right edge of the screen
Home,←	Moves the cursor to the left edge of the screen
Home,Home,↑	Moves the cursor to the top of the document
Home,Home,↓	Moves the cursor to the bottom of the document

COMPUTER BOOK SERIES FROM IDG

WordPerfect® For Dummies®

Cheat Sheet

General Information

Type WP at the DOS prompt to start WordPerfect:

```
C:\> WP
```

Then press Enter, and WordPerfect appears on the screen.

- ✔ Use the Insert key to switch between insert and typeover modes.
- ✔ Use the Backspace key to back up and erase.
- ✔ Use the Delete key to delete a character.
- ✔ Press the Enter key to start a new paragraph.
- ✔ Press the Tab key to indent or line up text.
- ✔ Press the F3 key to get help (press the Enter key when you're done with help).

Press Shift-F7 means to hold the Shift key and press the F7 key. Then release both keys. The same rule applies to the Alt and Ctrl keys: Press and hold that key and press the second key. Then release both keys.

Press the F7 key when you're ready to exit WordPerfect. Follow the instructions at the bottom of the screen and save the document to disk. Press Y when you're asked Exit WP?

Common WordPerfect Claw Commands

Command	Key(s)
Cancel	F1
Cut/Copy Block	Ctrl-F4
Exit	F7
Format Text	Shift-F8
Help	F3
List Files	F5
Mark Block	Alt-F4
Print	Shift-F7
Replace	Alt-F2
Retrieve	Shift-F10
Save	F10
Search	F2
Spell Check	Ctrl-F2
Thesaurus	Alt-F1

Document Filenames

A document must be saved to disk with a DOS filename. Here are the rules:

- ✔ The filename can be from one to eight characters long.
- ✔ The filename can contain letters and numbers in any combination.
- ✔ The filename cannot contain a space, a period, or any other symbol.
- ✔ Be brief and descriptive with filenames.

Helpful Tips

- ✔ Let the computer do the work. Let WordPerfect format pages and insert page numbers, headers, and footers. Don't ever do that stuff manually.
- ✔ Always save documents to disk: Press F10 to save.
- ✔ If a document has already been saved to disk, press F10, Enter, Y to update the document on disk.
- ✔ Press F5, Enter as an alternative to quitting to DOS and working with files.
- ✔ To start over with a clean slate, press F7, Enter, Enter, Y, N.
- ✔ If your document doesn't print, press Shift-F7, C and read the instructions on the screen.
- ✔ Never turn off or reset the computer when WordPerfect is on the screen. Always quit to DOS first.

. . . For Dummies: #1 Computer Book Series for Beginners

References for the Rest of Us! ®

COMPUTER BOOK SERIES FROM IDG

Are you intimidated and confused by computers? Do you find that traditional manuals are overloaded with technical details you'll never use? Do your friends and family always call you to fix simple problems on their PCs? Then the . . .*For Dummies*® computer book series from IDG Books Worldwide is for you.

. . .*For Dummies* books are written for those frustrated computer users who know they aren't really dumb but find that PC hardware, software, and indeed the unique vocabulary of computing make them feel helpless. . . .*For Dummies* books use a lighthearted approach, a down-to-earth style, and even cartoons and humorous icons to diffuse computer novices' fears and build their confidence. Lighthearted but not lightweight, these books are a perfect survival guide for anyone forced to use a computer.

> *"I like my copy so much I told friends; now they bought copies."*
>
> **Irene C., Orwell, Ohio**

> *"Quick, concise, nontechnical, and humorous."*
>
> **Jay A., Elburn, Illinois**

> *"Thanks, I needed this book. Now I can sleep at night."*
>
> **Robin F., British Columbia, Canada**

Already, hundreds of thousands of satisfied readers agree. They have made . . .*For Dummies* books the #1 introductory level computer book series and have written asking for more. So, if you're looking for the most fun and easy way to learn about computers, look to . . .*For Dummies* books to give you a helping hand.

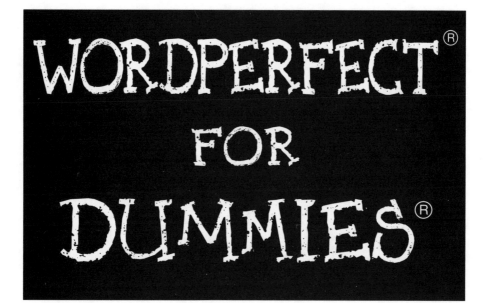

by **Dan Gookin,**
author of best-selling
DOS For Dummies and coauthor
of *PCs For Dummies*

IDG Books Worldwide, Inc.
An International Data Group Company

Foster City, CA ♦ Chicago, IL ♦ Indianapolis, IN ♦ Braintree, MA ♦ Dallas, TX

WordPerfect® For Dummies®

Published by
IDG Books Worldwide, Inc.
An International Data Group Company
919 E. Hillsdale Blvd.
Suite 400
Foster City, CA 94404

Library of Congress Catalog Card No.: 92-74323

ISBN: 1-878058-52-5

Printed in the United States of America

15 14 13 12 11 10

1B/QV/RS/ZV

Distributed in the United States by IDG Books Worldwide, Inc.

Distributed by Macmillan Canada for Canada; by Computer and Technical Books for the Caribbean Basin; by Contemporanea de Ediciones for Venezuela; by Distribuidora Cuspide for Argentina; by CITEC for Brazil; by Ediciones ZETA S.C.R. Ltda. for Peru; by Editorial Limusa SA for Mexico; by Transworld Publishers Limited in the United Kingdom and Europe; by Al-Maiman Publishers & Distributors for Saudi Arabia; by Simron Pty. Ltd. for South Africa; by IDG Communications (HK) Ltd. for Hong Kong; by Toppan Company Ltd. for Japan; by Addison Wesley Publishing Company for Korea; by Longman Singapore Publishers Ltd. for Singapore, Malaysia, Thailand, and Indonesia; by Unalis Corporation for Taiwan; by WS Computer Publishing Company, Inc. for the Philippines; by WoodsLane Pty. Ltd. for Australia; by WoodsLane Enterprises Ltd. for New Zealand.

For general information on IDG Books Worldwide's books in the U.S., please call our Consumer Customer Service department at 800-762-2974. For reseller information, including discounts and premium sales, please call our Reseller Customer Service department at 800-434-3422.

For information on where to purchase IDG Books Worldwide's books outside the U.S., contact IDG Books Worldwide at 415-655-3021 or fax 415-655-3295.

For information on translations, contact Marc Jeffrey Mikulich, Director, Foreign & Subsidiary Rights, at IDG Books Worldwide, 415-655-3018 or fax 415-655-3295.

For sales inquiries and special prices for bulk quantities, write to the address above or call IDG Books Worldwide at 415-655-3200.

For information on using IDG Books Worldwide's books in the classroom, or ordering examination copies, contact Jim Kelly at 800-434-2086.

For authorization to photocopy items for corporate, personal, or educational use, please contact Copyright Clearance Center, 222 Rosewood Drive, Danvers, MA 01923, or fax 508-750-4470.

is a trademark under exclusive license to IDG Books Worldwide, Inc., from International Data Group, Inc.

About the Author

Dan Gookin got started with computers back in the post slide rule age of computing: 1982. His first intention was to buy a computer to replace his aged and constantly breaking typewriter. Working as slave labor in a restaurant, however, Gookin was unable to afford the full "word processor" setup and settled on a computer that had a monitor, keyboard, and little else. Soon his writing career was underway with several submissions to (and lots of rejections from) fiction magazines.

The big break came in 1984 when he began writing about computers. Applying his flair for fiction with a self-taught knowledge of computers, Gookin was able to demystify the subject and explain technology in a relaxed and understandable voice. He even dared to add humor, which eventually won him a column in a local computer magazine.

Eventually Gookin's talents came to roost as he became a ghost writer at a computer book publishing house. That was followed by an editing position at a San Diego computer magazine, at which time he also regularly participated on a radio talk show about computers. In addition, Gookin kept writing books about computers, some of which became minor bestsellers.

In 1990, Gookin came to IDG Books with a book proposal. From that initial meeting unfolded an idea for an outrageous book: a long overdue and original idea for the computer book for the rest of us. What became *DOS For Dummies* blossomed into an international bestseller with hundreds and thousands of copies in print and many foreign translations.

Today, Gookin still considers himself a writer and computer "guru" whose job it is to remind everyone that computers are not to be taken too seriously. His approach to computers is light and humorous yet very informative. He knows that the complex beasts are important and can help people become productive and successful. Yet Gookin mixes his knowledge of computers with a unique, dry sense of humor that keeps everyone informed — and awake. His favorite quote is, "Computers are a notoriously dull subject, but that doesn't mean I have to write about them that way."

Gookin's most recent titles include the best-selling *DOS For Dummies*, 2nd Edition and *WordPerfect For Dummies*. All told, he's written over 30 books on computers and contributes regularly to *DOS Resource Guide, InfoWorld,* and *PC Computing Magazine*. Gookin holds a degree in Communications from the University of California, San Diego, and currently lives with his wife and boys in the Pacific Northwest.

Dedication

to Sandra and Baby Gookin

Acknowledgments

I would like to thank and acknowledge Lesa Roberts of WordPerfect Corporation. Yes, the big WordPerfect Corporation of Orem, Utah. She's the author liaison who, after I faxed her a sworn deposition that I'm really writing a WordPerfect book, sent me a copy of WordPerfect for Windows and new disks to update my old copy of WordPerfect 5.1. Thank you, Lesa.

I also would like to thank David Solomon and John Kilcullen at IDG Books for being really nice publishers; Sandy Blackthorn for being an even-handed editor; and Matt Wagner at Waterside Productions, who should really be a vice president. And a very special thanks to Mike McCarthy, formerly of IDG Books, for his inspiration and guidance with *DOS For Dummies*.

I would also like to thank Bill Murphy, without whom this book would not be possible. Hey, Bill, what can I say? You were there for me. I appreciate that.

(The Publisher would like to give special thanks to Patrick J. McGovern, without whom this book would not have been possible.)

Credits

**Senior Vice President
and Publisher**
Milissa L. Koloski

Associate Publisher
Diane Graves Steele

Brand Manager
Judith A. Taylor

Editorial Managers
Kristin A. Cocks
Mary Corder

Product Development Manager
Mary Bednarek

Editorial Executive Assistant
Richard Graves

Editorial Assistants
Constance Carlisle
Chris Collins
Stacey Holden Prince
Kevin Spencer

Production Director
Beth Jenkins

Production Assistant
Jacalyn L. Pennywell

**Supervisor of
Project Coordination**
Cindy L. Phipps

Supervisor of Page Layout
Kathie S. Schnorr

Production Systems Specialist
Steve Peake

Pre-Press Coordination
Tony Augsburger
Patricia R. Reynolds
Theresa Sánchez-Baker

Media/Archive Coordination
Leslie Popplewell
Kerri Cornell
Michael Wilkey

Editor
Alice Martina Smith

Technical Reviewer
Stuart J. Stuple

Graphics Coordination
Shelley Lea
Gina Scott
Carla Radzikinas

Production Page Layout
Elizabeth Cárdenas-Nelson
Patricia Douglas
Mark C. Owens

Proofreaders
Charles A. Hutchinson
Dwight Ramsey

Indexer
Anne Leach

Book Design
University Graphics

Cover Design
Kavish + Kavish

Contents at a Glance

Cartoons at a Glance

By Rich Tennant

Table of Contents

Introduction

Welcome to *WordPerfect For Dummies,* a book that's not afraid to say, "You don't need to know everything about WordPerfect to use it." Heck, you probably don't *want* to know everything about WordPerfect. You don't want to know all the command options, all the typographical mumbo-jumbo, or even all those special features that you know are in there but terrify you. No, all you want to know is a single answer to a tiny question. Then you can happily close the book and be on your way. If that's you, you've found your book.

This book informs and entertains. And it has a serious attitude problem. After all, I don't want to teach you to love WordPerfect. That's sick. Instead, be prepared to encounter some informative, down-to-earth explanations — in English — of how to get the job done by using WordPerfect. After all, you take your work seriously, but you definitely don't need to take WordPerfect seriously.

About This Book

This book is not meant to be read from cover to cover. If that were true, the covers would definitely need to be put closer together. Instead, this book is a reference. Each chapter covers a specific topic in WordPerfect. Within a chapter, you find self-contained sections, each of which describes how to do a WordPerfect task relating to the chapter's topic. Sample sections you encounter in this book include the following:

- Saving your stuff
- Cutting a block and pasting
- Making text italicized
- Doing a hanging indent
- Printing envelopes
- Changing text colors from hell
- Where did my document go?

There are no keys to memorize, no secret codes, no tricks, no pop-up dioramas, and no wall charts. Instead, each section explains a topic as if it is the first thing you read in this book. Nothing is assumed, and everything is cross-referenced. Technical terms and topics, when they come up, are neatly shoved to the side where you can easily avoid reading them. The idea here isn't for you to learn anything. This book's philosophy is look it up, figure it out, and get back to work.

How To Use This Book

This book helps you when you're at a loss over what to do in WordPerfect. I think that this situation happens to everyone way too often. For example, if you press Ctrl-PgUp, WordPerfect displays Variable: at the bottom of the screen. I have no idea what that means, nor do I want to know. What I do know, however, is that pressing F1 makes the annoying message go away. That's the kind of knowledge you find in this book.

WordPerfect uses *key combinations,* several keys you may press together or in sequence to get the job done. This book shows you those key combinations in the following manner:

Shift-F7, C, Enter

This setup means for you to press and hold the Shift key and press the F7 key. Release both keys. Then press the C key. Then press the Enter key. But don't type the commas or any period that ends a sentence.

Whenever I describe a message or information that you see on the screen, I present it as follows:

```
This is a message on-screen
```

Any details about what you type are explained in the text. And, if you look down at your keyboard and find ten thumbs — or scissors and cutlery — instead of hands, consider reading Chapter 3, "Using the Keyboard Correctly," right now.

This book never refers you to the WordPerfect manual or — yech! — to the DOS manual. It does refer you to a companion book in this series, *DOS For Dummies,* published by IDG Books Worldwide. However, most of what you need DOS for can be accomplished in WordPerfect, so you can happily keep your DOS knowledge to a minimum.

What You're Not To Read

Special technical sections dot this book like mosquito bites. They offer annoyingly endless and technical explanations, descriptions of advanced topics, or alternative commands that you really don't need to know about. Each one of them is flagged with a special icon or enclosed in an electrified, barbwire box. Reading this stuff is optional.

Foolish Assumptions

Here is my assumption about you: You use a computer. You use WordPerfect. Anything else involving the computer or DOS is handled by someone else, whom I call your personal guru. Rely on this person to help you through the rough patches; wave your guru over or call your guru on the phone. But always be sure to thank your guru. Remember that computer gurus enjoy junk food as nourishment and often accept it as payment. Keep a bowl of M&Ms or a sack of Doritos at the ready for when you need your guru's assistance.

How This Book Is Organized

This book contains six major parts, each of which is divided into three or more chapters. The chapters themselves have been Ginsu-knived into smaller, modular sections. You can pick up the book and read any section without necessarily knowing what has already been covered in the rest of the book. Start anywhere.

Here is a breakdown of the six parts and what you find in them:

Part I: Introducing WordPerfect (the Basic Stuff)

This is baby WordPerfect stuff — the bare essentials. Here you learn to giggle, teethe, crawl, walk, burp, and spit up. Then you can move up to the advanced topics of moving the cursor, editing text, searching and replacing, marking blocks, and spell-checking. (A pacifier is optional for this section.)

Part II: Making Your Prose Look Less Ugly

Formatting is the art of beating your text into submission. It's not the heady work of creating a document and getting the right words. No, it's "you will be italic" and "indent, you moron!" and "gimme a new page *here*." Often, formatting involves a lot of yelling. This part of the book contains chapters that show you how to format characters, lines, paragraphs, pages, and entire documents without raising your voice (too much).

Part III: Working with Documents

Document is a nice, professional-sounding word — much better than *that thing I did with WordPerfect. Document* is quicker to type. And you sound important if you say that you work on documents instead of admitting the truth that you sit and stare at the screen and play with the cursor. This part of the book tells you how to print, save, and shuffle documents.

Part IV: Making WordPerfect Less Than Ugly

One of my basic homeowner fears is that the people who decided green-on-pink text means italics in WordPerfect will one day show up to paint my house. WordPerfect is definitely not a charmer on the screen. This part of the book gives you hints about how to make WordPerfect look less ugly and how to deal with WordPerfect and Windows.

Part V: Help Me, Mr. Wizard!

One school of thought is that every copy of WordPerfect should be sold with a baseball bat. I'm a firm believer in baseball-bat therapy for computers. But, before you go to such an extreme, consider the soothing words of advice provided in this part of the book.

Part VI: The Part of Tens

How about "The Ten Commandments of WordPerfect" — complete with Charlton Heston bringing them down from Mt. Orem. Or consider "Ten Features You Don't Use but Paid for Anyway." Or the handy "Ten Things Worth Remembering." This section is a gold mine of tens.

Icons Used in This Book

This icon alerts you to overtly nerdy information and technical discussions of the topic at hand. The information is optional reading, but it may enhance your reputation at cocktail parties if you repeat it.

This icon flags useful, helpful tips or shortcuts.

This icon marks a friendly reminder to do something.

This icon marks a friendly reminder not to do something.

This icon flags information about using WordPerfect with a mouse (the computer kind — although if you like to work with the mammal variety, that's OK too).

This icon identifies the quick, no-commentary way to accomplish a WordPerfect task.

Where To Go from Here

You work with WordPerfect. You know what you hate about it. Why not start by looking up that subject in the table of contents and seeing what this book says about it? Alternatively, you can continue to use WordPerfect in the Sisyphean manner you're used to: Push that boulder to the top of the hill and, when it starts to roll back on you, whip out this book like a bazooka and blow the rock away. You'll be back at work and enjoying yourself in no time.

The 5th Wave

By Rich Tennant

"IT'S AN INTEGRATED SOFTWARE PACKAGE DESIGNED TO HELP UNCLUTTER YOUR LIFE."

Part I
Introducing WordPerfect
(the Basic Stuff)

The 5th Wave — By Rich Tennant

SO POORLY DOCUMENTED IS THE SOFTWARE THAT ROY IS BETA TESTING THAT HE FAILS TO NOTICE THAT THE GAME RULES TO "TWISTER" HAVE ACCIDENTALLY BEEN INCLUDED.

In this part...

Primitive persons first made their marks by slamming rocks into stone tablets. Then came the Egyptian papyrus, the clay tablets of the Babylonians, and the Greek and Roman scrolls. In the 1400s, Gutenberg's press ushered in a new era of printed communication. Then came the typewriter, the patented IBM Selectric, and the PC running WordPerfect word processing software. So how come, if we've made this much progress, you still feel like slamming a rock into the computer screen? The answer is that no one has ever bothered to explain it all to you in simple, clay-tablet terms. That's what happens in this part of the book — your basic WordPerfect stuff.

Chapter 1
Word Processing 101

● ●

In This Chapter

▶ Starting WordPerfect

▶ Reading the WordPerfect screen

▶ Entering text

▶ Editing a document on disk

▶ Getting help

▶ Understanding WordPerfect's imperfect commands

▶ Printing

▶ Saving your stuff

▶ Exiting WordPerfect

● ●

*T*his chapter offers an overview of how WordPerfect works — the way you probably use the program every day to get various word processing stuff done. The basics. More specific stuff happens in later chapters and is cross-referenced here for your page-flipping enjoyment.

Starting WordPerfect

To begin using WordPerfect, you must do the following:

1. Prepare yourself mentally.

Do I really want to do this? You know, the typewriter has always been my friend. And WordPerfect? DOS? A computer? OK. I'll try. I'll be brave. (Take a swig of your favorite beverage here.)

2. Turn on the computer, the monitor, and anything else of importance (or that has busy blinking lights on it) around the computer.

3. Contend with DOS or, if you're lucky, see a fancy menu system.

If you see a menu system, select the WordPerfect option. WordPerfect starts and you're done! If not, drearily move on to Step 4.

4. Start the WordPerfect program.

You've already started the computer. You've watched the miracle of DOS as it appears on the screen. Now you're probably staring at that horrid thing called the DOS prompt. Pain thyself no further! Type the following and press Enter:

```
C:\> WP
```

That is, type **WP** for WordPerfect (or word processing, take your pick) and press the Enter key. That's it! No excess punctuation, no kowtowing, and no mutterings in Latin.

WordPerfect starts on the screen, displaying an opening banner and other possibly helpful information that disappears too fast to be truly useful. Eventually, you see the initial blank page, which is discussed in the next section.

✔ Type **WP** to start WordPerfect. Don't type **WordPerfect** or **Oh, lordy, what am I doing here?** because it just won't work.

✔ If you know which document you want to edit, type its name after you type **WP**. For example, if you type **WP CHAP01** and press Enter, WordPerfect starts and automatically loads the document file CHAP01 for editing. Refer to "Editing a Document on Disk" later in this chapter for more information.

✔ If you see the dreaded error message Bad command or file name, then something is awry. Before loading your gun, refer to Chapter 22 and look for the section about what to do when you can't find WordPerfect.

✔ Your computer can be set up so that it automatically runs WordPerfect. Think of the time such a setup can save! If you want the computer set up thusly, grab someone more knowledgeable than yourself — an individual I call a *computer guru.* Direct your guru to "make my computer always start in WordPerfect." If your guru is unable to do as you ask, frantically grab other people at random until you find someone bold enough to obey you.

✔ You can find additional information on starting the PC and contending with the DOS prompt in *DOS For Dummies,* published by IDG Books Worldwide. That book does for DOS what this book does for WordPerfect: makes it understandable.

TECHNICAL STUFF

Don't read this stuff!

The actual name of the WordPerfect program is WP.EXE. You only need to know the first part: WP. The EXE means *executable,* and EXE is pronounced *ee-ecks-ee* (not *ecksee* or *ezzee* or *echcheey*).

When you type **WP** at the DOS prompt, DOS searches high and low through the hard drive for the program file named WP.EXE. It loads that file into memory and runs the WordPerfect software. This stuff all happens when you type **WP** at the DOS prompt. There's nothing else you need to do,

nothing more you need to buy, and no messy dyes or powders.

The horrid truth is that the WordPerfect program is more than just the WP.EXE file. Often, it's more like two or three dozen files, each of which contributes some small yet meaningful element of the WordPerfect program. All these files are stuffed into a special directory on the system.

Chapter 20 examines files and directories in detail — if you dare to look up this information.

Reading the WordPerfect Screen

After WordPerfect starts, you are faced with the electronic version of the blank page. This is the same idea-crippling concept that induced writers block in several generations of typewriter users. With WordPerfect it's worse; not only is the screen mostly blank, but no clues are offered as to what to do first.

Figure 1-1 shows the typical, blank WordPerfect start-up screen. Three things are worth noting about the screen:

1. **A large empty space, colored blue on some computer screens**

   This space is where the text you type and edit appears.

2. **The document name in the lower left corner of the screen**

   This fractured bit of text describes the name of the document. The name is listed in DOS language — a DOS pathname (which explains all the colons, backslashes, and other detritus). The filename is the last part of the text you see. The filename area is blank if you haven't yet saved a document to disk — a handy clue. (In the figure, the filename area is filled in with an example so you can see how it looks.)

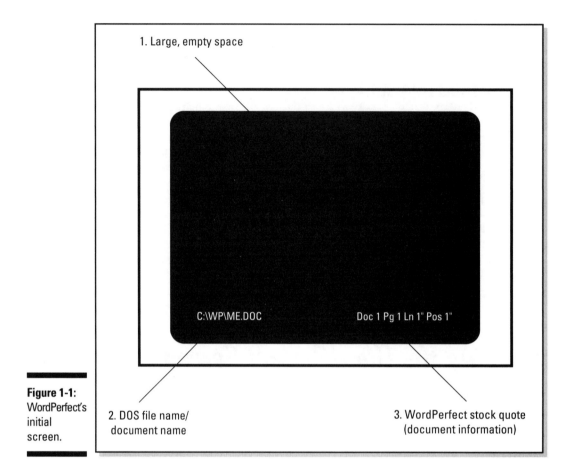

1. Large, empty space

C:\WP\ME.DOC

Doc 1 Pg 1 Ln 1" Pos 1"

Figure 1-1:
WordPerfect's
initial
screen.

2. DOS file name/
document name

3. WordPerfect stock quote
(document information)

3. The status line in the lower right corner of the screen

This gibberish explains where you are in the document. There are always
four word fragments followed by numbers (like a tenth-grade algebra
problem). Table 1-1 explains what these word fragments mean.

Table 1-1	Status Line Definitions
Word Fragment	**Description**
Doc 1	The document you're editing. This may be either Doc 1 or Doc 2.
Pg xx	The page number you're on. 1 is the first page, 8 is the eighth page, and so on.
Ln x.xx"	The line you're editing. Lines are measured in inches from the top of the page. (Ln 4.89" means that the cursor is on the line that's 4.89 inches from the top of the page.)
Pos x.xx"	The distance from the left edge of the page. (Pos 3.19" means that you're 3.19 inches from the left edge of the page.)

✔ My advice? Ignore all the weird numbers in the status line; concentrate instead on your writing. After all, only the truly disturbed whip out a ruler and measure a piece of paper in a typewriter as they go along. (The numbers come in handy later, telling you how much stuff you've written. Pretend that they don't exist for now.)

✔ The *cursor* is at the exact spot where text will appear when you type. The cursor is a blinking underline character somewhere in the large, empty space on the screen. The character you type appears right above where the cursor is flashing; the cursor then moves forward and waits for you to type the next character.

✔ WordPerfect displays text on color screens with white letters on a blue background. This color scheme can be changed, as can other weird colors you see; refer to Chapter 16 for information.

✔ If you have a mouse installed, move it around on the desktop. You see WordPerfect's mouse pointer block on the screen. The pointer block mimics on the screen the movements of the mouse on the desktop.

✔ The screen isn't blank if you've directed WordPerfect to load a document for editing when it starts. Refer to "Editing a Document on Disk" later in this chapter for details.

When WordPerfect is busy, `* Please wait *` appears in the bottom left corner of the screen. This message means please wait. The message disappears when you no longer need to wait and can get busy typing again. Other messages may appear in the bottom left corner of the screen from time to time.

Entering Text

To compose text in WordPerfect, use the *keyboard* — that typewriter-like thing sitting in front of the computer and below the monitor. Go ahead, type away. Let your fingers dance on the key tops! What you type appears on the screen, letter for letter — even derogatory stuff about the computer. (It doesn't care what you type, but that doesn't mean WordPerfect lacks feelings.)

New text is inserted right above where the cursor is flashing. For example, you can type the following:

Mother emphasized, "Don't say a thing about Grandma's moustache."

If you want to change *emphasized* to *reemphasized,* move the cursor to the start of *emphasized* and type **re.** Those two letters are inserted into the text. There's nothing to delete, and all the text after falls neatly into place.

✔ The way you compose text on the screen is to type. Every character key you press produces a character on the screen. This concept holds true for all letter, number, and symbol keys. The other keys, mostly the gray ones on the keyboard, do strange and wonderful things, which the rest of this book tries hard to explain.

✔ If you make a mistake, press the Backspace key to back up and erase. This key may actually be named Backspace on your keyboard, or it may have a long, left-pointing arrow on it.

✔ Moving the cursor around the screen is explained in Chapter 2.

✔ The Shift keys are used for producing capital letters.

✔ The Caps Lock key works like the shift lock key on a typewriter. After you press Caps Lock, everything you type appears in all capital letters.

✔ The Caps Lock light on the keyboard comes on when you're in All Caps mode. Also note that the word Pos in the bottom right corner of the screen becomes POS when Caps Lock is turned on.

✔ The number keys to the right of the keyboard make up the *numeric keypad*. To use those keys, you first must press the Num Lock key on the keyboard. If you don't, the keys take on their arrow-key functions (see Chapter 2).

✔ The Num Lock light on the keyboard comes on when you press the Num Lock key to turn on the numeric keypad. Most PCs start with this feature activated. Also note that the word Pos in the bottom right corner of the screen starts blinking when Num Lock is turned on. Most users keep Num Lock turned off.

✔ Refer to Chapter 3 for some handy tips on typing and using the keyboard.

✔ No one needs to learn to type to become a writer. But the best writers are typists. My advice is to get a computer program that teaches you to type. It can make a painful experience like WordPerfect a wee bit more enjoyable.

Typing away, la la la

Aeons ago, a word processor was judged superior if it had the famous *word-wrap feature*. This feature eliminates the need for you to press the Enter key at the end of each line of text — a requirement when you're using a typewriter. WordPerfect, and all other modern word processors, have this feature. If you're unfamiliar with it, you should get used to putting it to work for you.

With WordPerfect, when the text gets precariously close to the right margin, the last word is automatically picked up and placed at the start of the next line. There's no need for you to press Enter except when you want to end a paragraph.

- Press Enter to create a new paragraph. If you want to split one paragraph into two, move the cursor to the middle of the paragraph where you want the second paragraph to start and press Enter.

- Press Enter at the end of a paragraph only — not at the end of every line.

- As you start typing — actually, after you press any key — the mouse pointer block vanishes from the screen. To see it again, move the mouse on the desktop. (The disappearing pointer block is actually a feature; by making the pointer block disappear, WordPerfect makes the screen look less cluttered.)

- Don't be afraid to use the keyboard! WordPerfect always offers ample warning before anything serious happens. Also available is a handy Undo key, F1, which recovers anything you accidentally delete. Refer to Chapter 3 for details.

Getting used to that annoying line of hyphens

Occasionally, you see a line of hyphens stretching from one side of the screen to another — like one of those perforated cut-here things on a coupon. That thing marks the end of one page and the beginning of another — a *page break*. The text you see above the hyphens is on the preceding page; text below the hyphen is on the next page.

- You cannot delete the line of hyphens. Instead, just ignore it. Think of it as a useful way of telling where text stops on one page and starts on the next.

- You can see how the line of hyphens works by looking at the scrambled statistics in the lower right corner of the screen. For example, when the cursor is above the hyphens, the statistics may say Pg 5 for page 5. When the cursor is below the hyphens, you see Pg 6 for page 6.

- A row of equal signs marks a *hard page break*. This is a definite "I want a new page now" command given by the person who created the document. Refer to Chapter 10 for information.

Editing a Document on Disk

You use WordPerfect to create *documents*. The documents can be printed or saved to disk for later editing or printing. When a document has been saved to disk, it's considered a *file* on the disk (although you can still refer to it as a document).

Two ways are available for you to load and edit a document already on disk. You can specify the document's name when you start WordPerfect from DOS or retrieve a document after WordPerfect is running.

The easiest way to load a document is to specify the document's filename after typing **WP** to start WordPerfect. For example, to automatically load LETTER.WP when you start WordPerfect, type the following at the DOS prompt:

```
C:\> WP LETTER.WP
```

That is, type **WP** to start WordPerfect, then a space, and then the name of the document file you want to edit (in this case, **LETTER.WP**). Then press Enter. Notice that the command does not end with a period; you press the Enter key after the document name.

If you weren't as foresighted as you should have been when you started WordPerfect, you can always load a document after you start the program. You do so by using the Retrieve command. Follow these steps to load a document after WordPerfect is already running:

1. **Press Shift-F10, the Retrieve command key combination.**

   Press and hold the Shift key and then press the key labeled F10 near the top of the keyboard (or along the side if you have an older keyboard).

   After pressing Shift-F10, you see the following prompt in the lower left corner of the screen:

   ```
   Document to be retrieved:
   ```

2. **Type the name of the document you want to load.**

   Make sure that everything is spelled right; WordPerfect is finicky about filename spelling. You can type in uppercase or lowercase; it's all the same to WordPerfect.

3. **Press the Enter key.**

   The document is loaded and appears on the screen, ready for editing.

✔ Shift-F10 equals *retrieve?* The people in the WordPerfect Assigning Commands to Function Keys department were working late that night.

✔ The term *editing* means *to read, correct, or add to the text already composed and saved to disk.* Editing involves the use of the cursor-control keys, covered in Chapter 2. Also refer to Chapters 4, 5, and 6.

✔ When you're done editing a document, you print it or save it back to disk — or do one and then the other. Printing is covered in the section "Printing," later in this chapter; saving a document to disk is covered in the section "Saving Your Stuff," later in this chapter.

✔ Documents must be saved to disk with a DOS filename. If you think stuffing something clever into a 7-character vanity license plate is tough, wait until you try to save that letter to Aunt Velma! DOS is very limiting with how files are named. Refer to Chapter 14 for file-naming rules and regulations.

✔ If the document whose name you specified doesn't exist on disk, or WordPerfect can't find it, you see an error message:

```
ERROR: File not found—BLECH
```

In this example, the word *BLECH* is replaced by the name of the file you wanted to retrieve. Then WordPerfect redisplays the retrieve prompt. My advice is try again and check your spelling. Or refer to Chapter 14, which explains how to locate a file and retrieve it without using the Shift-F10 key combination.

Getting Help

Obviously, working with a computer program that believes Shift-F10 is a handy mnemonic for *retrieve* isn't going to be easy. This convention is akin to marking rest room doors with chromosome patterns rather than silhouettes of men and women. Sometimes, perhaps often, you will need help when using WordPerfect. If so, you only need to memorize one key: F3.

The F3 key is the Help key. Press F3 and you enter WordPerfect's help system. There, you can get information on all WordPerfect's commands and discover how things are done.

To make best use of the help system, try one of these two approaches:

Approach 1: Press F3 and then press the first letter of the thing you want help on.

```
Features [T]                              WordPerfect Key   Keystrokes

Tab                                       Tab               Tab
Tab Align                                 Tab Align         Ctrl-F6
Tab, Hard                                 Tab               Home,Tab
Tab Ruler                                 Screen            Ctrl-F3,1,23
Tab Set                                   Format            Shft-F8,1,8
Tab Type                                  Format            Shft-F8,1,8,t
Table                                     Columns/Table     Alt-F7,2
Table Box                                 Graphics          Alt-F9,2
Table of Authorities (Default)            Setup             Shft-F1,4,7
Table of Authorities, Mark (Block On)     Mark Text         Alt-F5,4
Table of Auth. (Define or Generate)       Mark Text         Alt-F5,5 or 6
Table of Contents, Mark (Block On)        Mark Text         Alt-F5,1
Table of Contents (Define or Generate)    Mark Text         Alt-F5,5 or 6
Target                                    Mark Text         Alt-F5,1,2
Text Box                                  Graphics          Alt-F9,3
Text Columns                              Columns/Table     Alt-F7,1
Text In/Out                               Text In/Out       Ctrl-F5
Text Quality                              Print             Shft-F7,t
Text Quality (Default)                    Setup             Shft-F1,4,8,4
Text Screen Type                          Setup             Shft-F1,2,3
More... Press t to continue.

Selection: 0                                        (Press ENTER to exit Help)
```

Figure 1-2:
One of
WordPerfect's
many help
screens.

For example, if you want help on tabs, press F3 and then press T. You see a
three-column display with a list of things that start with T (see Figure 1-2). Look
for the Tab entry (or whatever it is you want) in the first column and then
locate in the third column the key combination you must press to get that
feature. (The second column lists the official WordPerfect name for that key
combination.) Press the indicated key combination. For example, to get a tab,
press the Tab key, as shown in Figure 1-2.

Approach 2: Press F3 and then press the key combination for the command
you want help on.

For example, press F3 and then Shift-F8 to bring up the help menu for the
Format command. Of course, this method assumes that you know what Shift-F8
does in the first place. (If not, then you'll definitely find out!)

- WordPerfect's help isn't too helpful. Don't expect Dr. WordPerfect to pop
  out of the screen, put a calming hand on your shoulder, and point to the
  right key to press. This is WordPerfect — not a Disney cartoon.

- To quit the help system and return to the document, press the Enter key.
  This information is listed right on the help screen, in the lower right
  corner. Hard to miss, but many people do.

- Pressing the Cancel key, F1, stops anything run amok in WordPerfect —
  except for the help system. Press the Enter key to exit the help system.

✔ Press F3 twice to see a handy keyboard template, telling you which function keys do what on the keyboard. This book comes with its own keyboard template, which shows only the more popular keyboard commands. WordPerfect's template is grossly detailed.

 ✔ Some programs use F1 as the Help key. WordPerfect uses F3. F1 is the Cancel key in WordPerfect. As long as you never use another piece of software, you'll keep your marbles.

Understanding WordPerfect's Imperfect Commands

To create a document, you use the typewriter keys. OK, understood.

To edit a document, you use the arrow or cursor-control keys, most of which are located just to the right of the typewriter keyboard area. This is all right: Arrow keys us humans can deal with.

To do anything else in WordPerfect, you must use the *function keys.* Welcome to the land of Kryptic Key Kombinations. Time to put on those white jackets with the long sleeves and don those Napoleon party hats.

WordPerfect assigns its commands to the most unusual array of key combinations in the known galaxy. (On planet Zoon, however, the Zoonian version of WordPerfect also employs two foot pedals and an elbow switch.) There are 40 WordPerfect commands assigned to 10 function keys plus 3 shift keys:

Function keys by themselves:	F1 through F10
Shift key plus function keys:	Shift-F1 through Shift-F10
Ctrl key plus function keys:	Ctrl-F1 through Ctrl-F10
Alt key plus function keys:	Alt-F1 through Alt-F10

To activate a command, you must press the proper function key or function-key combination. For example, to press Ctrl-F2, press and hold the Ctrl (Control) key and then press the F2 key. This is the same action you use when you press Shift-F to get a capital F, but you're using the Ctrl and F2 keys instead. All the other key combinations work the same way.

There is nothing wrong with the mechanics of how this works: *F1 through F10* plus *3 shift keys times the 10 function keys* equals *40 key combinations.* The problem is, how do you remember which key does what?

✔ Some keyboards have two additional function keys: F11 and F12. Ha, ha! Boy, are you in trouble. WordPerfect doesn't use those keys. (Well, it does, but the functions are available on the standard F1 through F10 keys as well.)

✔ I remember the various unmemorable function-key commands by using what I call the *WordPerfect claw pattern.* I wax on and on about it in Chapter 3.

✔ WordPerfect's help system lists key combinations in the following manner:

```
Shift-F8,1,7
```

This list means press Shift-F8 (the key combination), then press 1, and then press 7. For goodness' sake, do not type the commas! If you need to press Enter, you see Enter listed like any other key. This book uses the same format.

✔ WordPerfect also has a *menu bar* where all its commands are stored in handy menus. The menu bar is primarily for use with the mouse. Refer to Chapter 17 for more information.

Do You Like It, No?

I hate going to those swanky French restaurants where the waiter asks, "Do you like it, no?" Nothing induces brainlock as quickly as a positive question ending in *no.* How do you answer? Does *no* mean you like it or don't like it? We'll leave this one up to the language gurus. For WordPerfect, you're often asked the following:

```
Do something? No (Yes)
```

Do something? is a question posed by WordPerfect — a *prompt* relating to a specific command. Your options are No and Yes, one of which is in parentheses. Here's what it means:

The first option, the one *not* in parentheses, is the safe option, called the *default* by computer geeks. Pressing Enter is the same as selecting the first option.

The second option, the one in parentheses, is the risky option. You must make an effort to select it; it does something serious to the document.

✔ Sometimes multiple options appear — not just Yes and No. Such a situation is called a *menu.* Item 0, meaning *none of the above,* is usually the automatically selected item, and it usually appears at the end of the list after a colon. Other numbered items in the list are separated by semi-colons. You can press the number associated with each item, or the highlighted letter in the item's name, to select that option.

✔ You can select Yes or No — or any menu option — by moving the mouse pointer block over the word you want and clicking the left mouse button.

✔ Pressing the Cancel key, F1, makes these and other annoying messages vanish. Too bad F1 doesn't work on the office gossip.

Printing

Suppose that after entering what you think is the best piece of written work since Tolstoy penned a line, you decide that you want to print it. After all, dragging the computer around and showing everyone what your prose looks like on the screen just isn't practical.

To print the document in WordPerfect — the document you see on the screen (all of it) — do the following:

1. **Make sure that the printer is turned on and ready to print.**

2. **Press Shift-F7.**

   The screen is cleared, and the Print menu is displayed. The Print menu is an overcrowded place where printing and related activities happen. (Don't worry about the document; it's still safe and happy — just hidden for the moment.)

3. **Press 1 to direct WordPerfect to print the full document.**

   The entire document that was on the screen is printed. Zip, zip, zip. The document comes out of the printer.

✔ Detailed information on printing is provided in Chapter 12. Included is information on making sure that the printer is ready to print.

✔ Pressing Shift-F7 brings up the Print menu. This is a good key combination, or claw pattern, to memorize.

✔ To print only part of the document (a paragraph, page, or block), refer to Chapter 6.

Here are the quick steps for printing an entire document in WordPerfect, do the following:

1. Make sure that the printer is on and ready to print. (OK, no quick steps here.)
2. Press Shift-F7, 1.

Saving Your Stuff

WordPerfect doesn't remember what you did the last time you used the computer. You must forcefully tell it to save your stuff. The document on the screen must be saved in a file on disk. To do this task, you need to use WordPerfect's Save command.

To save a document to disk, follow these steps:

1. Press the handy Save key, F10.

You see the following prompt:

```
Document to be saved:
```

If the document has been saved before, you see its name listed after the prompt — the same name you see all the time in the lower left corner of the screen. Skip to Step 3.

If you don't see a name after the prompt, the document hasn't yet been saved to disk. Your job now is to think of a name. Be clever; you have only eight characters (letters and numbers).

2. Type the document's name.

Watch what you type! Check out the technical sidebar in this chapter on selecting a proper filename. If you make a mistake, use the Backspace key to back up and erase.

3. Press Enter to save the file.

If you're editing an older, already saved document, you see the following prompt:

```
Replace filename? No (Yes)
```

Press Y for yes. This action replaces the original file on disk with the file you've just edited in WordPerfect. If you don't want to overwrite the original file, press N, go back to Step 2, and type a new name for the file. If you're saving a document for the first time, this message doesn't appear and the document is saved to disk.

- F10 is the Save key. F10 equals Save, F10 equals Save, ... Say it over and over until you're sure that you've memorized it.

- If you entered a forbidden filename, WordPerfect screeches this message at you: ERROR: Invalid filename. Try again (and read the technical sidebar about proper filenames).

- Save your documents to disk so that you can work on them later. Saved documents can be loaded into WordPerfect the next time you start. Refer to "Editing a Document on Disk," earlier in this chapter.

- After a document has been saved to disk, you see its name — actually, its complicated DOS pathname with almond clusters — displayed in the lower left corner of the screen. This is your clue that a file has been saved to disk.

- *There is nothing wrong* with replacing an older version of the file on disk. I do it all the time with everything I write. As the file is edited, I save it to disk, replacing the older version. That way, only the newest edition is saved, and my disk isn't littered with a bunch of old, not-yet-edited documents.

- *There is something wrong* with overwriting an unknown file on disk. For example, suppose that you decide to save a new letter document by using the filename LETTER, and you find that a file named LETTER already exists on disk. If you answer yes to the Replace LETTER? prompt, the new file overwrites the old one. There is no way to get the original back, so use another, more clever name instead.

- Refer to Chapter 14 for more information on filenames and such.

Here is how you can quickly save a document you're working on — something you should do all the time. Press the following:

   F10, Enter, Y

Use this command often as you work on a document.

Complicated — but important — information about DOS filenames

You must name the file according to DOS's file-naming rules. This task isn't as tough as memorizing stuff for a driving test, but it's darn close. Here are the rules:

1. A filename can be no more than eight characters long.

2. A filename can include letters and numbers and can start with either a letter or a number.

3. Filenames do not end with a period.

4. Filenames can be followed by an optional three-character *extension*. The extension is separated from the main filename with a period.

5. Common filename extensions for WordPerfect documents are WP and DOC.

Here are some sample filenames that are OK:

LETTER.DOC	A prim and proper filename, replete with optional period and three-character DOC extension. Mrs. Bradshaw, my third-grade computer science teacher, would be proud.
CHAP01.WP	Another OK filename, this time with the WP extension. Note how numbers and letters can be mixed — no oil and vinegar here!
01	Fine, upstanding DOS filename. Numbers are okey-dokey, and the extension is optional.
LTR2MOM4	No problems here.
STUFF.2DO	Just fine. The extension can contain numbers as well.

Here are some filenames you should avoid (with reasons why you should avoid them):

TO MOM	The filename contains a space. Heavens! Filenames cannot contain spaces.
BELLYBUTTON	This one is too long and morally offensive to certain groups of people.
1+1	Numbers are OK, but the + symbol is not; only use letters and numbers to name files.
I.LOVE.YOU	This is a weirdo filename because it contains two periods. The period is reserved for marking the filename extension only — nothing else.
CHOPSTIK.FOOD	The extension here is too long. Extensions can only be three characters maximum.

Exiting WordPerfect

It is the height of proper etiquette to know when to leave. This rule of etiquette was personally explained to me by the Queen of England in her response to my letter about Christmas-party crashing. Oh, well. Leaving WordPerfect is accomplished with the use of the Exit command. As you can guess, this command has a handy function key assigned to it: F7.

Pressing F7 doesn't quit WordPerfect immediately. First, WordPerfect asks whether you want to save the document. This is precautionary stuff: No sense quitting when you haven't saved your important words to disk. You see this prompt:

```
Save document? Yes (No)
```

Press Y to save the document. If you haven't yet saved your work, you are asked to enter a filename. If the document has been saved, you are asked whether you want to replace it. Press Y to replace the old document on disk. (Refer to "Saving Your Stuff," earlier in this chapter, for details about saving files.)

After the file is saved, you see the following prompt at the bottom of the screen:

```
Exit WP? No (Yes)
```

Press Y to quit and return to DOS. If you press N, you remain in WordPerfect but with a clean slate for starting a new document.

✔ The F7 key is the Exit key. In addition to quitting WordPerfect, pressing F7 also backs you out of various menus and returns you to the document. If you accidentally press F7, panic, and then press F1 to cancel.

✔ Pressing F7 is the proper way to exit from WordPerfect. Do not, under any circumstances, reset or turn off the PC to quit WordPerfect. This is an utterly irresponsible practice, and you go to computer etiquette jail for life if you're ever caught!

✔ If the document has already been saved to disk, and no modifications have been made since that time, you see (Text was not modified) in the lower right part of the screen.

✔ To start a new document, press F7. Save the current document if you want but press N for no when asked, Exit WP? Thus, you start over afresh — like when you cranked in a clean new sheet of erasable bond in the good ol' typewriter days. Here are the quick steps: F7, Enter, Enter, Y, N.

✔ If you say you don't want to save the document, but then change your mind, press the Cancel key, F1, when you see Exit WP? This instruction appears in the lower right corner of the screen (although Cancel to return to document doesn't exactly imply "Press F1 to admit you goofed").

✔ When you're at the DOS prompt again and see that friendly C:\>, you can start another program or safely shut off the computer, or you can give up, sell the computer, and start a new hobby like kayaking.

✔ A handy way to test whether a document has been saved to disk is to press the F7 key. Look in the lower right corner of the screen. If it says (Text was not modified), then the file has been saved. Press the Cancel key, F1, to return to the document.

The 5th Wave
By Rich Tennant

" UNFORTUNATELY, THE SYSTEM'S NOT VERY FAULT-TOLERANT."

Chapter 2
Navigating the Document

. . . .

. . . .

*A*fter you have something "in there," a document ready for you to work on, you need to get around that document. Navigating a document works like a big city bus system, but it doesn't cost you $1.25 in loose change and you don't have to sit next to anyone named Edna who hasn't bathed in a week. There are simple, but not quite obvious, ways to move around a document in WordPerfect. Being able to move around a document comes in handy because the screen only shows you a small part of what you're working on.

Using the Basic Arrow Keys

The most common way of moving around a document is to use the arrow keys on the keyboard. The term *arrow keys* is rather nonspecific. A better term is *cursor-control keys* because the keys move the little cursor/underline on the screen, which is important for viewing different parts of the document as well as for locating text when editing.

The cursor-control keys are located in two spots on the keyboard: They're located on the numeric keypad, and they're located between the keypad and the typewriter keys. The location of the cursor-control keys is shown in Figure 2-1. I know, it sounds redundant. Yet, by having two sets of cursor-control keys, you can activate the numeric keypad and rapidly type numbers while still having access to the duplicate cursor-control keys. Older PC keyboards lacked this luxury.

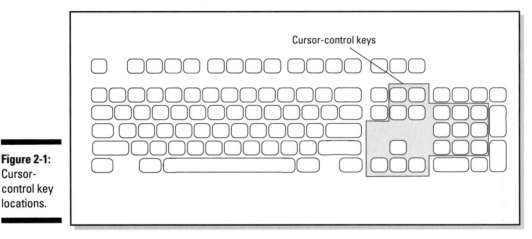

Cursor-control keys

Figure 2-1:
Cursor-
control key
locations.

The four basic cursor-control keys are the up, down, left, and right arrows. They are found in an inverted T pattern next to the typewriter keys and on the 8, 4, 6, and 2 keys on the keypad:

↑ Moves the cursor up one line of text

↓ Moves the cursor down to the next line of text

→ Moves the cursor right to the next character

← Moves the cursor left to the preceding character

✔ The cursor-control keys on the numeric keypad and the separate cursor-control keys work the same; you can use either set. But note that the Num Lock light on the keyboard must be off for the keypad cursor-control keys to work.

✔ You can move the cursor to any character on the screen by moving the mouse. When you move the mouse, the pointer block appears. Move it to where you want the cursor to be and then click the mouse's left button. The cursor instantly moves to that spot.

✔ If the cursor is on the top line of the screen, and you press the up arrow, the document scrolls down to reveal the preceding line of text. The cursor moves up to that preceding line.

✔ When the cursor is on the last line of the screen, and you press the down arrow, the document scrolls up to reveal the next line of text. The cursor moves down to that next line of text.

✔ Moving the cursor does not erase characters. The underline cursor slides under characters like a hockey puck under the goalie's legs.

✔ As you move the cursor around on the screen, the statistics in the lower right corner change to reflect your current position on the page. The Pos value tells you how how far away the cursor is from the left edge of the page, the Ln value tells you how far down you are from the top of the page, and the Pg value tells you which page you're on.

✔ The cursor only positions itself below characters and under spaces that appear between words. You can't move the cursor to outer space, which is any place on the screen that doesn't have any text characters.

✔ Older PC keyboards have only a numeric keypad. To use the cursor-control keys on such keyboards, turn the Num Lock light off by pressing the Num Lock key.

✔ Want to hop over eight characters at once? Press the Esc (Escape) key and then press an arrow key. The Esc key is the Repeat key. Any key or command you press after Esc is repeated — typically eight times. So pressing Esc, ← moves the cursor left eight places. The same is true for the other three arrow keys.

Using Ctrl with the Arrow Keys

If you press and hold the Ctrl (Control) key and then press an arrow key, the cursor jumps more than a single character:

Ctrl-↑	Moves the cursor up one paragraph
Ctrl-↓	Moves the cursor down to the next paragraph
Ctrl-→	Moves the cursor right one word
Ctrl-←	Moves the cursor left one word

✔ Press and hold the Ctrl key and then press an arrow key. Release both keys. You don't need to press hard; use the Ctrl key like you use the Shift key to produce a capital letter.

✔ Ctrl-→ and Ctrl-← always move the cursor to the first letter of a word.

✔ Ctrl-↑ and Ctrl-↓ always move the cursor to the start of a paragraph.

Moving Up and Down One Screenful of Text

The screen shows you only one small part of the document — not a full page. To see the next or preceding screen, use the plus and minus keys on the numeric keypad:

−   Moves the cursor to the top of the screen. If the cursor is already at the top of the screen, pressing the minus key moves you up to the preceding screen (the preceding 24 lines of text).

+   Moves the cursor to the bottom of the screen. If the cursor is already on the last line of the screen, pressing the plus key shows you the next screen (the next 24 lines in the document).

✔ Only the plus and minus keys on the numeric keypad move the screen up and down. The plus and minus keys next to the Backspace key on the typewriter keyboard produce the + and – characters.

✔ You also can move to the top and bottom of the screen, as well as the next and preceding screens, by using the Home key. Refer to "There's No Key Like Home," later in this chapter.

Moving Up and Down by Pages

The keys labeled PgUp and PgDn are the Page Up and Page Down keys, respectively. These keys move you around the document by pages, not by screens. Remember that there are more lines to a page than can be shown on the screen at once. Here's what PgUp and PgDn do:

PgUp   Moves the cursor to the top of the preceding page. If you're on page 1, this command moves you to the top of that page.

PgDn   Moves the cursor to the top of the next page. If you're on the last page in the document, PgDn moves you to the last line on that page.

✔ You can move to the bottom of the current page by using the Go To command. Refer to "Using the Go To Command," later in this chapter.

✔ To move to the tippy top of a document, use the Home key. Refer to "Moving to the Top of the Document," later in this chapter.

Moving to the End of the Line

Here's a quick one. To get to the end of a line of text, press the End key.

✔ Moving to the start of a line is accomplished with the Home key; see the next section.

✔ If you use the Ctrl key with the End key, you delete a line of text. Refer to Chapter 4.

There's No Key Like Home

One of the handiest keys in WordPerfect is the do-nothing Home key. I say *do-nothing* because, by itself, the Home key does nothing. (Well, for me *home* invokes images of Mom baking cookies and her screaming at me because my stubbed toe is getting blood on the new carpet.) Yet, when you press Home before pressing another navigation key, the Home key becomes a big key.

Here are the basic Home and arrow key sequences:

Home, ↑ Moves the cursor to the top of the screen

Home, ↓ Moves the cursor to the end of the screen

Home, → Moves the cursor to the right edge of the screen

Home, ← Moves the cursor to the left edge of the screen

Press the Home key once. Nothing happens. Then press an arrow key. Do not press and hold the Home key and use the arrow key as you do with the Ctrl key.

✔ Home is a prefix key — the big key. You're telling WordPerfect, "Move big in this direction."

✔ Home, → and the End key perform the same function.

✔ Home, ↑ and the minus key on the numeric keypad perform the same function.

✔ Home, ↓ and the plus key on the numeric keypad perform the same function.

Moving to the Top of the Document

Too many WordPerfect users press PgUp, PgUp, PgUp, and PgUp to get to the top of a document. This is akin to Mr. Spock using a ladder to get to the surface of a planet when he could just beam down.

To beam to the top of the document, press these keys:

Home, Home, ↑

Press the Home key twice and then press the up-arrow key. This action zaps you to the top of the document. No sweat.

Moving to the End of the Document

To move to theend of the document, press these keys:

Home, Home, ↓

Press the Home key twice and then press the down-arrow key. This action moves the cursor to the end of the document.

You can use this command to see how big the document is. Press Home, Home, ↓ and then look at the number next to the Pg hieroglyph in the bottom right corner of the screen. That number tells you how many pages are in the document.

Using the Go To Command

If you really want to fly around a document, you need the handy Go To command. This command is truly wings for the cursor. To issue the Go To command, press the Ctrl and Home keys together: Ctrl-Home.

That is, press and hold the Ctrl key and press the Home key. Release both keys. This command is how you powerfully direct WordPerfect to move by leaps and bounds all over the document. In the lower left corner of the screen, you see the following:

```
Go to
```

After this prompt appears, you can press the up-arrow or down-arrow key to zap yourself to the top or bottom of the current page:

↑ Goes to the top of the current page

↓ Goes to the bottom of the current page

You also can type a number after the prompt to go to the top of a specific page. For example, press 1 and press Enter to go to the top of page 1. Or press Ctrl-Home, 5 and press Enter to see what's on the top of page 5.

> ✔ If you type a specific character at the Go to prompt, WordPerfect moves you to the next occurrence of that character. But this is only a short-range command; WordPerfect may not find the character if it's too far away.

> ✔ Ctrl-Home, ↓ moves to the bottom of the current page. This is the only WordPerfect navigation command that does this action.

Getting Unlost

Has this ever happened to you? You want to move the cursor down to the next screen, but you press PgDn rather than the plus key. Or a stray elbow whacks a few cursor-control keys. You look up on the screen and discover that WordPerfect has moved itself elsewhere. Time to hunt for where you were . . . .

But wait! Here's a handy trick to getting back to where you were:

Ctrl-Home, Ctrl-Home

Pressing Ctrl-Home (the Go To command) twice in a row resets the cursor to its previous position.

> ✔ Press and hold the Ctrl key and press the Home key. Release both keys. At the Go to prompt, press and hold the Ctrl key and press the Home key again. This action moves you back to the previous cursor position.

> ✔ Pressing Ctrl-Home a third time moves you back to where you started.

> ✔ The Ctrl-Home, Ctrl-Home trick works great after search and search-and-replace operations. It repositions the cursor where it was when you started the search. It also works for spell checks and any other commands that reposition the cursor.

Chapter 3
Using the Keyboard Correctly

*S*ome people treat their computer keyboards as if there were land mines under half the keys. But, with the way things are in WordPerfect, the only way you can get anything done is to overuse the keyboard. The keys — a great deal of them used in combination with each other — are how you make WordPerfect do its stuff.

If this chapter has a theme, it is *be bold!* WordPerfect won't do anything perilous unless you tell it to. Even then, you are asked a yes/no question before the dangerous something happens. You can press the handy F1 key to cancel just about anything. Think of the F1 key as a little high-density uranium thimble that protects your fingers against those keyboard land mines.

Identifying Keys on the Keyboard

Welcome to Know Your Keyboard 101. Take a look at your keyboard and then take a look at Figure 3-1. Notice how the keyboard is divided into separate areas, each of which has a special function. These are the groups of keys you use in WordPerfect — either alone or in combination with other keys:

Function keys: These keys are along the top of the keyboard, labeled F1 through F12. WordPerfect only uses F1 through F10. You use these keys by themselves or in cahoots with the three different shift keys. (Note that on older PC keyboards, the function keys are not along the top; instead, the function keys are in two columns along the left side of the keyboard.)

Typewriter keys: These keys are the standard alphanumeric keys you find on any typewriter: A through Z, 1 through 0, plus symbols and other exotic characters.

Cursor-control keys: These are the arrow keys that move the cursor. Also lumped in are the Home, End, PgUp (Page Up), PgDn (Page Down), Insert, and Delete keys. Oh, and the big plus and minus keys on the keypad are counted as well.

Car keys: Don't leave these in the car and don't have any exposed valuables lying about. Buy *The Club* to help protect your car.

Numeric keypad: These keys switch between being cursor-control keys and number keys. Their split personality is evident on each key cap, which displays two symbols. The Num Lock key and its corresponding light are on if the numeric keypad is active. If the cursor-control keys are active, Num Lock is turned off.

Shift keys: These keys don't do anything by themselves. Instead, the Shift, Ctrl, and Alt keys are used in combination with other keys on the keyboard. In WordPerfect, all three keys are used with the ten function keys to give WordPerfect its memorable command list.

Enter key: This key is marked with the word *Enter* and sometimes a cryptic arrow thing: ↵

You use the Enter key to end a paragraph of text.

Esc (Escape) key: The Esc key is a handy key to use in WordPerfect, but its location may vary. Sometimes Esc is next to the Backspace key. Note its location on your keyboard.

> ✔ Be thankful: A piano has 88 keys — black and white with no labels. It takes years to master these keys. A computer keyboard, in comparison, is easy.

> ✔ Older PC keyboards have a different layout than the currently popular, 101-key Enhanced Keyboard. Some older models have the function keys to the side of the keyboard, and some lack the separate cursor-control keys. All keyboards work the same with WordPerfect, but this book assumes that you have the 101-key keyboard. (Go ahead and count 'em; there really are 101 keys on that baby.)

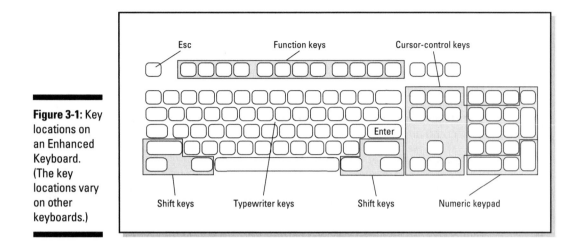

Figure 3-1: Key locations on an Enhanced Keyboard. (The key locations vary on other keyboards.)

Esc   Function keys   Cursor-control keys

Enter

Shift keys   Typewriter keys   Shift keys   Numeric keypad

✔ Laptop keyboards are all goofed up. Primarily, they lack the numeric keypad. This is OK, but you'll be missing the gray plus and minus keys, which enable you to move easily up or down a screen at a time. As a good substitute, I recommend using the following keys instead:

Home, ↑ = keypad minus

Home, ↓ = keypad plus

Pressing and Releasing

Sorry to disappoint all you budding third-world dictators. The title of this section is "Pressing and Releasing," and it refers to entering various WordPerfect key combinations. The title is not "Oppressing and Releasing," which sounds a bit liberal anyway.

In WordPerfect, key combinations are used to represent some commands. For example, if you press Shift-F7, you bring up the Print menu, which isn't really important right now. Instead, note that when I say "press Shift-F7," I mean "press and hold the Shift key and then press the F7 key; then release both keys."

You use key combinations all the time. Always press and hold the first key and then press the second key. Press and release.

✔ You press and release key combinations just like you press Shift-F to get a capital F. It's the same thing, but you use the odd Ctrl (Control) and Alt (Alternate) keys.

✔ Yeah, you really have to reach to get some of those function-key combinations. My advice? Use two hands. Or refer to the next section, "Using the WordPerfect Claw."

✔ There's no need for you to press hard. If you're having trouble working a command, pressing harder doesn't make the computer think, "Oh, lordy, she's pressing really hard now. I think she means it. Wake up, wake up!" A light touch is all that's required.

✔ Remember to release the keys. Press and hold the Shift key, press F7, and then release both keys. If you don't know which to release first, release the second key and then the shift key (Shift, Ctrl, or Alt).

✔ Some keys aren't used in conjunction with each other. For example, Home, ↑ moves you to the top of the screen. But, because these keys are separated by a comma, you first press and release Home, and then you press and release the up-arrow key. If you need to press two keys together, the keys are shown here (and in the WordPerfect manual) with hyphens: Shift-F10, for example.

Using the WordPerfect Claw

Don't be ridiculous. No one memorizes WordPerfect commands. But WordPerfect users do remember various claw patterns. *Claw patterns* are the finger gymnastics you use — the contortions you twist your fists into — to reach various shift-function key combinations.

For example, to press Alt-F1, I press the Alt key with the thumb on my left hand and press F1 with my middle finger. Pressing Alt-F4 is done with the same fingers but arched over the keyboard a bit. Pressing Shift-F10 is done with the left hand's pinky on the Shift key and the right hand's index finger on F10.

As you use WordPerfect, you become familiar with your own, personal claw patterns. After a while, you'll rely on them more than the keyboard template or the Help key.

✔ It's OK to use two hands for your various claw patterns. Notice that the three shift keys exist on both sides of the standard PC typewriter keyboard.

✔ Various WordPerfect users "claw" each other. For example, I hold up my hand in the Shift-F5 Date command pattern, and a fellow WordPerfect person tells me the current date.

Knowing When To Press Enter

On an electric typewriter, you press the Return key when you reach the end of a line. With a word processor, you need to press the Enter key only when you reach the end of a paragraph.

The reason you don't press Enter at the end of each line is that WordPerfect *word-wraps* to the next line on the page any words hanging over the right margin. Therefore, you need to press Enter only at the end of a paragraph, although having a short paragraph of just one line of text is still OK.

✔ Some people end a paragraph by pressing Enter twice; others press Enter only once.

✔ If you want to indent the next paragraph, press the Tab key after pressing Enter. This feature works just like it does on a typewriter.

✔ If you want to double-space a paragraph, you need to use a special line-formatting command, which is covered in Chapter 9. You do not double-space lines with the Enter key.

✔ If you press the Enter key in the middle of an existing paragraph, WordPerfect inserts a new paragraph, moving the rest of the text to the start of the next line. Inserting the Enter key is just like inserting any other key into the text. The difference is that you insert an Enter character, which creates a new paragraph.

✔ You can delete the Enter character by using the Backspace or Delete key. Removing the Enter character joins two paragraphs together; if you press Enter more than once between paragraphs, deleting an Enter character cleans up any extra blank lines.

Meaningless information about the Enter and Return keys

Enter or Return? Some keyboards label the Enter key *Return.* Most PCs use the word *Enter;* even so, some yahoos may call it the Return key. Why? (You really have to be hard up for trivia if you're continuing to read this stuff.)

The reason has to do with the computer's background. On a typewriter, the key is named Return. It comes from the preelectric days of typewriters when you had to whack the carriage-return bar to move the paper over to the other margin and continue typing. From the computer's calculator background, you pressed the Enter key to enter a formula into the calculator. This is the reason that some computer people can't make up their minds whether it's the Enter or Return key. My keyboard says Enter on that key — in two places. So that's what I use in this book.

Knowing When To Use the Spacebar

A major error committed by many WordPerfect users is to mistakenly use the spacebar rather than the Tab key. Allow me to clear the air on this one:

- ✔ Use the spacebar to insert space characters, such as you find between words or between sentences. You only need to press the spacebar once between each word or sentence, but some former touch typists (myself included) put two spaces between sentences. That's fine.

- ✔ Use the Tab key to indent, line up columns of information, or organize what you see on the screen. The Tab key indents text to an exact position. When you print, everything is lined up nicely and neatly, which doesn't happen with space characters.

If you're the doubting type and need to prove this point, open a WordPerfect document and press the Tab key. Then type the following:

Hello, I'm indented

Press Enter. On the next line, press the spacebar until the cursor is under the *H* in *Hello.* Then type the same sentence again. It looks lined up on the screen, but when it is printed, you see a definite difference. To prove this point without printing, move the cursor under one of the *H*s and check the Ln statistic in the lower right corner of the screen. Move to the other *H* and notice the difference. That's why you use the Tab key instead of spacing over.

✔ If you're using Courier, or some other monospaced font, then the spaces and tabs line up, just like you see them on the screen. But most of the time, you print in a fancier font. In that situation, nothing lines up, the printed document looks gross, and you'll reluctantly admit you should have paid attention here.

✔ Use the Tab key to indent. Use the spacebar to put spaces between words and sentences. I'm serious: Do not use the spacebar to indent or line up text. Your stuff will look tacky, tacky, tacky if you do.

✔ The reason that the Tab key and spacebar give different results is that the Tab character moves the cursor to a specific tab stop. The space character moves the cursor a fraction of an inch. These movements show up identically on the screen but print differently because the printed space is much thinner than what you see on the screen.

✔ To set tab stops in WordPerfect, refer to Chapter 9.

Using the Undo Key

Be bold! Why not? WordPerfect has a handy Undo key. And Undo remembers the last three things you deleted — not just the last thing.

To undelete any text you've just accidentally zapped, press F1, 1.

When you press F1, you see the following at the bottom of the screen:

```
Undelete: 1 Restore; 2 Previous Deletion: 0
```

On the screen, you see the last text you deleted highlighted and stuck at the cursor's current position. To restore the text at that position, press 1.

Often, what you see highlighted is not the text you remember deleting. If so, press 2. You see the next-to-the-last thing you deleted. If that still isn't what you want, press 2 again to see the next-to-the-next-to-the-last thing you deleted. Unfortunately, three deleted chunks of text are as far back as the Undo key remembers.

✔ Undo or Undelete? The key is really Undelete. It only undeletes text. Pressing F1 doesn't restore anything to a previous condition, nor does it undo any formatting or font changes. (I call it Undo anyway.)

✔ The Undelete key remembers only the last three chunks of text you deleted. Often, and to much chagrin, it isn't enough. For example, you may find a lot of little bits of text and single characters — not that previous paragraph you mistakenly murdered. The reason is that Undelete remembers each single-character deletion as well as big-chunk deletions. If the stuff you want can't be found, then it's lost forever. (Sniff, sniff.)

- Pressing both mouse buttons works the same as pressing the Undo/Cancel key, F1. On some mice, you must press all three buttons; with other mice, you press the two outside buttons.

- Yes! The F1 key is also WordPerfect's Cancel key. In a way, Cancel can be taken to mean Undelete. After all, if no command is running or no menu is on the screen, what else is there to cancel?

Using the Help Key

The handiest key on the keyboard is F3, the Help key. Here are some tips for using it in your fleeting moments of panic:

- Press F3 when you're doing something to display help and options available for that something. If you're just editing text, pressing F3 displays a couple of hints on how to use the help system.

- Press F3, F3 (that is, press F3 twice in a row) to see the detailed WordPerfect keyboard template. This template tells you which commands are associated with which keys. The commands are color coded to match the Shift, Alt, and Ctrl keys.

- Press F3 and then press the first letter of the command you need help with. A list of command names that start with that letter is displayed, along with their general category and key combination. Press the key combination for the particular command to see additional information.

- Press F3 and then press a key combination. WordPerfect tells you which command is associated with that key combination and offers additional details.

- Any time you're in the help system, a highlighted letter or number indicates that you can press that key for additional information.

- Press Enter to exit the help system and return to the document.

Using the Repeat Key

Here's a weird one: The Esc (Escape) key in WordPerfect is known as the Repeat key. One would think that Esc was the key that showed the way out. Wrong! The Esc key enables you to repeat a certain command a given number of times. That sounds dumb and useless and has little to do with escaping to or from anything, but it can really be a time-saver.

After pressing the Esc key, you see the following displayed at the bottom of the screen:

```
Repeat Value = 8
```

This message means that WordPerfect is ready for mass production. If you issue a WordPerfect command, press a cursor-control key, or type a character, that command, cursor-control key, or character is repeated eight times. Here are examples:

Esc, →	This command moves the cursor right eight places.
Esc, Ctrl- ←	This command moves the cursor left eight words.
Esc, PgUp	This command moves the cursor eight pages up in the document.
Esc, Delete	This command deletes the next eight characters.
Esc, Ctrl-End	This command deletes the next eight lines of text.
Esc, *	This command displays eight asterisks.

You can change the repeat value from 8 to any number from 1 to several hundred. You can do so on the fly or permanently. For on-the-fly changes, type the repeat value you want and then press the cursor-control key, command sequence, or letter you want repeated. Here are examples:

Esc, 10, -	This command displays 10 hyphens.
Esc, 5, Ctrl-Backspace	This command deletes the next 5 words.
Esc, 100, ↓	This command moves down 100 lines.

Press the Esc key, type a number for the new repeat value, and then type a command or press a cursor-control key or letter. (Don't type the commas shown in the preceding examples; they just mark where the number ends and the command, cursor-control key, or letter begins.)

To permanently change the repeat value, press Esc, type the new value, and then press Enter:

Esc, 10, Enter	This command changes the Repeat key's repeat value to 10.
Esc, 40, Enter	This command changes the repeat value to 40.
Esc, 8, Enter	This command changes the repeat value back to 8.

- ✔ In other programs, the Esc key is the Cancel key. Not in WordPerfect!

- ✔ You can follow the Esc key with any of the four arrow keys; the Ctrl-→ or Ctrl-← key; the PgUp, PgDn, or Delete key; or the Delete Word, Delete to End of Line, Delete to End of Page, or Macro command. You also can follow the Esc key with any individual character.

- ✔ The Esc key doesn't work with the Enter or Backspace key. And you can't use it to repeat a number key.

- ✔ If you follow Esc with a number and then press a cursor-control key, command, or character, the cursor-control key, command, or character is repeated that many times.

- ✔ If you follow Esc with a number and press Enter, you change the repeat value.

- ✔ Creating forms? Set the Esc key to a large value — say, 40. Then use Esc and the underline character to create fill-in-the-blanks items.

- ✔ I use the Esc key with the arrow keys to position the cursor in the middle of a large word.

Knowledge worth avoiding: selecting another keyboard

This is pure techie stuff here. I advise the casual WordPerfect user not to bother with this information because it changes the way the keyboard operates to a method not described in this book.

If you really, really — and I mean really — want to have F1 be the Help key, you can. WordPerfect uses one of several keyboard definition files on disk. These files describe how the keyboard behaves and which commands belong to which keys. To mess around with these files, press Shift-F1 and then press K.

You see a list of files describing several keyboard definitions available to your system. These definitions have reassigned certain commands on some keys and created new commands, or macros, for other keys.

For example, the SHORTCUT keyboard definition contains a lot of Alt-letter commands that do interesting and useful things. The ENHANCED keyboard definition assigns the Home key to move the cursor to the start of a line. The old Home key is replaced with the 5 key on the numeric keypad, and additional functions are added to the F11 and F12 keys.

To switch the functions of the F1 and F3 keys, you must create your own keyboard definition file, which isn't something I'd be foolish enough to describe in this book. But it can be done. If it's something you yearn for, have your computer guru sit down with the WordPerfect manual in his or her lap and slug it out. Remember to bribe your guru heavily with pizza and cola.

If you get fed up, you can restore the original keyboard's functions by selecting the Original option. Otherwise, everybody get out of here! Press F1 twice to cancel the keyboard setup options and return to the document.

Chapter 4
Deleting and Destroying Text

. . . .

In This Chapter

▶ Understanding insert and typeover modes

▶ Using the basic delete keys: Backspace and Delete

▶ Playing with the mystery delete grab bag

▶ Deleting a word

▶ Deleting to the end of the line

▶ Deleting to the end of the page

▶ Deleting odd shapes with blocks

▶ Undeleting

. . . .

*N*othing gives you such a satisfying feeling as blowing away text — especially if it's someone else's document you're editing. Of course, most of the destroying and deleting that goes on in WordPerfect is minor stuff: You delete the extra *e* in *potato,* slay a word here, and yank out a sentence there. It's much easier than using White Out on paper; because you delete text on the screen, it happens quickly and painlessly in the electronic ether. No mess and no white goop. And, if you change your mind, WordPerfect has a nifty Undelete command to bring the text back to glowing phosphorescent perfection.

Understanding Insert and Typeover Modes

The Insert key on the keyboard controls WordPerfect's two methods of putting text on the screen. Normally, new text is inserted at the cursor position. Any new text you type appears at the cursor's position, pushing any existing text to the right and down as you type. This setup is called *insert mode.*

If you press the Insert key, you enter *typeover mode.* The word Typeover appears in the lower left corner of the screen. Any text you next type overwrites existing text on the screen.

If you press the Insert key again, Typeover disappears from the screen and you're back in insert mode.

- ✔ The Insert key appears in two places on the 101-key Enhanced Keyboard. The word *Ins* appears on the zero key on the numeric keypad, and a second key, just to the right of the Backspace key, is labeled *Insert.* Both keys perform the same function.

- ✔ The new characters you type in insert mode appear right above the flashing cursor. Then the cursor moves to the right, awaiting the next character you type.

- ✔ When Typeover appears in the lower left corner of the screen, you're in typeover mode. Any new text you type overwrites existing text. I point this out because a stray finger or elbow can press the Insert key and put you in that mode when you don't want it.

- ✔ Leaving WordPerfect in insert mode all the time is a good idea. If you want to overwrite something, just type in the new text and then delete the old.

- ✔ You can get back any text you've overwritten in typeover mode by using the Undelete key, F1. See "Undeleting," later in this chapter.

Using the Basic Delete Keys: Backspace and Delete

You can use two keys on the keyboard to delete single characters of text: Backspace and Delete.

The Backspace key deletes the character to the left of the cursor.

The Delete key deletes the character above the cursor (the one the cursor is flashing on). Consider, for example, the following sentence:

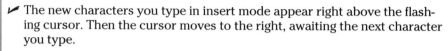

```
No one will notice those white socks, Dan.
```

In this sample sentence, the cursor is flashing under the *s* in *those*. Pressing the Backspace key deletes the *o* in *those;* pressing the Delete key deletes the *s.*

- ✔ After you delete a character, any text to the right of or below the character moves up to fill in the void.

- ✔ If you're in typeover mode, the Backspace key does not pull the rest of the text to the right. Instead, pressing Backspace replaces the deleted character with a space character and moves the cursor one notch to the left.

- ✔ Backspace works like the Backspace key on a typewriter. The difference is that when you press Backspace in WordPerfect, it backs up and erases. (The WordPerfect equivalent of the typewriter's Backspace key is the left-arrow key.)

✔ You can press and hold either Backspace or Delete to continuously, machine-gun delete characters. Release the key to stop your wanton destructive rampage.

Playing with the Mystery Delete Grab Bag

There's more to a WordPerfect document than what you see on the screen. Lots of hidden, secret codes are littered about the document. These codes change the font, center text, and boldface, italicize, underline, and format the document. You don't see these codes on the screen, but you see their effects.

When you press the Delete or Backspace key, you may stumble over one of these codes. For example, you may see the following:

```
Delete [BOLD]? No (Yes)
```

The word in the square brackets is the secret code you encountered while pressing the Backspace or Delete key. In this example, the code is the [BOLD] code, which WordPerfect uses to mark the start of boldfaced text in a document. In real life, you may see a variety of secret codes displayed, depending on how you formatted the document.

If you press Y in response to this question, you delete the secret code. Press N to leave it intact. My advice? Press N.

✔ Don't be surprised by the mystery codes in the document. You put them there as you create and format your text.

✔ If you really do want to get rid of stray codes — and sometimes a lot of them are junking up the document — refer to Chapter 11.

Deleting Text

WordPerfect is flexible enough to enable you to delete text one word at a time, delete text from the cursor to the end of the current line, and delete text from the cursor to the end of the page. In addition, you can block an odd shape of text (two paragraphs, one sentence, and three words, for example) and then delete the whole chunk in one devastating act.

Deleting a word

WordPerfect enables you to gobble up entire words at a time by using one of two Delete Word commands:

Ctrl-Backspace   This is the traditional Delete Word command.

Ctrl-Delete   This is an alternative Delete Word command, popular in European countries.

To delete a word with Ctrl-Backspace, position the cursor at the first letter of the word or any letter in the word. Press Ctrl-Backspace, and the word is gone! The cursor then sits at the start of the next word or the end of the line (if you deleted the last word in a paragraph).

- ✔ Both of these key commands perform the same function. Most people use Ctrl-Backspace. Ctrl-Delete has another function when used with blocks; refer to Chapter 6.

- ✔ If the cursor is positioned on a space character between two words, Ctrl-Backspace deletes the word to the left.

- ✔ If the cursor is sitting in space, Ctrl-Backspace doesn't delete anything. You really must be on or right next to a word to delete it.

- ✔ To delete several words at once, press the Esc key before pressing Ctrl-Backspace. Refer to the discussion of the Repeat key in Chapter 3.

Other ways to delete words (that you don't need to know about)

You have two additional ways to delete words in WordPerfect, both of which involve the handy Home key:

Home, Backspace   This command deletes from the cursor position to the start of the previous word — no matter where you are in the paragraph.

Home, Delete   This command deletes from the cursor position to the start of the next word.

Home, Backspace deletes backward; Home, Delete deletes forward. In both cases, the cursor is placed at the start of a word when you're done.

Deleting to the end of the line

No command is available in WordPerfect for deleting a line of text (at least, not a single command). Instead, there's a handy command that deletes from the cursor's position to the end of a line: Ctrl-End.

The Ctrl-End command deletes from where you are to the end of the line.

- ✔ The Ctrl-End command *does not* delete to the end of a paragraph. If you have any additional text in the paragraph, it wraps up after the cursor to replace the deleted text.

- ✔ Ctrl-Home is the Go To command. Refer to the discussion of the Go To command in Chapter 2.

- ✔ Unfortunately, no command is available for deleting from where you are to the beginning of the line. If one was available, think of how handy it would be in the Post Office or your bank.

- ✔ To delete a complete line of text, first move the cursor to the start of the line by pressing Home, ← . Then press Ctrl-End. So the keystrokes are as follows:

  Home, ← , Ctrl-End

  These keystrokes delete a whole line of text.

Deleting to the end of the page

To delete all the text from the cursor's position to the end of the page, use the Delete to End of Page command: Ctrl-PgDn.

After pressing Ctrl-PgDn (either of the two Page Down keys), you see the following at the bottom of the screen:

```
Delete Remainder of page? No (Yes)
```

Press Y to delete text from the cursor's position to the end of the page; press Enter or N — and go *whew!* — to avoid deleting the text.

- ✔ Of all the delete commands, I seem to stumble over this one most often. Thankfully, pressing any key but Y prevents the text from being deleted. (And, if you do accidentally delete text, press the Undelete key, F1, to bring it back; refer to "Undeleting," later in this chapter.)

- ✔ The *end of the page* is defined as all the text between the cursor's position to just above that row of hyphens across the screen, which WordPerfect uses to identify the end of the page. If you don't quite have a full page, then Ctrl-PgDn deletes to the end of the document.

- ✔ The Ctrl-L key combination also works like Ctrl-PgDn.

Deleting odd shapes with blocks

WordPerfect can delete characters, words, lines, and to the end of the page all by itself. To delete anything else, you need to mark the text to be axed as a *block* of text and then delete the block.

To delete a block of text, follow these steps:

1. **Mark the block.**

   Move the cursor to the start of the block, press Alt-F4 to start the block, and move the cursor to the end of the block.

2. **Press the Delete key.**

   The following prompt is displayed at the bottom of the screen:

   ```
   Delete Block? No (Yes)
   ```

3. **Press Y to delete the block.**

If you press N to not delete the block, the text remains marked as a block (highlighted) on the screen. Press F1 to cancel the block highlighting.

- Notice that the block is not deleted right away; you see a yes/no prompt first. Deleting blocks can be deadly, so WordPerfect wants to make sure that you're sure before proceeding.

- You also can use the Backspace key to delete a block after it's marked.

- You can find more information on marking blocks in Chapter 6.

- If you want to cut the block and move it elsewhere in the document, refer to the discussion of cutting blocks in Chapter 6.

Undeleting

Deleting text can be traumatic — especially for the timid WordPerfect beginner. But editing is editing, and mistakes happen. If you want some of your freshly deleted text back, you can use the Undelete command, F1. It usually works like this:

1. **Panic!**

   Oh, lordy! I just deleted cousin Jimmy from the will!

2. Press the F1 key.

You see the following at the bottom of the screen:

```
Undelete: 1 Restore; 2 Previous Deletion: 0
```

The last bit of text you deleted appears at the cursor's position, high-lighted (like a block).

3. If you want to restore the highlighted text, press 1 (Restore). (You also can press R.)

This action should put cousin Jimmy back in line.

Or, if the highlighted text isn't what you want to restore, press 2 (Previous Deletion).

WordPerfect shows you the next-to-the-last thing you deleted; press 1 to restore that text.

If you still don't like what you see, press 2 again.

WordPerfect shows you the next-to-the-next-to-the-last thing you deleted; press 1 if you want to restore that text.

If you still don't see what you want to restore, then it's long gone. The Undelete command only remembers the last three things you deleted.

✔ The Undelete command works for anything you deleted, no matter which delete command you used.

✔ The Undelete key is also the Cancel key, used for backing out of menus and for canceling yes/no questions. It acts as a general panic key.

✔ The Undelete command does not reverse formatting or font changes. To see how to undo those kinds of changes, refer to Part II of this book, the individual formatting chapters (Chapters 8 through 11) for assistance.

✔ After the program shows you the next-to-the-next-to-the-last thing you deleted, pressing 2 again shows you the last thing you deleted (the thing it showed you when you first pressed F1).

✔ The amount of text the Undelete command remembers includes whatever you deleted with any delete command up until the point you typed some new text, used a cursor-control key, or entered a WordPerfect command. Therefore, pressing Home, Backspace four times to delete four words is considered one chunk of deleted text by the Undelete command.

✔ You must be quick with the Undelete key. It only remembers the last three things you deleted — everything from single characters to full pages and more.

The 5th Wave

By Rich Tennant

"I TOLD HIM WE WERE LOOKING FOR SOFTWARE THAT WOULD GIVE US GREATER PRODUCTIVITY, SO HE SOLD ME A WORD PROCESSOR THAT CAME WITH THESE SIGNS."

Chapter 5
Searching and Replacing

Little Bo Peep has lost her sheep. Too bad she doesn't know about WordPerfect's Search and Replace commands. She could find the misplaced ruminants in a matter of microseconds. Not only that, but she could search and replace — say, replace all the sheep with Mazda Miatas. It's a cinch after you force the various purposes of the F2 key into your head. Sadly, only words are replaced. If WordPerfect could search for and replace real things, there'd be a lot less sheep in the world.

Finding Text

No matter where you are in a document, you can search for text either up (in previous paragraphs) or down (in following paragraphs). If you think you saw some sheep in text you just read through, you can tell WordPerfect to look up; if you think the sheep are hiding in text you haven't yet read, tell WordPerfect to look down. After you find one of those tricky little animals, you can continue your search for more sheep in the same direction. All the looking you have to do is for the F2 key on the keyboard.

Finding text down

With WordPerfect, you can locate any bit of text anywhere in the document. Well, not really. You can really only locate text above or below the cursor position. Two commands are available for doing this task. The first and most common is the Search Down command, accessed with the F2 key. Use this command to find text from the cursor's position to the end of the document.

Here's how the Search Down key, F2, works:

1. **Think of some text you want to find.**

   For example, how about *sheep*.

2. **Press the F2 key.**

   The F2 key means *search from here to thither*, where *here* means where the cursor is and *thither* means to the end of the document. After pressing F2, you see the following at the bottom of the screen:

   ```
   -> Srch:
   ```

3. **Type the text you want to find.**

   For example, type **sheep**. Always type the text in lowercase letters. (You find out why if you dare to read the technical-information sidebar about finding uppercase and lowercase text.)

4. **Press F2 again to start the search.**

   This step is important. *Do not press Enter to start the search.* Press F2 to search from the cursor's position to the end of the document. (If you do press Enter, press Backspace to delete the `[HRt]` code that appears.)

If any text matching what you entered is found, it appears in the middle of the screen. The cursor is positioned right after the matching text. (If it were only this easy for Miss Peep and her stray ovines.)

- Type the text you want to find, exactly as you think it appears in the document. Do not end the text with a period unless you want to look for the period too.

- If the text isn't found, you see the message `* Not found *` displayed at the bottom of the screen. Alas. You can try again or just accept the fact that the text doesn't exist and continue with your daily struggle.

- To find any additional occurrences of the text, press the F2 key twice: F2, F2. This shortcut works because you've previously searched for text, so that text appears after the prompt when you press the F2 key. You can edit the text by using the cursor-control keys if you like.

✔ If WordPerfect can't find the text, consider using the Search Up command, described in the next section. Also check to make sure that the text you are searching for was typed in lowercase letters.

✔ To search the entire document, start at the top. Press the following keys to move to the top of the document:

Home, Home, ↑

These keystrokes position you at the tippy top of the document. From there, you can use the Search Down command, F2, to search through all the text.

✔ You can search for a variety of things by using the F2 key — not only text, but spaces, the Enter character, and formatting codes. Searching for these kinds of noncharacters is covered in "Finding secret codes," later in this chapter.

✔ Do not press Enter after the Srch prompt. Press the F2 key to start the search. (If you do press Enter, the Enter character appears at the Srch prompt. Refer to "Finding secret codes," later in this chapter, for details.)

✔ To return to where you started searching for text, use the Go To, Go To command. Press Ctrl-Home twice in a row: Ctrl-Home, Ctrl-Home.

✔ To cancel the Search Down command and return to the document, press the Cancel key, F1.

Annoyingly technical information for finding upper-case and lowercase text

WordPerfect finds any matching text in the document — provided that you type it in lowercase letters. If you type a capital letter, WordPerfect then matches the word only with capital letters. Here are examples:

-> Srch: ruminant   Matches all instances of the word — uppercase and lowercase: *ruminant, Ruminant,* and *RUMINANT*

-> Srch: Ruminant   Matches all instances of the word when the first letter is capitalized: *Ruminant* and *RUMINANT*

-> Srch: RUMINANT   Matches only a word that has all capital letters: *RUMINANT*

Incidentally, my sister, who is a veterinarian, tells me most ruminants are ungulates. She says, "A *ruminant* is an animal with a four-part stomach, which contains a population of bacteria and protozoa capable of fermenting cellulose to utilizable nutrient substances." In other words, a sheep.

Finding text up

Just as your VCR's remote has a reverse button, WordPerfect's Search command has a backward mode. The standard F2 Search command searches down, and the Shift-F2 Search command searches from the cursor's position to the top of the document. This command isn't as popular as the Search Down command, but both work the same way:

1. **Think of some text you want to find.**

   Think of something you remember a few pages back — for example, *ungulate* to look for a hoofed mammal.

2. **Press the Shift-F2 key combination.**

   Shift-F2 works just like F2, but it means *search from here to hither,* where *hither* means to the start of the document. After pressing Shift-F2, you see the following at the bottom of the screen:

   ```
   <- Srch:
   ```

   Note how the arrow cleverly points backward. In case your pinky finger is numb, and you forgot that you pressed Shift-F2 rather than only F2, the arrow is your clue that you are searching backward.

3. **Type the text you want to find.**

   For example, type **ungulate** if you want to look for a hoofed mammal. Type the text in lowercase letters.

4. **Press F2 to start the search.**

   Oh, you can press Shift-F2 if you want. Either way, the F2 key starts the search.

If WordPerfect finds the text, it appears in the middle of the screen, with the cursor blinking at the start of the matching text.

- ✔ Note that you need to press only F2 to start the search, but Shift-F2 works as well. As with the Search Down command, avoid the temptation to start the search by pressing Enter.

- ✔ If WordPerfect can't find the text, you see the message * Not found * displayed.

- ✔ All other rules and regulations for finding text up are the same as for finding text down. Refer to the preceding section for details.

- ✔ Most ungulates are herbivores, and many are horned.

Finding the next matching text

WordPerfect doesn't have a feature for counting the number of text matches in a document. However, if you want to continue looking down for the same text after the initial find, press the F2 key twice: F2, F2.

If you're looking up, press Shift-F2 and then F2: Shift-F2, F2.

You don't have to press Shift-F2 a second time; F2 works fine and keeps the direction upward: Shift-F2, F2.

Finding secret codes

Laced throughout a document are secret codes and printing instructions. You don't see these codes on the screen, but they affect how the document looks and is printed. You read about these codes in detail in Part II of this book — specifically, in Chapter 11. Basically, secret commands like boldface, underline, center, and new page, as well as special characters like Enter and Tab, can be searched for like any other text.

To search for a secret code, first press the proper Search command: Press F2 to search from the cursor's position to the end of the document or Shift-F2 to search from the cursor's position up.

At the Srch prompt, type the characters or WordPerfect commands you want to search for. For example, to search for the Enter key, press Enter. You see the following at the bottom of the screen:

```
-> Srch: [HRt]
```

The [HRt] code is the way WordPerfect represents the Enter-key character. Likewise, pressing the Tab key causes [Tab] to appear when you're looking for tab characters.

Press F2 to search for the character or formatting command.

- ✔ This feature is the reason that you don't press Enter to start a search; if you do, you tell WordPerfect to find the Enter key. Press F2 to start searching.

- ✔ To search for a WordPerfect command, you need to know the proper keys to press to start the command. For example, to search for the [Center] code, which centers text, press Shift-F6, the Center formatting command. The Srch prompt then shows [Center] and looks for that secret code when you press F2.

✔ When you search for some of the advanced, confusing commands, you see their menus displayed at the bottom of the screen to assist you. Don't expect much; the menus are extremely brief. For example, to search for the [ITALC] code that marks the start of italic text, you press the following keys at the Srch prompt:

Ctrl-F8, A, I

After you press Ctrl-F8, the Font menu appears at the bottom of the screen. From there you select A (Appearance). The Appearance menu appears. From the Appearance menu, you select I (Italc). You need to type all these keystrokes to put the[ITALC] code after the Srch prompt so that you can search for that formatting. (If you bother to do this stuff, keep in mind that all the vowel keys were broken on WordPerfect's programming computer that day.)

✔ I strongly advise anyone who wants to search for the advanced, confusing commands to review how they work. Formatting commands are covered in Part II of this book.

✔ HRt means *hard return,* which is what happens when you press the Enter key. When WordPerfect wraps a line of text, it inserts what it calls a *soft return.* The softness comes from WordPerfect's capacity to juggle words in a paragraph so the text continues to fit on the page after you edit it. The hard return produced by the Enter key is a definite, I-want-a-new-paragraph command.

Using Super Find

Amazing things are hidden inside a WordPerfect document. You can search for secret and hidden codes by using the basic Search commands. But, if you want to search through such things as headers, footers, footnotes, end notes, and the mysterious text boxes, you need to use the Super Find command. (Hum triumphant theme music here.)

This is a cinch: You use the Super Find command just like F2 and Shift-F2. The difference is that before pressing either of those keys, you press the Home key. Yes, Home boosts the power of the normal Search commands. It's akin to Captain Picard saying, "Put sensors on maximum." Here are the Super Find commands:

Home, F2   The Super Find Down command

Home, Shift-F2   The Super Find Up command

✔ The Super Find commands work just like the regular Search commands do. The only difference is that text in the header, footer, footnotes, end notes, text boxes, captions — all the text, everything — is searched in addition to the text in the document.

✔ You also can use Super Find with the Replace command, Alt-F2. Just press the Home key before you press Alt-F2, and WordPerfect searches and replaces through headers, footers, and so on.

✔ To use the Super Find command through the entire document, press these keys:

Home, Home, ↑, Home, F2

Pressing these keys moves the cursor to the top of the document and then starts the Super Find Down command. If the text is in the document, it will be found.

✔ Refer to the section "Finding text down," earlier in this chapter, for details on how the Search command works.

Searching for and Replacing Text

Search and replace is the art of finding a bit of text and replacing it with something else. For example, you can replace the word *goat* with *caprine* (yet another ungulate). With WordPerfect, you can do it in a snap by using Alt-F2, the Replace command:

1. **Position the cursor where you want to start searching for text.**

   The search always happens from the cursor's position down to the end of the document.

2. **Press Alt-F2, the Replace command.**

   You see the following at the bottom of the screen:

   ```
   w/Confirm? No (Yes)
   ```

3. **Do you want WordPerfect to ask your permission before replacing each bit of found text? If so, press Y; if not, press N.**

   Pressing Y is a good idea. If you press N in response to this prompt, text is found and replaced automatically. If you press Y, WordPerfect stops and displays a yes/no prompt, which enables you to decide whether or not to replace that occurrence of text. My advice? Press Y.

   Then WordPerfect displays the Search Down prompt:

   ```
   -> Srch:
   ```

4. Type the text you want to find and replace with something else.

Any previously searched-for text appears at the prompt. Edit it, if you like, or type new text or secret codes to search for. For example, if you want to search for *goat* and replace it with *caprine*, type **goat** at this prompt.

5. Press the F2 key.

Do not press Enter. WordPerfect prompts for the replacement text:

```
Replace with:
```

6. Type the text you want to use as a replacement.

For example, if you're replacing *goat* with *caprine,* type **caprine** here. Type it exactly the way you want it: no quotation marks and no period (unless you want to replace with these characters). *Do not press Enter.*

7. Press F2 to start the search-and-replace operation.

WordPerfect displays the message ⋆ Please wait ⋆ as it scans for text.

✔ If no text can be found for replacement, WordPerfect doesn't display anything. Your clue that no text has been found is that the cursor does not move after the ⋆ Please wait ⋆ message disappears.

✔ If you've directed WordPerfect to confirm each text replacement, it stops each time it finds the search-for text, blinks the cursor at the start of the text, and displays the following at the bottom of the screen:

```
Confirm? No (Yes)
```

Press N to keep the text as is; press Y to replace it.

✔ Press the Cancel key, F1, to stop the search-and-replace operation at any time.

✔ Always type something at the Replace with prompt. If you don't type something here, you systematically delete all the search-for text in a wanton round of wholesale slaughter. This feature is called *search and delete* and is covered in "Searching and deleting," later in this chapter.

✔ To return to your starting position, the place where the cursor was when you activated the Replace command, press Ctrl-Home twice: Ctrl-Home, Ctrl-Home.

✔ My advice is to press Y (yes) in response to the w/Confirm prompt. Only if you're replacing something and you're *certain* (a rare occurrence, at least in my book) should you press N (no). Because . . .

✔ There is no way to undelete text you've searched for and replaced. Sorry.

✔ A good way to restore a document after an adverse search and replace is to save the document *before* you do a search and replace. If you make a mistake, you can exit the document (press F7, N, N) and then reload the older document from disk by using the Shift-F10 command.

✔ The Replace command works from the cursor's position to the end of the document. To replace all occurrences of text in a document, start at the top of the document. Press the following keys:

Home, Home, ↑, Alt-F2

The double-Home, up-arrow keystrokes move the cursor to the top of the document. Alt-F2 starts the search-and-replace operation.

✔ To perform a search and replace through the entire document, including headers, footers, footnotes, end notes, references, and so on, press the Home key before starting the Replace command:

Home, Alt-F2

Refer to "Using Super Find," earlier in this chapter, for additional information about using the Home key with the Replace command.

Searching for and replacing spaces

This section provides you with a practical use for the Replace command. Too many WordPerfect users litter their documents with excessive spaces. The most harmless of all these spaces come at the end of a line of text, after the period and before you press Enter. I put spaces there too. Yet the extra spaces serve no purpose. Here is how to get rid of them:

1. **Move to the top of the document by pressing the following keys:**

   Home, Home, ↑

2. **Start the Replace command by pressing Alt-F2.**

3. **At the** w/Confirm **prompt, press N (no).**

   I know, I said always press Y. It's OK this time. But, if you'll feel better, press Y if you want.

4. **At the** Srch **prompt, type a space and then press the Enter key.**

   The search-for text should look like this:

   ```
    -> Srch: [HRt]
   ```

   (Trust me, there's a space character before the [HRt].) This setup means WordPerfect will look for spaces before the Enter key was pressed — excess junk you don't need.

5. **Press the F2 key.**

   You see the Replace with prompt.

6. **Press the Enter key.**

   The prompt should look like this:

   ```
   Replace with: [HRt]
   ```

This setup tells WordPerfect to replace all space-Enter sequences with just Enter. The end result is to remove the spaces before the Enter character in the document.

7. Press F2 to start the operation.

In a few seconds, it is over, and the excess spaces are removed from the document.

If the cursor didn't move, there probably were no extra spaces in the document. If it did move, extra spaces abound. Go back to Step 1 and start all over to continue removing them. Repeat these steps until all the excess spaces in the document are gone.

- ✔ To confirm whether any spaces exist before trying this exercise, use the Search command, F2, to search for the space-Enter sequence. If none exist, you see `* Not found *` displayed.

- ✔ A quick way to transform extra spaces into a tab character is to search for five spaces in a row and replace them with a tab character. At the `Srch` prompt, press the spacebar five times. At the `Replace with` prompt, press the Tab key. The `[Tab]` character appears, meaning that the spaces will be replaced with tabs, which are much easier to line up.

Searching and replacing in a block

Although WordPerfect doesn't let you search through a block of marked text, it does let you search and replace inside a block. This feature is great if you just want to change some text in a paragraph, page, or some other odd grouping of words. Follow these steps:

1. Rope off the block of text you want to search.

Move the cursor to the start of the text you want to block, press Alt-F4 to start marking the block, and then move the cursor to mark the end of the block.

2. Press Alt-F2.

The Replace command now works only with the text in the block. The rest of the document is unaffected.

3. Follow steps 2 through 7 in "Searching for and Replacing Text," earlier in this chapter.

When you press F2 at the `Replace with` prompt, WordPerfect searches only the block of text you've marked.

TIP

✔ Use the Replace command on a block of text when you want to change text in only a small part of the document. The rest of the document is unaffected by the Replace command.

✔ The text block is searched from the start to the end. When the last item has been found and replaced (or not), the block is unhighlighted.

✔ If the search-for text was not located in the block, the block is unhighlighted and the cursor appears at the end of the block.

✔ Detailed information on marking a block of text is offered in Chapter 6.

Searching and deleting

If you don't type anything at the `Replace with` prompt, WordPerfect's Replace command systematically deletes all the text it finds. This is a scary thing, so be sure to press Y when you're asked whether you want confirmation. Otherwise, you could zap the document irrevocably.

Suppose that Bo Peep wants to get rid of her sheep. (She wants to be a truck driver.) Here's how to delete the sheep from a WordPerfect document:

1. **Position the cursor at the beginning of the document or at the spot from which you want to search down.**

   Remember that the Replace command always works from the cursor's position down.

2. **Press Alt-F2 to start the Replace command.**

3. **At the** `w/Confirm?` **prompt, press Y.**

   If you're particularly ruthless — or just very sure of yourself — press N for no confirmation.

4. **At the** `Srch` **prompt, type the text you want to find.**

   Here is an example:

   ```
   -> Srch: sheep
   ```

   Type the text exactly as you want to search for it. Any previously searched-for text appears at the prompt. Edit it or type new text, secret codes, or whatever you want to search for.

5. **Press the F2 key.**

   Do not press Enter.

6. **At the** `Replace with` **prompt, press F2.**

   In moments, all the sheep are gone. Bo Peep's sheep go pop, pop, popping away! If you've asked to confirm each find, the process takes a bit longer because you have to squint at the screen and press the Y or N key on the keyboard.

✔ As with any search-and-replace operation, the text you replace — delete, in this case — cannot be recovered with the Undelete key, F1.

✔ As with any massive replacement operation, you may want to save the document to disk *before* you start the replace operation. To do so, press the following keys:

  F10, Enter, Y

F10 is the Save command. If the document hasn't yet been saved, type a name. If it has been previously saved, press Enter when the name is displayed and then press Y to overwrite the old copy on disk.

Go ahead with the search-and-destroy operation. If you goofed, you can reload the saved, presearch document by pressing the following keys:

  F7, N, N

Press F7 to exit WordPerfect, N to not save the now-corrupted document, and N to stay in WordPerfect. Then use the Shift-F10 command to reload the presearch document back into memory. Try, try again.

✔ Wish Miss Bo Peep good luck in her new profession.

Chapter 6
Working with Text Blocks, Stumbling Blocks, and Mental Blocks

●　●

In This Chapter

▶ Marking a block with the cursor-control keys

▶ Marking a block with the Search command

▶ Copying a block and pasting

▶ Cutting a block and pasting

▶ Copying, cutting, and pasting fast with the Move command

▶ Pasting a previously cut or copied block

▶ Deleting a block

▶ Undeleting a block

▶ Formatting a block

▶ Spell-checking a block

▶ Searching and replacing in a block

▶ Printing a block

▶ Saving a block to disk

●　●

A major advantage of a word processor over, say, a stone tablet is that you can work with blocks of text. Stone tablets, no way: You can break them up into blocks, but gluing them back together again is *tres gauche*. Hand such a thing with a report on it to your boss, and she'll shake her head, muttering, "Tsk, tsk, tsk. This is tacky, Jenson."

A block in a word processor is a marvelous thing. You can rope off a section of text — any old odd section (a letter, word, line, paragraph, page, or rambling polygon) — and then treat the text as a unit, a *block*. You can copy the block, move it, delete it, format it, spell-check it, use it to keep the defensive line from getting to your quarterback, and on and on. Think of the joy: Years after childhood, WordPerfect has made it OK for us to play with blocks again.

Marking a Block

You can't do anything with a block of text until you mark it. Marking a block tells WordPerfect, "OK, my block starts here. No, *here*! Not over there. Here, where I'm looking, where the cursor is." Use the Start Block command, Alt-F4. That command drops anchor, marking the start of the block. You then can use the cursor-control keys or the Search command to find the other end of the block. WordPerfect highlights the selected block of text by using reverse text on the screen. After the block is marked, you're ready to do something with it.

Marking a block with the cursor-control keys

To mark a block of text with the cursor-control keys, follow these handy steps:

1. **Move the cursor to the start of the block.**

   Place the cursor under the first letter of the text you want in the block. Be very specific. Tell the computer, "I want my block to start here" as you position the cursor.

2. **Press the Mark Block key combination, Alt-F4.**

   Press and hold the Alt key and press the F4 key. Release both keys. You see the following at the bottom left corner of the screen:

   ```
   Block on
   ```

   This message blinks incessantly. WordPerfect is telling you, "You're in block-marking mode. You're in block-marking mode. You're in . . . ."

   Block-marking mode is active until you give a block or formatting command, or press F1 to cancel. So let the message blink.

3. **Use the cursor-control keys to mark the block.**

   Position the cursor where you want the block to end. Refer to Chapter 2 for various key combinations you can use to move the cursor.

   As you mark the block, the text included inside the block is *highlighted,* or shown in reverse text on the screen (see Figure 6-1). That's OK; the text stays that way, and Block on continues to blink until you issue a block command.

   When you've moved the cursor to the end of the block, you're ready to issue a block command.

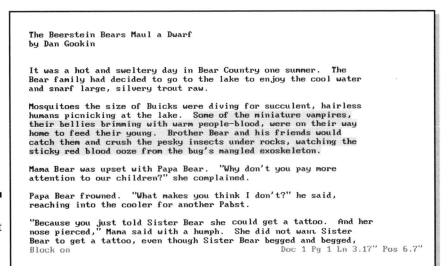

The Beerstein Bears Maul a Dwarf
by Dan Gookin

It was a hot and sweltery day in Bear Country one summer. The
Bear family had decided to go to the lake to enjoy the cool water
and snarf large, silvery trout raw.

Mosquitoes the size of Buicks were diving for succulent, hairless
humans picnicking at the lake. Some of the miniature vampires,
their bellies brimming with warm people-blood, were on their way
home to feed their young. Brother Bear and his friends would
catch them and crush the pesky insects under rocks, watching the
sticky red blood ooze from the bug's mangled exoskeleton.

Mama Bear was upset with Papa Bear. "Why don't you pay more
attention to our children?" she complained.

Papa Bear frowned. "What makes you think I don't?" he said,
reaching into the cooler for another Pabst.

"Because you just told Sister Bear she could get a tattoo. And her
nose pierced," Mama said with a humph. She did not want Sister
Bear to get a tattoo, even though Sister Bear begged and begged,
Block on   Doc 1 Pg 1 Ln 3.17" Pos 6.7"

Figure 6-1:
A block of text
marked on
the screen.

You can copy the block, cut it and paste it elsewhere, format the block, print it, spell-check it, or do a dozen other interesting things, all covered in this chapter. Refer to the appropriate section later in this chapter for instructions on what to do with the block.

- ✔ On some keyboards, the F12 key performs the same function as Alt-F4. Pressing F12 only requires one finger and no claw pattern.

- ✔ Yes, until you issue a block command, the block remains highlighted and Block on continues to blink. This is OK; marking a block is an active thing.

- ✔ On some systems, the Block on message does not blink but is shown highlighted in reverse text. This is OK, too; not every computer is capable of making text blink.

- ✔ Before pressing Alt-F4, position the cursor where you want the block to start.

- ✔ After pressing Alt-F4, you can move the cursor up or down from the block's anchor point. Most people move the cursor down.

- ✔ Instead of using the cursor-control keys to mark a block, you can type a character. WordPerfect locates the next occurrence of that character and highlights all the text between it and the start of the block. You can do this action several times to make the block as large as you like.

✔ To mark a block by using the mouse, position the mouse pointer at the start of the block. Press and hold the mouse button and drag to the end of the block. WordPerfect scrolls the screen if you drag down (toward yourself) with the mouse. Release the mouse button when you're done defining the block.

✔ To cancel a block, press F1. You also can press Alt-F4 again to turn off block-marking mode.

✔ To mark a paragraph, position the cursor at the start of the paragraph, press Alt-F4, and then press Enter. Because Enter marks the end of the paragraph, these keystrokes mark a paragraph block for you.

Marking a block with the Search command

Marking a block can get sloppy with the cursor-control keys — especially if you use the PgDn or gray + key to mark large acres of text. A better way is to use the Search command to locate the end of the block:

1. Position the cursor at the start of the block.

The cursor must be blinking right under the first character you want to include in the block. Be precise.

2. Press the Alt-F4 key combination.

This action turns on the annoying Block on blinking message in the lower left corner of the screen. You're in block-marking mode.

3. Press the F2 key.

You see the Srch prompt displayed at the lower left corner of the screen:

```
->Srch:
```

Yes, you're still in block-marking mode, but now you can use the Search command to locate the end of the block.

4. Type the text you want to search for.

This text will mark the end of the block. *Do not press Enter.*

5. Press F2 to search for the matching text.

WordPerfect stretches the block highlighting down to that point in the text and includes the found text in the block.

When the cursor is at the end of the block, you're ready to use a block command.

Refer to the appropriate section later in this chapter for details about using block commands. Notice that until you issue a block command, the block remains highlighted and Block on continues to blink.

- ✔ If no text is found when you use the Search command, you see * Not found * displayed in the lower left corner of the screen. You are still in block-marking mode.

- ✔ To find the next occurrence of the matching text, or to search for additional text to include in the block, you can press F2 again.

- ✔ There's no point in searching for individual characters with the Search command; WordPerfect does that automatically any time you press Alt-F4 to mark a block.

- ✔ You can still use the cursor-control keys to mark the block, either before or after pressing F2 to find text. Blocking is a liberal thing: You're not limited to using only the cursor or Search-command method to mark a block.

- ✔ You can find more details about the Search command in the discussion about the Search Down command in Chapter 5.

- ✔ You also can use the Search Up command, Shift-F2, to mark a block upward in the document. This feature is called *marking an Australian block.*

Doing Things with Blocks

The rest of this chapter explains what you can do with a block after you've marked it.

Copying a block and pasting

After a block is marked, you can copy and paste that block into another part of a document. The original block remains untouched by this operation:

1. **Mark the block.**

   Locate the start of the block by using the cursor. Press Alt-F4 to start the block. Use the cursor or Search command to locate the end of the block.

2. **Press Ctrl-F4 to start the Move command.**

   F4 is also the Copy command, and it does other things as well (yet another vague, multipurpose WordPerfect function key). You see the following displayed at the bottom of the screen:

```
Move: 1 Block; 2 Tabular Column; 3 Rectangle: 0
```

Who knows what a tabular column or rectangle is? Our worries are about blocks, so . . .

3. Press B for Block.

You see yet another prompt:

```
1 Move; 2 Copy; 3 Delete; 4 Append: 0
```

4. Press C for Copy.

The block's highlighting disappears. This is OK. What happened was that WordPerfect read the block and stored it in memory. It won't forget the block, but now it's up to you to find a location for the copy. Another prompt has appeared at the bottom of the screen:

```
Move cursor; press Enter to retrieve
```

5. Move the cursor to the position where you want the block copied.

Don't worry if there isn't any room there; WordPerfect inserts the block into the text just as if you typed it there manually.

6. Press Enter to paste the block.

You now have two copies of the block in the document.

✔ About the most annoying thing with copying (or cutting) and pasting a block is that you can't do anything after the Move cursor; press Enter to retrieve message appears. You must immediately find the block's destination and press Enter. If you see anything interesting along the way, you can't stop to fix it; you have to go back and hit it after you paste the block.

✔ Additional information on marking a block is found in the first part of this chapter.

✔ After you paste the block, you may have to do a bit of editing to clean things up. Although WordPerfect makes room for the block, it doesn't add punctuation, move a period or quotation mark, or format the block. You may have to do those things manually.

✔ After you copy a block, you can paste it into the document a second time. This procedure is covered in the section "Pasting a previously cut or copied block," later in this chapter.

Here are the quick steps for copying a block in WordPerfect:

1. Mark the block.

2. Press Ctrl-F4, B, C.

3. Move the cursor to where you want to insert the block.

4. Press Enter.

Cutting a block and pasting

Cutting a block is like deleting it, but nothing is really gone. Instead, like an article you snip out of the newspaper, the cut block can be pasted into the document at another location. This feature is technically called a *move;* you move a block of text from one spot to another in the document. (Talk about writing moving text!)

Cutting a block of text is very similar to copying a block. Follow these steps:

1. **Mark the block of text you want to move.**

   Locate the start of the block by using the cursor. Press Alt-F4. Use the cursor-control keys or Search command to locate the block's end.

2. **Press Ctrl-F4 to start the Move command.**

   You see the following displayed at the bottom of the screen:

   ```
   Move: 1 Block; 2 Tabular Column; 3 Rectangle: 0
   ```

   You want to move a block, so . . .

3. **Press B for Block.**

   Yet another prompt appears:

   ```
   1 Move; 2 Copy; 3 Delete; 4 Append: 0
   ```

4. **Press M for Move.**

   The block disappears! That's OK. It has been stuffed into WordPerfect's electronic storage place, nestled deep in the computer's memory. Another prompt appears at the bottom of the screen:

   ```
   Move cursor; press Enter to retrieve
   ```

5. **Move the cursor to where you want the block pasted.**

   Don't worry if there isn't any room for the block; WordPerfect makes room as it inserts the block.

6. **Press Enter to paste the block at the cursor's location.**

   ✔ You can find additional information on marking a block in the first part of this chapter.

   ✔ Copying a block works just like moving a block, but the original isn't deleted. Refer to "Copying a block and pasting," earlier in this chapter.

   ✔ Moving a block is not the same as deleting a block. You can only recover a moved block by positioning the cursor and pasting the block with the Enter key. The Undelete command does not recover a block you've moved.

✔ The F1 key does not undo a block move.

✔ You can use any cursor-control key combination when you're hunting for the location at which you want to paste the block. You cannot, however, edit text before you press Enter to paste the cut block. Moving a block is an immediate thing. WordPerfect does not enable you to leisurely edit as you search for the block's new location.

✔ The pasted block may not look the way you want it. The reason is that pasting is rough; a wee bit of editing is always required to make the pasted block look just right.

✔ After a block has been cut and moved, you can paste it into the document a second time. This procedure is explained in the section "Pasting a previously cut or copied block," later in this chapter.

Here are the quick steps for moving a block in WordPerfect:

1. Mark the block.

2. Press Ctrl-F4, B, M.

3. Move the cursor to where you want to insert the block.

4. Press Enter.

Copying, cutting, and pasting fast with the Move command

When a block isn't marked on the screen, you can use the Move command, Ctrl-F4, to quickly move a line, paragraph, or page. This method can be very handy and is less time-consuming than going through the rigmarole of marking, cutting, and pasting a block:

A weird WordPerfect shortcut that may come in handy

Cutting a block and pasting it can be easier than you think — but only if you have the special 101-key Enhanced Keyboard. To cut and paste a block with this keyboard, follow these steps:

1. Mark the block.

2. Press Ctrl-Delete. This action cuts the block and immediately puts you into paste mode.

3. Locate a new position for the block by using the cursor-control keys.

4. Press Enter to paste.

This quickie technique removes a lot of the bothersome WordPerfect commands and rituals. I like it. But it only works if you have a newer keyboard, which is why I stuffed it off here into a box.

1. **Position the cursor in the middle of the sentence, paragraph, or page you want to copy or cut.**

2. **Press Ctrl-F4 to start the Move command.**

   You see the following at the bottom of the screen:

   ```
   Move: 1 Sentence; 2 Paragraph; 3 Page; 4 Retrieve: 0
   ```

3. **Press 1, 2, or 3, depending on what you want to move or copy.**

   For example, press 2 to move or copy a paragraph.

   The sentence, paragraph, or page is highlighted, and another menu appears:

   ```
   1 Move; 2 Copy; 3 Delete; 4 Append: 0
   ```

4. **Press M to move the block or C to copy the block.**

   If you press M, the block vanishes; if you press C, the block is unhighlighted. Either way, the following prompt appears at the bottom of the screen:

   ```
   Move cursor; press Enter to retrieve
   ```

5. **Move the cursor to the place in the document where you want the block pasted.**

   As with the other block Move and Copy commands, WordPerfect makes room in the document for the pasted block.

6. **Press Enter to paste the block.**

   ✔ Press F1 to cancel this command at any time. However, note that the Undelete key, F1, does not yank back a block you've moved. Refer to the next section, "Pasting a previously cut or copied block," for additional information.

   ✔ When you use the quick Cut or Copy command, you dispense with the block-marking phase, but you're limited to cutting or copying sentences, paragraphs, or pages.

   ✔ A *sentence* is not the same thing as a *line of text*. When you use the quick Cut or Copy command, a sentence starts at the first line of the paragraph or after a period; a sentence ends with a period. All the spaces after the period and up to the start of the next sentence are included in the block.

Pasting a previously cut or copied block

Whenever a block of text is cut or copied, WordPerfect remembers it. You can yank that block back into the document at any time — sort of like pasting text again after it has already been pasted. You do this procedure with the Move command, Ctrl-F4. (Don't ask me why. I assume that if a Blorf or Fragus shift key existed on the keyboard, WordPerfect would use it with the function keys, too: Blorf-F4 pastes a block of text. Forget it!)

To paste a previously cut block of text, follow these exciting steps:

1. **Position the cursor at the spot where you want the block of text to be pasted.**

   You should always do this step first. The block appears right at the cursor's position, just as if you typed it in yourself.

2. **Press Ctrl-F4 to start the Move command.**

   You see the following displayed at the bottom of the screen:

   ```
   Move: 1 Sentence; 2 Paragraph; 3 Page; 4 Retrieve: 0
   ```

   Ten bonus points if you recognize this prompt from the preceding section! But, instead of pressing 1, 2, or 3, you want 4 or R for the Retrieve option.

3. **Press R to retrieve the block.**

   You see another prompt at the bottom of the screen:

   ```
   Retrieve: 1 Block; 2 Tabular Column; 3 Rectangle: 0
   ```

4. **Press B to get back the block.**

   Zap. There is the block, back on the screen.

   ✔ If nothing has yet been copied or cut with the other block commands, nothing can be pasted with this command. Duh.

   ✔ WordPerfect has a small brain. It only remembers the last cut or copied block. Anything cut or copied before that is gone, gone, gone.

   ✔ Here's yet another ungulate fact: Cows must eruct two liters of gas an hour, or they bloat and die. This is caused by the fermentation process that takes place in their rumens. (You'd be the same way if you had to eat grass.)

Here are the quick steps for retrieving a previously copied or cut block in WordPerfect:

1. Position the cursor where you want the block pasted.

2. Press Ctrl-F4, R, B.

Deleting a block

Two ways are available for deleting a block: the complex way and the easy way. What say we do it the easy way, huh? Follow these steps:

1. Mark the block.

Position the cursor at the start of the block. Press Alt-F4 to turn on block-marking mode. Move the cursor to the end of the block.

2. Press the Backspace key.

You see the following prompt:

```
Delete Block? No (Yes)
```

3. Press Y to delete the block.

No problemo.

✔ You also can press the Delete key to delete the block.

✔ Additional information on marking a block is covered in the first part of this chapter.

✔ When you delete a block with the Delete or Backspace key, you can recover it by using the Undelete key, F1. This feature is what makes deleting a block different from cutting and pasting a block.

✔ Chapter 4 explores the interesting subject of deleting and destroying text. Look there to quench your destructive thirsts.

The hard way to delete a block, if you care to read it

Deleting a block with the Backspace or Delete key seems simple, right? And would you expect WordPerfect to leave things simple? Of course not. So you have an alternative: a more complex and devious way to delete a block. We're not talking straightforward information here:

1. Mark the block.

2. Press Ctrl-F4, the multipurpose do-anything-with-a-block key combination.

3. Shake your head. Mutter to yourself, "Why didn't I just press the Backspace key?"

4. Press B for Block.

5. Press D for Delete. The block is gone.

This method avoids the `Delete Block?` prompt and goes ahead to obliterate the block you marked. But who wants to commit all this to memory? Sheesh.

Undeleting a block

This task is simple. Suppose that you delete a block and — oops! — you didn't mean to. The handy F1 key comes to the rescue. Refer to the discussion of undeleting text in Chapter 4 for details.

Formatting a block

After you rope off a section of text as a block, you can format the text and characters as a single unit. Formatting is covered in detail in Part II of this book. So, instead of repeating the details, I'll list the various things you can do to a block for formatting:

1. You can boldface the text, underline it, or change the font with the Font command, Ctrl-F8. This command enables you to alter the text's size and appearance.

2. You can change the position of the block by centering it or right-justifying it. Centering is done with the Shift-F6 command; Alt-F6 is the Flush Right command.

3. You can convert text in the block between uppercase and lowercase letters by using the Switch command, Shift-F3.

✔ To make any of these changes on a block of text, you must first mark the block. Then select the proper formatting command. The formatting command affects only the text roped off in the block.

✔ Be aware that some of the function keys operate differently when a block is marked. I agree that this is weird, but WordPerfect gears its commands toward blocks when that blinking Block on message is on the screen.

✔ Information about changing the text style, boldfacing, underlining, italicizing, and all that is offered in Chapter 8. Information on shifting between uppercase and lowercase is presented in the same chapter.

✔ Changing the position of a block — its justification — is covered in Chapter 9.

Spell-checking a block

If you want to spell-check a small or irregularly sized part of a document, you can block it off and then use WordPerfect's Spell command. Using this method is a lot quicker than going through the pain of using the Spell command on the full document.

To see whether your spelling is up to snuff, follow these steps:

1. **Mark the block.**

   Move the cursor to the start of the block. Press Alt-F4 to begin the block-marking process. Move the cursor to the end of the block.

   Note: The highlighted area marked by the block is the only part of the document that will be spell-checked.

2. **Press Ctrl-F2 to start the Spell command.**

   WordPerfect compares all the words in the block with its internal dictionary. If a misspelled or unrecognized word is found, it is highlighted and you have the chance to correct or edit it.

   When the spellcheck is completed, WordPerfect displays summary information at the bottom of the screen:

   ```
   Word count: xxx   Press any key to continue
   ```

3. **Press Enter to continue working with the document.**

✔ Chapter 7 covers WordPerfect's spell checker in glorious detail. Refer to that chapter for additional information on changing or correcting your typos.

✔ Marking a block and pressing Ctrl-F2 not only checks the spelling in the block but also provides a count of the number of words in the block. You can go ahead and get excited if this is a feature you've been craving.

✔ For checking only a few words, it's quicker to activate the Spell command and press W to check one word at a time. Refer to the discussion of spell-checking one word in Chapter 7 for more information.

Searching and replacing in a block

You cannot search for text in a marked block, but you can use WordPerfect's Replace command in a block. When a block is defined, Replace searches for and replaces text only in the marked block. The rest of the document is unaffected.

A full description of the Replace command is offered in Chapter 5. I'm too lazy to rewrite all that stuff here.

Printing a block

WordPerfect's Print command only enables you to print one page, several pages, or an entire document at once. If you only want to print a small section of text, you must first mark it as a block and then print it. Here's the secret:

1. **Make sure that the printer is turned on and ready to print.**

   Refer to Chapter 12 for additional information.

2. **Mark the block of text you want to print.**

   Move the cursor to the start of the block, under the first character you want to print; press Alt-F4 to turn on block-marking mode; and move the cursor to the end of the block.

3. **Press Shift-F7 to start the Print command.**

   You see the following at the bottom of the screen:

   ```
   Print block? No (Yes)
   ```

4. **Press Y to print the block.**

   In a few moments, you see the hard copy sputtering out of the printer.

   ✔ You can find additional information on marking a block of text in the first part of this chapter.

   ✔ The block you print appears on the page in exactly the same location and position — and with any headers or footers — as it would if you printed the whole document, which explains why it takes longer to print a block located at the end of a document than at the beginning.

   ✔ The full subject of printing is covered in Chapter 12. Refer to that chapter for information on printing options and setting up the printer.

Saving a block to disk

With WordPerfect, you can mark a block of text and then save that block to disk. The block isn't deleted from the document; its contents are just put into another WordPerfect document file on disk. This feature can be really handy for saving stuff you want to delete but may need later. The procedure follows:

1. **Start by marking the block.**

   Move the cursor to the start of the block, press Alt-F4 to activate block-marking mode, and move the cursor to the end of the block.

2. **Press F10 to start the Save command.**

   You see the following prompt at the bottom of the screen:

   ```
   Block name:
   ```

3. Type a filename for the block.

This filename must be an acceptable filename: Use only letters and numbers and keep the filename from one to eight characters long.

4. Press Enter.

A few grinds of the disk drive later, the block is saved to disk.

✔ The block is saved as a WordPerfect document file, complete with formatting information and such. It's not an ASCII file or a text file (just in case you were wondering).

✔ A block is not deleted when you save it to disk.

✔ You must enter a proper filename for the block. Information on naming a file can be found in Chapter 14.

✔ If the file to which you're saving the block already exists, you see the prompt `Replace filename? No (Yes)` at the bottom of the screen. Press N. If you press Y, you overwrite the file already on disk, which is probably not what you want to do.

✔ To load a block from disk into memory, use the Retrieve command, Shift-F10. This command is covered in Chapter 13 in the section about loading one document into another document.

You don't have to read this stuff on appending a block to a disk file

Sometimes you may want to write several blocks of stuff to the same file. If you use the mark-block-F10 technique described in the "Saving a block to disk" section, you can't do that. Each new file overwrites the existing file and you're stuck. However, an Append command is available, hidden in the — can you guess? can you guess? — Move command, which is Ctrl-F4. (If that key combination isn't a can of worms . . . .)

To append a block of text to an existing WordPerfect document file on disk, follow these steps:

1. Mark the block.

2. Press Ctrl-F4 to start the Move command.

3. From the list, select B for Block.

4. Select A for Append.

5. Type the name of the file to which you want to append the block.

6. Press Enter.

These steps stick the current block at the end of the specified file on the disk (which is what *append* means anyhow).

Chapter 7
Getting Along with the Electronic Mrs. Bradshaw

· ·

In This Chapter

▶ Checking your spelling

▶ Checking only one word

▶ Looking up a word in the dictionary

▶ Adding words to the dictionary

▶ Doing a word count

▶ Using the thesaurus

· ·

*E*veryone should have a third-grade teacher like Mrs. Bradshaw. The woman was a goddess in the annals of proper English, pronunciation, and, of course, spelling. Nothing pleases an eight-year-old more than a smile from Mrs. Bradshaw: "Very good, Danny. There is no *e* at the end of *potato.*" The woman could probably correct the Queen.

What ever happened to Mrs. Bradshaw? The folks at WordPerfect somehow scooped out the essence of her brain, sliced it thin, and distributed it on the WordPerfect disks. Every copy of WordPerfect comes with a spell checker that's as efficient and knowledgeable as Mrs. Bradshaw (but without the little red check marks). Not only that, but her vast knowledge of the English vocabulary has been included as well: WordPerfect's thesaurus offers alternative word suggestions quicker than Mrs. Bradshaw could disapprovingly frown over the misuse of the word *boner.*

Checking Your Spelling

One of the miracles of modern word processing is that the computer knows English spelling better than you do. Thank goodness. I really don't know how to spell. Not at all. The rules are obtuse and meaningless. There are too many exceptions. With WordPerfect, you don't have to worry about being accurate. Just be close, and the Spell command does the rest.

To check the spelling of words in a document, press Ctrl-F2, the Spell command key combination. Follow these steps:

1. Press Ctrl-F2.

The following menu appears at the bottom of the screen:

```
Check: 1 Word; 2 Page; 3 Document; 4 New Sup. Dictionary; 5 Look-up; 6 Count: 0
```

2. Press 3 to check the spelling of all the words in the document.

You don't have to be at the top of the document; WordPerfect automatically moves you there to start testing the spelling of each word.

Or, if you want to check the spelling of words on a single page, press 2 (Page) at this menu.

The screen splits in two.

WordPerfect displays the document in the top part of the screen as it compares each word in the document against the words in its dictionary. The split screen is shown in Figure 7-1.

```
of it.
      Just then they smelled smoke.  Judy said, "Are you wearing
your  inflamable  underwear?"  She recalled that steamy August
night they spent in the asbestos factory.
      Steve looked down, still embarrassed by her earlier comment
                                        Doc 1 Pg 2 Ln 2" Pos 1.5"
{    ▲    ▲    ▲    ▲    ▲    ▲    ▲    ▲    ▲    ▲    ▲    ▲    }    ▲
    A. inflammable          B. inflatable




Not Found: 1 Skip Once; 2 Skip; 3 Add; 4 Edit; 5 Look Up; 6 Ignore Numbers: 0
```

Figure 7-1:
Spell-checking
a document.

Any misspelled or unknown words appear highlighted (shown in reverse text). Alternative words, correctly spelled, appear in the bottom part of the screen.

Also at the bottom of the screen is this menu:

```
Not Found: 1 Skip Once; 2 Skip; 3 Add; 4 Edit; 5 Look Up; 6 Ignore Numbers: 0
```

3. **Read the highlighted word in context in the top window and then look for the properly spelled word in the bottom window.**

4. **Press the letter associated with the properly spelled word (A through Z).**

   Note that if more choices are available, you see the prompt `Press Enter for more words`; press Enter to see a new batch of suggested corrections.

   If the word is misspelled but you don't mind, press 1 (Skip Once).

   This action skips over the word and moves the program on to the next misspelling.

   If you don't want WordPerfect to stop when it encounters that misspelled word again, press 2 (Skip).

   This action directs WordPerfect to ignore that word whenever it's found in the rest of the document.

   If the word is spelled correctly and WordPerfect doesn't know it, press 3 (Add) to add it to your personal dictionary.

   If you know how to quickly correct the spelling by yourself, press 4 (Edit).

   This option enables you to edit the highlighted word on the screen. Use the left- and right-arrow keys, and Backspace and Delete, to help you edit. Press F7 (Exit) when you're done editing (a message to this effect appears at the bottom of the screen).

   After replacing a misspelled word, WordPerfect hunts down the next suspect word.

5. **Repeat steps 3 and 4 for every misspelled word.**

   Wordperfect continues in this manner until the end of the document.

   When the spell check is complete, WordPerfect displays a total word count for the document. An example follows:

```
Word count: 5484   Press any key to continue
```

6. **Press Enter and you're done.**

✔ To check the spelling of only one word — which does come in handy — refer to "Checking only one word," later in this chapter.

✔ To check the spelling of a paragraph or an irregularly shaped block of text, refer to the discussion on spell-checking a block in Chapter 6.

✔ To cancel the Spell command, press F1. You may need to press F1 a second (or even a third) time to get rid of the Spell menu at the bottom of the screen.

✔ To return to the position in the document from which you started the spell check, press Ctrl-Home, Ctrl-Home.

✔ If you just want to see the total word count, refer to "Doing a Word Count," later in this chapter.

✔ The WordPerfect dictionary is not a substitute for a real dictionary. Only in a real dictionary can you look up the meaning of a word, which tells you whether you're using the proper word in the proper context. No computer writer works with an electronic dictionary alone; usually a good, thick Webster's dictionary is sitting right within arm's length.

✔ WordPerfect assumes that any word with a number in it is misspelled. Press 6 (Ignore Numbers) at the Spell menu if this situation happens and starts to bug you. Pressing 6 shuts off number checking. (I press 6 all the time — especially in this book where every function key is considered a misspelling by WordPerfect.)

✔ If you encounter a word that WordPerfect doesn't recognize but that is spelled correctly, press 3 (Add). This option adds the word to your personal dictionary. WordPerfect accepts that word as spelled correctly from here on out. The Add option differs from the Skip options, which only work until the spell check is complete. Refer to "Adding words to the dictionary," later in this chapter.

✔ If two identical words are found in a row, WordPerfect highlights them as a double word. Error, error! The Double Word menu appears at the bottom of the screen; from it, you can press keys to tell WordPerfect how to treat the duplicate word: Press 1 or 2 to ignore the double word, press 3 to delete the second word, press 4 to edit, and press 5 to disable the double-word checking feature (my advice is that leaving it on is a good idea).

✔ My, but this is a long list.

✔ The Spell command also locates words with weird capitalization — for example, *BOner.* You see the Irregular Case menu at the bottom of the screen: Press 1 or 2 to ignore the weird word, press 3 to replace it with a word that's capitalized properly, press 4 to edit the word, or press 5 to disable the weird-word feature. In the computer industry, where weird capitalizations abound, this disable feature is a boon to productivity.

✔ Here are the keys you press to spell-check a document:

Ctrl-F2, 3

✔ The WordPerfect dictionary is good but definitely not as good as Mrs. Bradshaw. For one thing, it doesn't check your words in context. For example, *your* and *you're* are both correct spellings as far as WordPerfect is concerned, but you may be using them improperly. The same thing goes for *its* and *it's*. For that kind of in-context checking, you need something called a *grammar checker,* which doesn't come with WordPerfect but is available as a separate product. Go visit a software store for more details.

✔ *Spell* here refers to creating words by using the accepted pattern of letters. It has nothing to do with magic. Many people assume that a spell checker instantly makes their document better. Wrong! You need to read what you write, edit, look, and read again. Pressing Ctrl-F2 doesn't fix things up other than finding rotten words and offering suggested replacements.

Checking only one word

You don't have to spell-check an entire document when all you want to check is one word. Actually, this is a great way to mentally deal with English spelling: Go ahead and spell the word the way you think it *should* be spelled. Then check only that word. WordPerfect looks up the accurate, wretched English spelling, and you're on your way. And the cool part is that you don't need to learn a thing!

To check the spelling of a single, suspect word, do the following:

1. **Put the cursor somewhere on the word or just before it.**

2. **Press Ctrl-F2 to start the Spell command.**

3. **Press W to select the Word option from the menu at the bottom of the screen.**

   You only want to proof one word.

   WordPerfect checks that word. If it's OK (and the way I spell, the odds are 50-50), the cursor jumps to the next word and you're done. If it's not OK, you see a half-screenful of possible alternative spellings and suggestions.

4. **Select a word from the suggested spellings and press the letter by that word.**

   WordPerfect replaces the word you thought was correctly spelled with its proper and nonintuitive English spelling.

If you're in the mood — or if you have a terrible parade of mangled and misspelled words — continue to press W to spell-check the next word. Press F1 to cancel the single-word spell-check feature.

- ✔ Refer to the first section in this chapter for additional information on working WordPerfect's Spell feature.
- ✔ Single-word checking is often a good way to immediately tackle a word you know is hopelessly wrong. Of course, my philosophy (or *filosofy*) is to spell any old which way and then run the spell checker for the whole document to catch everything at once.

Looking up a word in the dictionary

A handy feature of the WordPerfect spell checker is its Look-up command. OK, it isn't handy; it's more curious. The Look-up command enables you to find a word in the dictionary that you're thinking of but may not know how to spell. To use this command, follow these steps:

1. **Press Ctrl-F2.**

2. **From the list at the bottom of the screen, press 5 (Look-up).**

   The screen splits in half; the bottom half is blank except for the following prompt:

   ```
   Word or word pattern:
   ```

3. **Type a word you want to look up in the dictionary.**

   If you don't know how the letters go, replace them with an asterisk. Or just type a similar word. The examples in Table 7-1 explain how everything works.

- ✔ WordPerfect cannot look up a specific word in a document; you must directly type the word at the `Word or word pattern` prompt. I know, it sounds stupid. What do you expect?

- ✔ The word you find with the Look-up command cannot be pasted into the document. However, if you start the spell checker for a misspelled word by pressing Ctrl-F2 and then press 1 (Word) at the first Check menu, you can press 5 (Look Up) from the Not Found menu and then replace the misspelled word in the document with a word found by this version of the Look Up command. (Notice the difference in hyphenation and capitalization between these two commands: Look-up and Look Up.) This is a convoluted way of doing things, but it works.

Table 7-1	Spell Checker Look-Up Examples
Example	*Explanation*
dan	This entry displays the word *dan* plus all the words that look, sound, or are spelled similarly. (It works with any name; try it with yours.)
bonnet	This entry displays such interesting words as *bayonet, beaned, buoyant,* and *boned.*
rec*	This entry displays all the words in the dictionary that start with *rec.*
*ing	This entry displays all the words in the dictionary that end with *ing.* It comes in handy for budding poets.
s*itis	This entry displays all the words in the dictionary that start with *s* and end with *itis* — lots of medical terms.

Adding words to the dictionary

There are common words that don't appear in WordPerfect's dictionary — *Gookin,* for example. Perhaps your last name is as unique as mine, or maybe your first name, city, business name, and so on, are all spelled correctly yet unknown to WordPerfect. Therefore, each time you spell-check a document, the spell checker comes up with alternative suggestions for those words. Two options are available for avoiding this tautological conundrum.

The first, and more stupid, option is to press 2 (Skip) when the spell checker finds the word. WordPerfect ignores that word during this spell-check run, but the next time you spell-check the document, you have to do the same thing. Dumb, dumb, dumb.

The second, and wise, option is to add said word to your *supplemental dictionary.* This dictionary is a list of words that WordPerfect skips every time you run the spell checker because you've told it that these words are all OK. Here's how to add words to your supplemental dictionary:

1. **Start the spell checker as you normally do.**

   Refer to the first section of this chapter for the persnickety details.

   Lo, you stumble across a word unbeknownst to WordPerfect yet beknownst to you.

2. **The word is spelled just fine, so press 3 (Add) at the Not Found menu at the bottom of the screen.**

   That action stuffs the word into the supplemental dictionary, and you'll never have to mess with it again.

- ✔ After a word is in the supplemental dictionary, WordPerfect knows and recognizes it like it does the words that come in the real dictionary — the one they made from Mrs. Bradshaw's brain.

- ✔ Be careful when you decide to add a word to the supplemental dictionary. Make sure that you don't press 3 when you really mean to press 2. Because . . .

- ✔ No way is available to unadd a word from the dictionary, which is something you may want to do if you commit a flub and inadvertently put a seriously misspelled word into the dictionary. (I once added *fo* to the dictionary and spent three weeks in the WordPerfect penalty box — and that's in Utah of all places!) You actually *can* get the word out again, as covered in the nearby technical sidebar (optional reading).

- ✔ You can actually maintain several supplemental dictionaries on disk. To select or create a new dictionary, press Ctrl-F2 and choose option 4 (New Sup. Dictionary). Type the filename of the supplemental dictionary you want to use. If it exists, WordPerfect uses it for the spell-check process. If the file doesn't exist, WordPerfect creates it.

No need to bother with this trivial drivel on the supplemental dictionary

The supplemental dictionary is actually a WordPerfect document on disk. It contains, in alphabetic order, all the words you added to the dictionary. And, as a special bonus, you can edit the list, removing any deleterious words you may have added.

The filename for the standard WordPerfect supplemental dictionary is WP{WP}US.SUP — an ugly filename, no? It's actually a WordPerfect document that you can edit by using WordPerfect. The file can be found in the WordPerfect directory or sometimes in the SPELL or SPELLER subdirectory. (Refer to Chapter 14 for information on how to locate the WordPerfect directory.)

The reason you want to edit this file is to remove extra words from the supplemental dictionary. For example, suppose that you accidentally stuck *fo* in the dictionary. Only by editing the WP{WP}US.SUP file can you get *fo* out of there.

My advice is to make a duplicate copy of the WP{WP}US.SUP file before you edit it. That way, if the edited copy gets fouled up, you can restore the duplicate. Needless to say, this procedure isn't something for the timid.

Doing a Word Count

The spell checker has an interesting feature that counts the number of words in a document. This feature comes in handy for free-lance writers who are paid by the word or told to produce a document with a specific word length. For everyone else, it's a good way to gauge how big a document is getting because margins, font sizes, and spacing can affect page count.

To see how many words are in a document, follow these steps:

1. **Press Ctrl-F2 to start the Spell command.**

2. **From the list of options displayed at the bottom of the screen, press 6 (Count).**

   You see `* Please wait *` displayed.

   WordPerfect rapidly counts all the words in the document, from top to bottom. When it's done, WordPerfect displays the total in the following format:

   ```
   Word count: xxx    Press any key to continue
   ```

   The *xxx* is replaced with the total number of words in the document.

3. **Press Enter.**

   The Spell menu reappears.

4. **Press F1 to return to the document.**

   ✔ Performing a word count moves the cursor to the bottom of the document. To return to your previous position, press Ctrl-Home, Ctrl-Home.

   ✔ To get a word count for only a page, a paragraph, or another specific-sized portion of text, first mark the text as a block. Then spell-check the entire block. When the operation is finished, you see the total word count for the block. Refer to the discussion of spell-checking a block in Chapter 6 for the gripping details.

   ✔ A page of single-spaced text runs about 400 words; double-spaced text is about 200. An article in a magazine contains anywhere from 1,500 to 6,000 words. There are about 60,000 words in the typical paperback novel. A larger novel may contain 120,000 to 350,000 words. This book contains about 85,000 words.

Using the Thesaurus

If you think I'm smart enough to have been using all the big words in this chapter, you're grievously mistaken. Witness: *tautological conundrum.* That ain't me talkin'. That's WordPerfect's thesaurus in action. An amazing tool, or astounding utensil, or marvelous implement. You get the idea. The thesaurus helps you find *synonyms,* which are other words that have the same meaning but more weight or more precision.

Here's how to instantly become a master of big, clunky words in English:

1. **Hover the cursor on a simple word, say *big*.**

   Adjectives are best for the thesaurus, but the WordPerfect statistical department tells me that the thesaurus contains more than 120,000 words.

2. **Press Alt-F1 to start the thesaurus.**

   Instantly, the bottom two-thirds of the screen convert into a three-column window. You can still see the original word, highlighted in context, at the top of the screen (see Figure 7-2).

   WordPerfect displays several alternatives for the word. The words are grouped into numbered categories, and each alternative has a letter by it.

3. **To replace the word in the document, press 1 (Replace Word).**

4. **Press the letter next to the new word you want.**

   If the new word you want is in the second or third column, press the right-arrow key to move the letters over to that column; then press 1 (Replace Word) and select the proper letter.

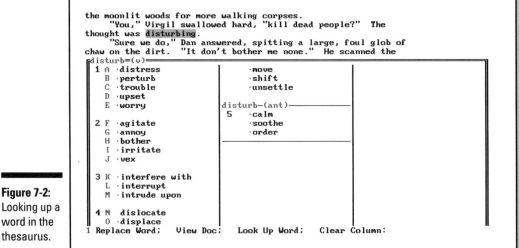

Figure 7-2:
Looking up a word in the thesaurus.

After selecting a word, you return to the document. If you don't find an appropriate word, press F1 to cancel the thesaurus and return to the document.

✔ A thesaurus is not a colossal, prehistoric beast.

✔ If one of the alternative words is close to what you want but not exactly what you want — and the word has a dot in front of it — press its letter key without first pressing 1 (Replace Word). WordPerfect displays synonyms for that word in the next column. If you find a word you like in the new list, press 1 (Replace Word) and press the letter next to the desired word. (This feature doesn't work unless the word has a dot in front of it.)

✔ If no synonyms are available for the word you selected, the thesaurus displays Word not found. Then you see a Word: prompt. Type a new, similar word or press F1 twice to get back to the document.

✔ To look up a related word, press that word's letter key. To look up a new word, press 3 (Look Up Word) and, at the prompt, type the word to look up.

✔ If the columns get junky, you can press 4 (Clear Column) to remove some definitions.

✔ Use the down-arrow key to see some of the longer definitions displayed.

✔ Press 1 and then the letter key to replace a word. If you just press the letter key, and that word has a dot next to it, you see additional definitions for that word.

✔ After inserting a new word, you may need to do a bit of editing: Add *ed* or *ing* to the word, replace *a* with *an* — that kind of thing. Usually, a bit of editing is required whenever you replace one word with another.

Part II
Making Your Prose Look Less Ugly

The 5th Wave   By Rich Tennant

"NOPE - I'D BETTER WAIT 'TIL ALL MY FONTS ARE WORKING. A HATE LETTER JUST DOESN'T WORK IN *Filigree Flowerbox Extended*."

In this part...

Formatting is what makes WordPerfect documents shine. It's what makes you boast when you show your labors to Microsoft Word users and they snivel, "Gosh, how'd you get it to print all on one page?" Few other things in life can make you swell with such pride.

Yet formatting isn't without its dark side. It involves a lot of invisible stuff and a lot of secret things that you really don't see on the screen. This part describes the intricacies of how formatting works in WordPerfect and how to make your documents look oh so purty.

Chapter 8
Formatting Characters

● ●

In This Chapter

▶ Making text boldfaced

▶ Making text underlined

▶ Making text italicized

▶ Affecting text attributes

▶ Affecting text size

▶ Making text normal

▶ Changing the font

▶ Converting uppercase and lowercase letters

▶ Inserting oddball characters

● ●

*T*he most basic of all things you can format in a document is the character. *Characters* include letters, words, text in paragraphs, and weird uncle Lloyd who trims the hair in his ears with a butane lighter. You can format characters to be boldfaced, underlined, italicized, little, big, or in different fonts. WordPerfect gives you a lot of control, but there are pitfalls: First, don't expect to see your text with all these bells and whistles on the screen. Second — a disappointment you should be used to by now — there is no one-key approach to formatting characters.

Applying Character Attributes

When you change the way a character looks, you apply an *attribute* to that character. You can apply all kinds of character attributes to text in WordPerfect; you can boldface text, underline it, italicize it, change the text size, return text to "normal," and apply some less common attributes like shadow, strikeout, small caps, double underline, outline, and redline. Most of these attributes will have their places in your documents, and you're probably eager to start changing the boring old computer-looking text into text with zest and zing.

Making text boldfaced

Bold

To emphasize a word, you make it boldfaced. Boldfaced text is, well, bold. It's heavy. It carries a lot of weight, stands out on the page, speaks its mind at public meetings, wears a cowboy hat — you know the type.

To make your text stand out, follow these steps:

1. Press the F6 key.

This action turns on the boldface character format.

2. Type the word or characters you want boldfaced.

The next text appears on the screen in a bold color — usually brighter than the other characters. Also, the numbers after the Pos indicator (in the lower right corner of the screen) take on the bold color as well.

3. Press the F6 key again to turn off the boldface character format.

That takes care of formatting new text as boldface. But, if you have text already on the screen, and you want to make it boldfaced, you have to block it first. Follow these steps:

1. Mark the block of text you want boldfaced.

Move the cursor to the start of the block, press Alt-F4 to turn on block-marking mode, and move the cursor to the end of the block. The block appears highlighted on the screen.

2. Press the F6 key.

This action makes all text in the block boldfaced, and the block highlighting disappears.

TIP

A quick way to rehighlight a block

If you're applying multiple character formats to the same block, here's a handy tip you can use to rehighlight that block:

After you issue a character-formatting command, the block is unhighlighted. Don't despair and don't type any other keys before you . . .

1. Press Alt-F4. This action reactivates block-marking mode.

2. Press Ctrl-Home, Ctrl-Home (The Go To command twice). The same block is rehighlighted on the screen. It's magic!

3. Issue the next character-formatting command to apply that format to the text in the block.

This tip works best if you press Alt-F4, Ctrl-Home, Ctrl-Home right after you finish with the first character-formatting command.

🖝 These steps apply to the use of all character formats. Use these basic steps as you create new text and as you format blocks of existing text. The only difference in the steps is the command key you press to apply a specific format. The other keys you need to press in order to apply other formats are covered in the rest of this chapter.

🖝 You're lucky: Boldfaced text shows up brighter on the screen. That's acceptable. Other character formats don't show up that way. Instead, on color monitors, expect to see red, blue, orange, grape, and other flavors of screen colors to represent different text formats and attributes. It can drive you nuts! (Also refer to Chapter 16.)

🖝 You can mix and match character formats; text can be boldfaced *and* underlined or boldfaced *and* italic. To do so, you need to press the proper keys to turn on those formats before typing the text. Yes, this means that you have to issue the WordPerfect character-formatting commands *before* you type the text. It's a hassle, but everyone has to do it that way.

🖝 Refer to the section on marking a block in Chapter 6.

🖝 To remove the boldface character format from the text, refer to the section on undoing character formatting in Chapter 11.

Making text underlined

| Underline |

Underlined text just isn't as popular as it used to be. Instead, people now use italicized text for subtle emphasis. Still, underlined text does have its place. I just don't know where, or I'd come up with a cheesy example here.

To underline your text, follow these steps:

1. Press the F8 key.

This action turns on the underline character format.

2. Type the text you want underlined.

Here's the weird part: The text you see on a color monitor takes on a specific color. You don't see the text actually underlined. (However, you *do* see underlined text on a monochrome monitor. And you thought they were cheap!) For the standard configuration of WordPerfect, underlined text shows up on the screen as inverse blue characters on a white background.

3. Press the F8 key again to turn off underlining.

If you already have text on the screen and want it underlined, you must mark the text as a block and then press the F8 key. Here are the steps to take:

1. **Mark the block of text you want to underline.**

    Position the cursor at the start of the block, press Alt-F4 to activate block-marking mode, and move the cursor to the end of the block. The block appears highlighted on the screen.

2. **Press the F8 key.**

    This action underlines the entire block, turning it into that special under-line color. The highlighted block disappears.

✔ Blue text on a white background means underline? Get out of here!

✔ On monochrome monitors, you actually get to see underlined text on the screen. Swell with pride. On color monitors, underlined text shows up as a different color. Turn to Chapter 16 to discover some tricks for changing the color or even — gasp! — producing underlined text on a color monitor.

✔ To add another character format to the same text, you must issue the proper character-formatting commands *before* you type. Or, if you're ap-plying text formats to a block, re-mark the block and issue another text-formatting command. See the sidebar about rehighlighting blocks for a nifty shortcut.

✔ Chapter 6 contains a section on marking blocks, which tells you more about marking blocks.

✔ To remove the underline text format, read the section about undoing char-acter formatting in Chapter 11.

Making text italicized

Italicized

Replacing underline as the preferred text-emphasis format is italics. I'm not em-barrassed to use italics to emphasize, to highlight a title, or just because it looks so much better than shabby underlined text. It's light and wispy, poetic and free. Underlining is what the Department of Motor Vehicles does when it feels creative.

To italicize your text, follow these steps:

1. **Press the Ctrl-F8 key combination.**

    This is the Font key combination. You see the Font menu displayed at the bottom of the screen:

```
1 Size; 2 Appearance; 3 Normal; 4 Base Font; 5 Print Color: 0
```

2. Press A (Appearance).

You see the Appearance menu displayed:

```
1 Bold 2 Undln 3 Dbl Und 4 Italc 5 Outln 6 Shadw 7 Sm Cap 8 Redln 9 Stkout: 0
```

Behold! This menu lists all the character-appearance formats supported by WordPerfect. Frustrating how they're abbreviated, eh?

3. Press I (Italc).

Italc is how you spell *italic* when the little *i* key is broken. This action activates the italic character format.

4. Type away.

The text you type prints in italics. On the screen, you see a horridly bizarre color, which the folks at WordPerfect's Color and Attribute Center for Disease Studies have selected as best representing italics on the screen: bright yellow. Ugh.

Whatever color is selected (I have no idea how it shows up on a monochrome screen), the Pos indicator in the lower right corner of the screen takes on that same color. This indicator means that you're in italics-typing mode.

5. To turn off italics-typing mode, press the right-arrow key once.

This is a shortcut. Technically, you're supposed to press Ctrl-F8, A, I again to switch off italics. But, hey, pressing the right-arrow key once does the job a lot easier.

If the text you want to italicize is already on the screen, you must mark it as a block and then change its character format. Follow these steps:

1. Mark the block of text you want to italicize.

Move the cursor to the start of the block, press Alt-F4 to switch on block-marking mode, and move the cursor to the end of the block. The block appears highlighted on the screen.

2. Press Ctrl-F8, then A, and then I.

This action italicizes the block, displaying it in the garish yellow color (or the italics *color du jour* for your monitor).

✔ Think over and over to yourself, "Bright yellow is italics, bright yellow is italics . . . ." Actually, you can make it any color you want or even see the text in true italics on some monitors. Refer to Chapter 16 for more information.

✔ If you want to double-up on a character font — say, make something italics *and* boldface — press both character-formatting keys before you type the text. If you're applying the formats to a block, re-mark the block and issue the second formatting command. Refer to the sidebar earlier in this chapter for a fun shortcut.

> ✔ Refer to the discussion about marking blocks in Chapter 6 for more information on marking blocks.
>
> ✔ To remove the italics format from the text, refer to the section about undoing character formatting in Chapter 11.

Here are the keys to press to activate the italics text format:

Ctrl-F8, A, 4

Use this same key sequence to turn italics off and to mark a block as italic text.

Affecting text attributes

The most common character formats are boldface, underline, and italics. Those formats were described in the preceding sections. WordPerfect has six other text formats, not so common, which work through the Ctrl-F8 key combination to format characters or blocks of text. All the text formats are listed in Table 8-1, along with examples of what they look like and their key commands.

Table 8-1	Text Formats, Examples, and Commands	
Character Format	*Sample Text*	*Key Command*
Boldface	Don't **bleed** on the rug!	Ctrl-F8, A, 1
Underline	Don't <u>bleed</u> on the rug!	Ctrl-F8, A, 2
Double Underline	Don't bleed on the rug!	Ctrl-F8, A, 3
Italics	Don't *bleed* on the rug!	Ctrl-F8, A, 4
Outline	Don't bleed on the rug!	Ctrl-F8, A, 5
Shadow	Don't bleed on the rug!	Ctrl-F8, A, 6
Small Caps	Don't BLEED on the rug!	Ctrl-F8, A, 7
Redline	Don't ~~bleed~~ on the rug!	Ctrl-F8, A, 8
Strikeout	Don't ~~bleed~~ on the rug!	Ctrl-F8, A, 9

Bold
Underline
Double Underline
Italicized
Outline
Shadow
Small Caps
Redline
Strikeout

✔ To apply one of these weird text formats to characters as you type or to a block of already typed text, refer to "Making text italicized," earlier in this chapter, and substitute the appropriate key-command number from Table 8-1. For example, to make text italicized, you press Ctrl-F8, 4; to put text in small caps, you press Ctrl-F8, 7.

✔ Don't expect the printer to handle all these attributes. Small caps usually comes out OK. Strikeout works on most printers. But the redline format has a red line through it, which you can't get on most black-and-white printers (duh). And, on my printer, I can get the shadow format but not the outline format.

✔ Removal of these character formats is covered in Chapter 11.

Affecting text size

Super ^script

Fine Small Normal Large Very Large Extra Large

Sub ₛ꜀ᵣᵢₚₜ

Attributes — boldface, italics, underline, and so on — are only some of the character formats you can apply in WordPerfect. The others deal with the text size. With text-size formatting commands, you can make your text superscript, subscript, teensy-weensy, or very large.

To change the size of text as you type, follow these steps:

1. Press the Font key combination, Ctrl-F8.

You see the following menu displayed at the bottom of the screen:

```
1 Size; 2 Appearance; 3 Normal; 4 Base Font; 5 Print Color: 0
```

2. Press S (Size).

You see the Size menu at the bottom of the screen:

```
1 Suprscpt; 2 Subscpt; 3 Fine; 4 Small; 5 Large; 6 Vry Large; 7 Ext Large: 0
```

The Suprscpt and Subscpt items produce superscript and subscript text. The other items, numbered 3 through 7, change the size of the text. Lucky for us, they're labeled nicely from smallest to largest.

3. Select the size format you want by pressing the appropriate key.

4. Type the text you want in the selected text size.

5. When you're done, press the right-arrow key.

This is a shortcut. The WordPerfect propriety meisters want you to go through steps 1 through 3 again to turn off that attribute. Now you know better.

If you want to apply a size format to text already on the screen, mark the characters as a block and then issue the appropriate formatting command. Follow these steps:

1. **Mark the block of text you want to modify.**

   Position the cursor at the first character in the block, press Alt-F4 to activate block-marking mode, and move the cursor to the last character in the block. The block appears highlighted on the screen.

2. **Press Ctrl-F8, then S, and then the proper size command.**

   The text in the block takes on that size format — and the appropriately garish color.

   ✔ If you think the text colors for underline and italics are weird, they're nothing. WordPerfect has a special color for each of the size attributes. And, if you combine attributes, stand back for a trip to the psychedelic '60s.

   ✔ *Superscript* is text above the line — for example the *10* in 2^{10}. To produce this effect, press Ctrl-F8, S, 1 and then type the text you want in superscript. Alternatively, mark a block of text and press Ctrl-F8, S, 1 to superscript the text in the block.

   ✔ *Subscript* is text below the line — for example, the *2* in H_2O. To subscript text, press Ctrl-F8, S, 2 and then type away. If you mark a block of text and then press Ctrl-F8, S, 2, all the text in the block is subscripted.

   ✔ Refer to the sidebar earlier in this chapter for a handy way to apply several attributes to the same block of text.

   ✔ Removing text attributes is twist-your-arm-off painful. Refer to Chapter 11 for details.

Making text normal

Sometimes you have so many character attributes going you don't know what to press to get back to normal text. This situation can be very frustrating. Fortunately, WordPerfect has lent a tiny ear to your cries for help. You can use the Normal text-formatting command to shut off everything — size and attribute formats — and return text to normal. Here's how:

1. **Press Ctrl-F8 to start the Font command.**

2. **From the menu at the bottom of the screen, press N (Normal).**

   Everything you type from that point on is normal (or at least has the normal attributes).

If you mark a block and then press Ctrl-F8, N, all text in the block is returned to normal. Refer to the discussion on marking blocks in Chapter 6 for more information on marking blocks of text.

You can always keep an eye on the color of the numbers in the Pos indicator to see, more or less, what kind of goofy attributes are being applied. Granted, no one memorizes the colors used to indicate attributes. But, if you see colors splashing around the screen, and you want normal text rather than all of that, use the Normal command: Ctrl-F8, N.

Changing the Font

Text can be boldfaced, italicized, underlined, made big, made little, and on and on. But the text *font* — the basic characteristics of the text you see printed — is controlled by the printer, not by WordPerfect.

Your printer has stuffed inside its brain certain fonts or character sets. WordPerfect selects the basic character set, which usually looks like typewriter output (not too fancy), when it prints a document. You can change the character set, however, at any point in the document, selecting a different font as appropriate. (And I'm not going to tell you what's appropriate; you'll have to guess.)

To switch to a different font, follow these steps:

1. **Press Ctrl-F8.**

   This action displays the Font menu at the bottom of the screen.

2. **Press 4 (Base Font).**

   You see a screenful of font names. The number of fonts you see depends on the capabilities of the printer. Some printers have only a few fonts; others have scores.

3. **Use the arrow keys to select a font from the list.**

   The currently selected font has an asterisk by it.

   Note that fonts can have their own attributes: boldface, italics, and boldface and italics, for example. These attributes are in addition to any character formats you add with WordPerfect. For example, if you select the Times Roman Italic font, the text is italicized even though you don't see green or whatever on the screen.

4. Press Enter to select the font.

For some fonts, you may see a prompt at the bottom of the screen:

```
Point size: xxx
```

The *xxx* indicates the current *point size* — the height of the letters in the font, as measured in points. There's no need for me to explain what *points* are; just know that 12-point text is average; larger numbered point sizes give you larger text.

5. Press Enter to exit the Font screen menu and start using that new font.

Alternatively, you can press F1 (once or twice) to cancel the font change.

✔ A *font* is a character set. For example, Times Roman is a font. Helvetica is a font — one that uses straighter lines than the Times Roman font. This book is printed with the Cheltenham font for body text. The headings are in the Cascade font.

✔ You can switch to an italics, a boldface, a small, or a large font, and the color of the text on the screen does not change. Selecting a new base font is different from selecting a new character format. My advice? Stick to character formats first; then play with the Font command later, when you have time to goof off.

✔ You cannot use the Font command (Ctrl-F8, 4) to change a highlighted block. Instead, move to the start of the block where you want the font to change; press Ctrl-F8, 4; and select the new font. Then move to the end of the block; press Ctrl-F8, 4 again; and select the font you were using before.

✔ To change the font for an entire document, move to the absolute tippy top of the document before pressing Ctrl-F8, 4. Move to the top of the document with the triple-Home command: Home, Home, Home, ↑. After pressing those keys, press Ctrl-F8, 4 to change the font for the entire document.

✔ If you change the font in the middle of a document and want to change it back, use the Font command twice. Press Ctrl-F8, 4 once to select a new font. Then, when you're ready to switch back, press Ctrl-F8, 4 again to change the font back to the original.

Converting Uppercase and Lowercase Letters

Uppercase and lowercase letters aren't considered part of a font, character attribute, or format. Anyway, WordPerfect enables you to switch from all capital letters to all lowercase letters with a fun feature: the Switch Case feature. It can come in handy.

To switch text to all capital letters, follow these steps:

1. Mark the text you want to convert as a block.

Position the cursor at the start of the block, press Alt-F4 to switch on block-marking mode, and move the cursor to the end of the block. The block is highlighted on the screen.

2. Press the Switch Case key combination, Shift-F3.

You see the following menu at the bottom of the screen:

```
1 Uppercase; 2 Lowercase: 0
```

3. Press 1 (Uppercase).

The block highlighting disappears, and the text is converted to all uppercase letters.

To switch your text to all lowercase letters, follow the preceding steps, but press 2 (Lowercase) in Step 3. That action converts the text in the highlighted block to lowercase letters.

✔ The Switch Case key combination, Shift-F3, only works if a block is marked. Otherwise, this key combination sends you off into Document 2. If that happens, press Shift-F3 again to return to Document 1. Also, refer to the section on working on two documents at once in Chapter 13.

✔ Alas, no way is available for you to switch text to initial caps or mixed case. Sniff, sniff.

Inserting Oddball Characters

Look over your keyboard's keys. Yeah, there are the letters of the alphabet, plus numbers, and some weird symbols and such. WordPerfect can display all those characters just fine; you see them on the screen every day. But there are several dozen additional, interesting characters you can display. Some you can see on the screen; others can only print. These are WordPerfect's *oddball characters*.

You insert oddball characters by using the Ctrl-V command. You need to know the character's secret code numbers, which are stored in the WordPerfect manual, but I've included the most popular ones in this book's Appendix A (and on the instant reference card). Here is how you work the Ctrl-V command:

1. **Position the cursor where you want the oddball character to appear.**

2. **Press Ctrl-V.**

   You see the following at the bottom of the screen:

   ```
   Key =
   ```

3. **Type the secret code number.**

   The secret code is two numbers, each hugging a comma. Table 8-2 lists some common and interesting characters you can use.

4. **Press Enter.**

   The oddball character is inserted into the text.

Table 8-2   Some Common and Useful Oddball Characters

Code	Symbol	Name
4,0	•	Dot
4,2	■	Square
4,17	½	One-half
4,18	¼	One-quarter
4,19	¢	Cents
4,23	©	Copyright symbol
4,41	™	Trademark symbol
5,26	☹	Mr. Grumpy

✔ You may not see the oddball character show up on the screen. Instead, you most likely see a small block, which is WordPerfect's way of saying, "I sure wish I could display this character. But, hey, you swallowed bright-yellow text for italics, so you'll probably believe that this little block is a happy face."

✔ There's no need for you to memorize any of the oddball-character secret code numbers. Everyone looks them up.

✔ The first number in the secret code — the one before the comma — represents a special character set. WordPerfect has a dozen character sets, including math symbols, box drawing, Greek, Hebrew, and Cyrillic (Russian) letters. A document named CHARACTR.DOC comes with WordPerfect and contains all the secret codes and their symbols. Load it into WordPerfect and print it to see what the codes look like and whether the printer is capable of printing them all.

No need to read this information if you're just passing by

The Ctrl-V key combination is called the Compose command. Note that it's *Compose* not *compost.* In addition to typing secret code numbers, you can also create special characters by welding two keyboard characters together. This can be fun.

For example, to create the plus-minus sign, ±, do the following:

1. Press Ctrl-V.

2. Type a plus and a minus: + −.

You don't need to press Enter; the plus-minus character automagically appears on the screen.

You can add accents above characters by typing that letter and then the ', `, ~, or ^ key. For example, do the following:

1. Press Ctrl-V.

2. Type n~, the N key and then the tilde.

This action produces the ñ, en-ay, character, which is common in Spanish. Similarly, pressing Ctrl-V and then typing u" produces ü, which makes an oo-ey sound in some languages.

Chapter 9
Formatting Sentences and Paragraphs

- -

In This Chapter

▶ Centering text

▶ Making text flush right

▶ Changing the justification

▶ Changing the line spacing

▶ Working with tabs

▶ Using alignment tabs

▶ Setting the margins

▶ Indenting a paragraph

▶ Double-indenting a paragraph

▶ Using the margin release

▶ Doing a hanging indent

- -

*A*fter you format characters or text, the next biggest things you can format in a document are sentences and paragraphs. This kind of formatting involves the position of text on the page, its margins, lining things up with tabs or indents, and line spacing. This stuff can be done on the fly, but I recommend doing it just before printing (along with page formatting, covered in the next chapter). That way you can pull your hair out while you struggle with spelling and grammar and getting your ideas on paper. Then, when that's perfect and your blood pressure has dropped, you can pull out the rest of your hair while you struggle anew with WordPerfect's line and paragraph formatting. Ugh. Will it never end?

Centering Text

WordPerfect enables you to center either a single line of text or a block of text. And, as a special bonus (probably because the sun was shining in Utah that day), you can see the text centered right on the screen. Glory be!

If you just want to center a single line, follow these steps:

1. **Start on a new line, the line you want to be centered.**

   If the line is already typed on the screen, skip to the second set of directions, following this set.

2. **Press the Center key combination, Shift-F6.**

   The cursor zips to the center of the screen (or thereabouts).

3. **Type the title or heading.**

   Try to limit what you type to one line of text.

4. **Press Enter when you're done.**

   The line you typed is centered.

If you want to center more than a line — say, a paragraph or more — first type the text and then follow these steps, which are the same steps for centering text already in the document:

1. **Mark the text you want to center as a block.**

   Move the cursor to the start of the block, press Alt-F4 to start block-marking mode, and move the cursor to the end of the block. The block is highlighted on the screen.

2. **Press the Center key combination, Shift-F6.**

   You see the following displayed at the lower left corner of the screen:

   ```
   [Just:Center]? No (Yes)
   ```

   Er, I believe that means "center this block?" (I don't think you can get any more cryptic than this message, but at least they remembered the vowels.)

3. **Press Y to center the block.**

   The highlighting disappears, and the block is centered on the screen — and centered on the page when you print the document.

A quick way to rehighlight a block

If you need to apply character formatting to the block you've just centered, here's a quick way to rehighlight the block. Do these steps immediately after centering the block:

1. *Don't move the cursor.*

2. Press Alt-F4 to turn on block-marking mode.

3. Press Ctrl-Home, Ctrl-Home.

The block is rehighlighted. Now you can assign a text attribute to the block: make it boldfaced, bigger, and so on. All that's covered in Chapter 8.

- ✔ The Center command, Shift-F6, only centers one line of text. For anything larger, you must first type the text, mark it as a block, and then center it.

- ✔ If you press Shift-F6 and the title or heading turns out to be longer than a line, don't despair! Keep typing. When you're done, go back and mark the text as a block and then press Shift-F6 to center the block. (Follow the second set of steps.)

- ✔ [Just:Center] refers to the cryptic and secret formatting code WordPerfect hides in the document when you center text. Refer to Chapter 11 for more information on these secret codes.

- ✔ To uncenter a block, refer to the section on undoing paragraph formatting in Chapter 11.

Making Text Flush Right

Oh, I could really have a field day with the title of this section and my potty-mouth mentality. But I'm going to cut my editor some slack here. *Flush right* describes the way text is lined up on the screen. Normally, text is *flush left,* with each line starting even with the left margin. Flush right text is where a line starts even with the right margin. In other words, the text is slammed against the right side of the page — like if you could pick up the paper and jerk it wildly until the text slides over.

You can flush right a single line of text or mark any lump of text as a block and flush it right. If you just want to flush a single line, follow these steps:

1. Position the cursor where you want to type a line flush right.

The cursor is on the same line but still at the left side of the screen. Don't use the spacebar or Tab key to move the cursor; the Flush Right command will move the text in just a second.

If the text you want to flush right is already on the screen, skip to the second set of instructions, following this set.

2. Press the Flush Right key combination, Alt-F6.

The cursor skips over to the right margin, at the right side of the screen.

3. Type the line of text.

The characters push to the left, always staying flush with the right side of the document.

4. Press Enter when you're done.

To flush right more than a single line or to format text you already have in the document, you must first mark it as a block. Follow these steps:

1. Mark the text you want to flush right as a block.

It's best to use the Flush Right command on full paragraphs or sentences only. If you mark an odd section of text, it's going to look darn weird on the screen and print even weirder.

Mark the text by moving the cursor to the start of the block, pressing Alt-F4 to turn on block-marking mode, and moving the cursor to the end of the block.

2. Press the Flush Right key combination, Alt-F6.

You see the following prompt in the lower right corner of the screen:

```
[Just:Right]? No (Yes)
```

No, WordPerfect isn't asking you whether the block is just right. This technical mumbo-jumbo refers to *right justification,* which in English means "do you want to slam this block against the right side of the page?"

3. Press Y to flush away.

The block is lined up on the right side of the page. (No sound effects, please.)

✔ The Flush Right command, Alt-F6, works best when you're only typing one line of text. For anything larger, enter the text first, mark it as a block, and press Alt-F6, as described in the second set of instructions just presented.

✔ If a single line of text gets longer, just keep on typing. After you're done, go back, mark everything you want flush right as a block, and then refer to the second set of instructions for flushing that block to the right.

TIP

Making the date flush right at the top of the document

A neat-o thing to flush right at the top of a document is the date. This setup is the way most people start their letters. To flush right the date at the top of a document, follow these handy steps:

1. Move to the top of the document, to the line where you want to put the date. It must be a blank line.

2. Press the Flush Right key combination, Alt-F6. The cursor zooms over to the right side of the page.

3. Press Shift-F5, 1. The current date is inserted into the document.

You now can continue editing. The current date is proudly flushed right at the top of the page.

TECHNICAL STUFF

✔ [Just:Right] is the name of the hidden WordPerfect formatting code inserted into the document that actually flushes text to the right. Chapter 11 contains all the information you really don't need to read about this. The next section in this chapter goes into detail on the whole concept of justification.

✔ To unflush a block of text, turn to the section on undoing paragraph formatting in Chapter 11.

Changing the Justification

Left Justification

When you want to change the justification from the cursor's current position to the end of the document, follow these steps:

1. Move the cursor to the position in the text where you want the new justification format to take effect.

It's best if this place is at the beginning of a new paragraph or the top of a page. Wherever you choose, the justification from that point down in the document is changed.

Center Justification

2. Press the Format key combination, Shift-F8.

You see a nifty, full-screen menu displayed. Marvel at it for a moment.

3. Press L (Line).

Right Justification

A second, nifty, full-screen menu is displayed — the Format: Line menu. The item you want this time is Justification, the third one down in the list.

Full Justification

4. Press J (Justification).

You see the following menu at the bottom of the screen:

```
Justification: 1 Left; 2 Center; 3 Right; 4 Full: 0
```

5. Press the key associated with the justification you want.

For example, for full justification, press F (Full).

You see the word for the justification you selected (left, right, center, or full) up by the word Justification in the Format: Line menu.

6. Press the Exit key, F7, to return to the document and enjoy your new justification.

✔ If you change the justification with the Shift-F8 key combination, the rest of the document is affected. The new justification takes over from the cursor's position to the end of text or until another justification command is encountered.

✔ To change justification later in the document, repeat these steps after you position the cursor where you want the new justification to start taking place.

✔ You cannot change the justification for a single block of text. If you press Shift-F8 when a block is highlighted, you see the prompt Protect block? I have no idea what that means, but it sure isn't anything to do with justification. Press F1 to make the obnoxious prompt go away.

✔ To change the justification for the entire document, move to the very top *before* you do these steps. Press Home, Home, Home, ↑ to move to the top and then follow these steps.

✔ If you want the new justification to start on a new page, first issue the New Page command by pressing Ctrl-Enter. Then go through these steps to start the new page with the justification you want.

✔ Typographers do not always limit their labels for these different formats to *justification.* They occasionally use the word *ragged* to describe how the text fits. For example, left justification is *ragged right;* right justification is *ragged left.* A *rag top* is a vehicle with a soft top (a convertible), and a *rag bottom* is any child still in diapers.

Here are the quickie keys you press to change justification in a document:

For left justification	Shift-F8, L, J, L, F7
For center justification	Shift-F8, L, J, C, F7
For right justification	Shift-F8, L, J, R, F7
For full justification	Shift-F8, L, J, F, F7

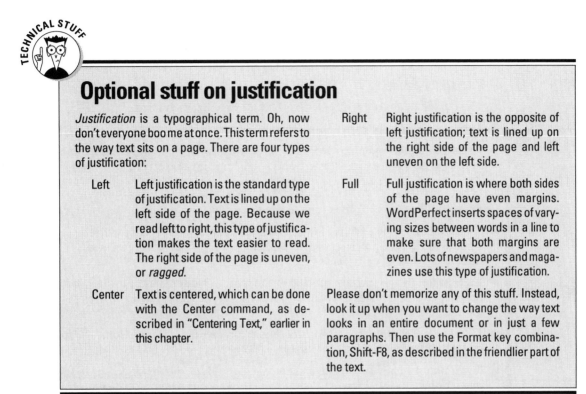

Optional stuff on justification

Justification is a typographical term. Oh, now don't everyone boo me at once. This term refers to the way text sits on a page. There are four types of justification:

Left   Left justification is the standard type of justification. Text is lined up on the left side of the page. Because we read left to right, this type of justification makes the text easier to read. The right side of the page is uneven, or *ragged.*

Center   Text is centered, which can be done with the Center command, as described in "Centering Text," earlier in this chapter.

Right   Right justification is the opposite of left justification; text is lined up on the right side of the page and left uneven on the left side.

Full   Full justification is where both sides of the page have even margins. WordPerfect inserts spaces of varying sizes between words in a line to make sure that both margins are even. Lots of newspapers and magazines use this type of justification.

Please don't memorize any of this stuff. Instead, look it up when you want to change the way text looks in an entire document or in just a few paragraphs. Then use the Format key combination, Shift-F8, as described in the friendlier part of the text.

Changing the Line Spacing

On a typewriter, you change the line spacing with a double or triple whack of the carriage-return bar. Sadly, while whacking the computer twice or thrice may help your attitude, it won't do diddly for the document's line spacing. Instead, you need to use WordPerfect's Line Spacing command, which is nestled in there with the other format commands clinging to the Shift-F8 key combination.

To change the line spacing, follow these steps:

1. **Move the cursor to the spot in the document where you want to change the line spacing.**

   For example, move to the top of the document to change the line spacing for the entire document or move to the beginning of a line or paragraph. (You can change the line spacing at any position in a document, but it's best to do it at the start of a line.)

2. **Press the Format key combination, Shift-F8.**

   You see the full-screen Format menu.

3. Press L (Line).

The Format: Line menu appears. The Line Spacing item is the sixth one down. The current line-spacing value is shown in the column on the right.

4. Press S (Spacing).

The cursor hops to the number by the Line Spacing menu item.

5. Type a new line-spacing value.

Press 1 for single spacing, press 1.5 for one-and-a-half spacing, press 2 for double spacing, press 2.5 for two-and-a-half spacing, and so on.

6. Press Enter to lock in the new line-spacing value.

7. Press the Exit key, F7, to return to the document.

- ✔ Line spacing is one of those few formats that actually shows up on the screen. Although "half spacing" doesn't show up properly, you will see double or triple spacing as is.

- ✔ It's best to change the line spacing at the start of a document, the start of a page, or the beginning of a paragraph. Changing the line spacing in the middle of a random bit of text looks ugly and weird.

- ✔ To move to the tippy top of the document, press Home, Home, Home, ↑. To move to the start of a line, press Home, Home, ←.

- ✔ If you want to change the line spacing a second time, move the cursor to the proper place in the document and follow these steps again. You can have several different types of line spacing in a single document if you like.

- ✔ The Line Spacing command affects all text in a document from the cursor's position to the end of the document — unless another Line Spacing format command exists to change it. It's possible for a single document to contain several line-spacing commands, if you like. But don't be a line-spacing glutton.

- ✔ The Format command hides a secret line-spacing code in the document. You can delete this code to return the line spacing to normal. Refer to the section on undoing line formatting in Chapter 11.

The command for changing the line spacing has a terrific mnemonic: L,S for Line Spacing. Here are the quick steps:

1. Press Shift-F8, L, S.

2. Type the new spacing value.

3. Press Enter.

4. Press F7 to return to the document.

Playing with Tabs

It's not a good idea to shove information around the page with the spacebar. To put text in columns or to indent paragraphs, using the Tab key is much better because you can assign different values to the tab. (And Tab has only one calorie more than water.) Just as on the typewriter where you can make one tab scoot the carriage three inches, you can make WordPerfect take different-sized leaps across a line every time you press the Tab key.

The tab stops here

When you press the Tab key, WordPerfect moves the cursor over to the next tab stop. Normally, the tab stops are set every half inch. You can change this value to any interval to customize the tab stops if you like. But I beg you, don't! This is really a knotty thing to do. But, because you insist, follow closely:

1. **Position the cursor in the document before the place where you want to change the tabs.**

   The new tab stops will be in effect only from that position to the end of the document (or until a spot where you change the tab stops again).

2. **Press the Format key combination, Shift-F8.**

3. **Press L (Line) to bring up the Format: Line menu.**

4. **Press T (Tab Set).**

   You see the document again, but at the bottom of the screen is a tab-stop menu and a little tab bar (see Figure 9-1).

   The numbers 0, +1, and so on, show you how far the tabs are set from the left margin. The row of dots and the Ls show you where the tabs are. Any changes you make to the tabs are immediately shown in the window above the tab-stop bar, so you can actively see what effects your changes have on the document.

5. **Press Ctrl-End to delete all the tab stops.**

   The document collapses a bit because all the tab stops have just been sent to WordPerfect hell.

6. **Use the left-arrow and right-arrow keys to help place new tab stops on the tab-stop bar; press the L key where you want a tab.**

   Continue to do this step until all the tabs are set.

7. **Press the Exit key, F7, when you're done setting tabs.**

   This action returns you to the Format: Line menu.

```
aliens?"
       Parker cleared his throat.  "We ate them."
       A sea of hushed voices crested and ebbed back into silence.
The press ate it up.  "We ate them," they wrote.  Some of the
seedier reporters already left to file their stories.  This was
sensational stuff: Government Team Devours Friendly Aliens.
       "You ate them," the Director said, matter-of-factly.
       "We didn't mean to," Parker countered.
       "No, I'm sure you didn't," the Director nodded.  He raised
an eyebrow, adding, "But you did."
       The press glued their eyes to Parker, standing rigidly in
the dock.  He nodded.  They jotted down the reaction on their pen
pad computers.
       In a quiet voice, the Director finally asked, "Why?"
       Parker cleared his throat again.  He looked down, and then back
at his lawyer who sat patiently, not giving a signal one way or
the other.  Finally, Parker looked back up to the Director, yet
hung his head low.  He said, "We ate them.  They smelled so good.
They smelled like, like steak and eggs.  We just had to eat them.
Their heads cut open like butter.  It was the most delicious
L....L....L....L....L....L....L....L....L....L....L....L....L....L.
!    ^    !    ^    !    ^    !    ^    !    ^    !    ^    !    ^    !
0"        +1"       +2"       +3"       +4"       +5"       +6"       +7"
Ctrl-End (clear tabs); Enter Number (set tab); Del (clear tab);
Type; Left; Center; Right; Decimal; .= Dot Leader; Press Exit when done.
```

Figure 9-1:
The tab-stop
bar at the
bottom of the
screen.

8. Press F7 again to return to the document.

You may have to scroll down with the cursor to make the new formatting visually line up on the screen.

✔ You know, I really hate messing with tabs. Keeping them at half-inch intervals — which WordPerfect does all by itself — is just fine for me.

✔ Each time you reset the tab stops, they affect the rest of the document — up until the point where you set the tab stops again. A single document can have several different tab stops in it. In fact, experimenting with tab stops usually leads to the insertion of several tab-stop bars in a row. Refer to Chapter 11 for information on expelling the excess tab-stop nonsense from the document.

✔ If you don't want to delete all the tab stops with Ctrl-End, use the cursor to locate only the tab stops you don't want and then press the Delete key to remove specific stops.

✔ When I'm working with a lot of tabs, I usually press the Tab key only once between each column of information. Then I follow these steps to reset the tab stops so that my columns line up. Using one tab rather than two or three makes editing a lot easier. And moving the tab stops around makes the document look perfect-o.

A dreary explanation of the tab stop types, which you don't have to read

In the tab-stop menu, at the bottom of the screen, are several letters for different types of tabs.

The most common tab is L, the left tab. This tab works like the Tab key on a typewriter: Press Tab and the new text appears at the next tab stop. No mental hang-ups here.

The R tab is a right tab. Press the Tab key with this type of tab, and text lines up right-justified at that tab stop. The text is right-justified until you press the Tab key again or press Enter.

The C tab causes text to be centered on the tab stop. The text is centered until you press the Tab key again or press Enter.

The D tab is a decimal tab; it lines up numbers by their decimals. The number is right-justified before you press the period key and then left-justified afterward.

The dot-leader tab (the . tab) is used for producing a row of dots when you press Tab. You see this setup all the time in tables of contents:

Using Dot Leader Tabs 119

After you set a dot-leader tab, pressing the Tab key produces the dots and lines up the numbers right-justified.

✏ The tab stops are measured from the left margin (see Figure 9-1). If you want to set tab stops relative to the right side of the page, press T to select the Type item from the tab-stop menu at the bottom of the screen. Press A (Absolute) to have the inch indicators represent the distance from the right side of the page. If you press R (Relative), the tab stops are measured from the right margin, which won't always be 1 inch — especially if you re-set the margin.

Alignment tabs

The *alignment tab* differs from normal tabs in that it lines up text at any tab stop — not just a simple L or an R or any of the other dorky things you can do in the overly complex Tab menu. Forget all that! Instead, do the following:

1. Press Ctrl-F6.

This key combination is the Tab Align command, and pressing it works just like pressing the Tab key; the cursor jumps to the next tab stop. You see the following displayed at the bottom of the screen:

```
Align char = .
```

This message tells you that WordPerfect lines up text based on the period character. (You can change this character, as described later in this section.)

2. Type something.

The text pushes to the left. It continues to do that until you type a period — the align character. From that point on, the text moves right as it always does.

3. Press Enter.

4. On the next line, type something again, typing a period and then typing some more as you did in the preceding line.

See how the two lines align themselves on the period? That's the alignment tab. Oh, happy day.

You can change the align character if you like. If you change the align character, you can line up other types of text — not just values. To change the align character, follow these steps:

1. Press Shift-F8, O, D.

2. Type a new alignment character — say, a colon or a hyphen.

3. Type the thousands separator.

It's a requirement: Press the comma key.

4. Press F7 to exit the menu and return to the document.

The new character you typed is the character WordPerfect uses to align the text when you press Ctrl-F6.

The Tab Align command enables you to line up text that may not be all the same length. It's best suited for lining up numbers or prices, which usually have a period in them.

Indenting Text

Text that's all flush left or flush right is boring. It makes your work look like it came from the DMV. So this section explains how you can set margins to make your work look more exciting. But note that you don't want to change your margins too much or your text will look like a fat guy wearing a belt.

This section also covers other things you can do to jazz up the look of your work. You can indent paragraphs, double-indent paragraphs, release margins, and do hanging indents.

Setting the margins

Every page has left and right *margins,* which serve as the air around the document — that inch of breathing space that sets the text off from the edges of the page. WordPerfect automatically sets margins one inch in from the right and one inch in from the left sides of the page. This setup is how most English teachers and book editors want things because they love to scribble in margins. But you can adjust both the left and right margins to suit any fussy professional.

To change the margins for a document, follow these steps:

1. **Move the cursor to the place in the text where you want the new margins to start.**

   Setting the new margins at the top of the document, the top of a page, or the start of a paragraph is best.

2. **Press the Format key combination, Shift-F8.**

   You see the Format menu displayed.

3. **Press L (Line).**

   You see the Format: Line menu. The seventh item down enables you to change the left and right margins. The current margins are listed in the column on the right.

4. **Press M (Margins).**

   The cursor hops to the value next to `Left`.

5. **Type an indent value for the left margin.**

   You're setting the margin relative to the left edge of the page. For example, a value of 1 sets the left margin in 1 inch. A value of 2.5 sets the left margin in 2 ½ inches. You don't need to type the inch symbol (").

   If you don't want to change the left margin, don't type anything. WordPerfect does not reset the value when you press Enter, which you do in the next step.

6. **Press Enter after setting the left margin.**

   The cursor drops down to the value next to `Right`.

7. **Type an indent value for the right margin.**

   This value is measured in from the right edge of the paper. For example, a value of 1 sets a 1-inch margin; a value of 1.5 sets a 1½-inch margin. You don't need to type the inch symbol (").

8. **Press Enter after setting the right margin.**

   The cursor drops down to the `Selection` prompt.

9. Press the Exit key, F7, to return to the document.

✔ You get some visual feedback on the screen regarding the new margin settings. The Pos indicator in the lower right corner of the screen starts at the value specified as the left margin. And, if several margins exist in a single document, you see the text vary from wide to narrow on the screen. (Thank goodness they didn't decide to use different colors to show different margins. But don't write any letters; you never know what they may be thinking.)

✔ To move to the top of the document before setting left and right margins, press Home, Home, Home, ↑. To move to the left side of the page before setting left and right margins, press Home, Home, ←.

✔ To set the margins at the top and bottom of the page, refer to the section on adjusting the top and bottom margins in Chapter 10.

✔ If you don't want to change one or the other margin, just press Enter in Step 5 or 7 of the preceding instructions. This action tells WordPerfect to continue using the present margin setting.

✔ The margin change affects the document from the current cursor position to the end of the document. If you want to change the margins again, move to the place where you want new margins in the document and start with Step 1 of the preceding instructions. A single document can have several margin changes.

✔ Laser printers cannot print on the first half-inch of a piece of paper (top, bottom, left, and right). This first half-inch is an absolute margin; although you can tell WordPerfect to set a margin of 0 inch right and 0 inch left, text still does not print there. Instead, specify a minimum of 0.5 inch for the left and right margins.

✔ If you want to print on three-hole paper, set the left margin to 2 or 2.5 inches. Doing so allows enough room for the little holes, plus it offsets the text nicely when you open up something in a three-ring notebook or binder.

✔ If your homework comes out to three pages and the teacher wants four, bring in the margins. Set the left and right margins to 1.5 inches each. Then change the line spacing to 1.5. Refer to "Changing the Line Spacing," earlier in this chapter. (You also can select a larger font; check the section on text sizes in Chapter 8.)

Indenting a paragraph

To offset a paragraph of text, you can indent it. I don't mean just indent the first line, which you can do with the Tab key. Instead, you can indent the entire paragraph, lining up its left edge against a tab stop. Here's how:

1. **Move the cursor to the start of the paragraph.**

   The paragraph can already be on the screen, or you can be poised to type a new paragraph.

2. **Press the Indent key, F4.**

3. **Type your paragraph if you haven't already.**

   Otherwise, the paragraph is indented to the next tab stop.

   ✔ F4 is the Indent key. It works like the Tab key but indents the entire paragraph's left margin to the next tab stop.

   ✔ To indent the paragraph to the second tab stop, press F4 again.

   ✔ To indent both the right and left sides of a paragraph, refer to the next section, "Double-indenting a paragraph." Also check out "Doing a hanging indent," later in this chapter.

   ✔ If you're in a fair mood, refer to "The tab stops here," earlier in this chapter, for information about setting tab stops.

Double-indenting a paragraph

Sometimes an indent on the left just isn't enough. Sometimes you have days when you need to suck a paragraph in twice: once on the left and once on the right — when you lift a quote from another paper but don't want to be accused of plagiarism, for example. I do this stuff to Abe Lincoln all the time. When I quote his stuff, I follow these steps:

1. **Move the cursor to the start of the paragraph.**

   If the paragraph hasn't been written yet, move the cursor to where you want to write the new text.

2. **Press the Double Indent key combination, Shift-F4.**

3. **Type your paragraph if you haven't already.**

   Otherwise, the paragraph is indented to the next tab stop on the right and left margins.

- ✔ To suck up the paragraph even more, press Shift-F4 again.

- ✔ To indent only the left side of a paragraph, refer to the preceding section, "Indenting a paragraph."

- ✔ Refer to "The tab stops here," earlier in this chapter, for information on setting tab stops — but only after a few swigs of Geritol.

Releasing the margins

A margin release is a mystery. It was that MAR REL key you'd stab during a lazy moment in typing class. What does it do? Why is it there? The world may never know. WordPerfect has a Margin Release command, but you'd never know it. That's because the margin release in WordPerfect is really what's called a *back-tab*. Note that this feature isn't the same thing as a *back-stab*.

The back-tab key, a.k.a. the *Margin Release* key, is Shift-Tab.

Whereas the Tab key indents the text one notch to the right, the back-tab (formerly called *margin release*) extends the text one notch to the left. I guess they call this feature a margin release because if you're at the left margin and press the back-tab, text sticks out into the margin, looking like a diving board in the middle of a cliff.

- ✔ The only true and practical use for the Margin Release command is when you create a hanging indent. That excitement is bundled up in the next section.

- ✔ Hoo boy, nothing messes up text on the screen like a stray margin release. If you accidentally press Shift-Tab whilst in the middle of a paragraph, you notice that the text looks funny and reads weird. Unless you've turned into a new-age poet, you probably pressed the Shift-Tab key combination accidentally. Keep pressing Backspace until you delete it.

Doing a hanging indent

A *hanging indent* has committed no felonious crime. Instead, it's a paragraph where the first line sticks out to the left and the rest of the paragraph is indented. To create such a beast, follow these steps:

1. **Move the cursor to the beginning of the paragraph you want to hang and indent.**

   Alternatively, position the cursor where you want to type a new, hanging-indent paragraph.

2. **Press the Indent key, F4.**

   This action moves the left side of the paragraph over to the first tab stop. (See "Indenting a paragraph," earlier in this chapter.)

3. **Press Shift-Tab, the back-tab or Margin Release key combination.**

   That action moves the first line of the paragraph back one tab stop. Ta-da! You have a hanging-indented paragraph.

✔ If you want to indent the paragraph even more, press F4 more than once. You should also press Shift-Tab an equal number of times if you want to even up the first line of the paragraph with the rest of the text.

✔ Slapping on a hanging indent must be done individually to each paragraph in a document. There is no Universal Hanging Indent formatting command in WeirdoPerfect.

Chapter 10
Formatting Pages and Documents

*A*t last, the formatting three-ring circus has come to this. Formatting pages and documents isn't as common as formatting characters or even formatting paragraphs. This is major-league stuff that affects the entire document, and it can really be handy: adding headers and footers, page numbers — even footnotes. This is the stuff of which professional-looking documents are made. This chapter explains it all so carefully that even amateurs like you and me can fool them, too.

Starting a New Page

Two ways are available for you to start a new page in WordPerfect:

1. Keep pressing the Enter key until you see the row o' hyphens, which denotes the start of a new page. Needless to say, this way is tacky and wrong.

2. Press Ctrl-Enter, the Hard Page key combination. Pressing Ctrl-Enter inserts a row of equal signs, also denoting the start of a new page. This is the preferred way to start a new page.

> ✔ A hard-page break works just like a regular page break, but you control where it is in the document. Move the cursor to where you want the hard-page break to be and press Ctrl-Enter.

> ✔ Pressing Ctrl-Enter inserts a hard-page character in the document. That character stays there, always creating a hard page no matter how much you edit the text on previous pages. The first approach to creating a page break doesn't take into account any editing you may do on text.

> ✔ You can delete a hard-page break with the Backspace or Delete key. If you do so accidentally, just press Ctrl-Enter again or use the F1 key to undelete.

Adjusting the Top and Bottom Margins

WordPerfect likes a one-inch margin all around the page: top, bottom, left, and right. You learned how to adjust the left and right margins in Chapter 9. If you want to adjust the top and bottom margins to something other than an inch, follow these steps:

1. Position the cursor at the top of the document or at the top of the page where you want to start using the new top and bottom margins.

2. Press the Format key combination, Shift-F8.

You see the full-screen Format menu displayed, along with the several categories of things you can format. You want the Margins Top/Bottom item, located under the Page heading.

3. Press P (Page).

You see the Format: Page menu displayed. The Margins Top/Bottom setting is five options down. You see the current margin values, in inches, in the second column.

4. Press M (Margins).

The cursor hops to the value next to Top, the top margin setting.

5. Type a new value for the top margin.

The number you type is the number of inches from the top of the page that WordPerfect starts printing text. A value of 1 sets a 1-inch margin, a value of 1.5 sets a 1½-inch margin, and so on. You don't need to type the inch symbol (").

If you want to leave the top margin alone, don't type anything. WordPerfect does not reset the value when you press Enter in the next step.

6. Press Enter after setting the top margin.

The cursor drops down to the value next to `Bottom`, the bottom margin setting.

7. Type a new value for the bottom margin.

The number you type is the number of inches from the bottom of the page that you want WordPerfect to stop printing text. A value of 1 sets a 1-inch margin, a value of 2 sets a 2-inch margin. You don't need to type the inch symbol (").

8. Press Enter after setting the bottom margin.

The cursor drops down to the `Selection` prompt.

9. Press the Exit key, F7, to return to the document.

✔ To move the cursor to the very top of a document before resetting the top and bottom margins, press Home, Home, Home, ↑. To move the cursor to the top of a page, press PgUp, PgDn. Keep an eye on the page numbers in the lower right corner of the screen to make sure that you're on the proper page.

✔ The top and bottom margins are relative to the edges of the paper. A one-inch margin means that the text starts one inch from the paper's edge.

✔ The `Ln` indicator in the lower right corner of the screen reflects the new value for the top margin each time you start a new page. Other than that, there is no visual feedback when you change the top and bottom margins (although if you move up and down too far, you notice that the pages get shorter on the screen).

✔ If you want to center text up and down on a page, refer to "Centering a Page, Top to Bottom," later in this chapter.

✔ Laser printers cannot print on the first half-inch of a piece of paper. Therefore, you shouldn't set top or bottom margins to any value less than 0.5 (half an inch). Although WordPerfect accepts values less than that, the text beyond the half-inch margin doesn't print on the laser printer.

✔ To undo a top and bottom margin change, you can do these steps again later in the document. To delete the margin change altogether, refer to the section on undoing page formatting in Chapter 11.

Setting the Page Size

Most printing takes place on a standard, 8½-by-11-inch sheet of paper. But WordPerfect enables you to change the paper size to anything you want, from an envelope to some weird-sized sheet of paper. The degree of weirdness I'll leave up to you; printing envelopes is covered in Chapter 12. The following steps describe how you change the paper size to a wide, 11-by-8½-inch sheet of paper:

1. **Position the cursor at the top of the document or at the top of the page where you want to start using the new paper size.**

2. **Press the Format key combination, Shift-F8.**

   You see the Format menu.

3. **Press P (Page).**

   The Format: Page menu appears. The item you're interested in is the seventh one down: Paper Size. The right column tells you the current paper size, which should be 8.5 x 11, Standard, unless you've been goofing around.

4. **Press S (Paper Size).**

   You see the Format: Paper Size/Type menu. Four options are displayed:

Envelope - Wide	The item for printing envelopes, as covered in Chapter 12
Standard	The typical, 8½-by-11-inch sheet of paper (and this item should be highlighted)
Standard - Wide	The 11-by-8½-inch sheet of paper — the wide format
[ALL OTHERS]	Custom formats you can create in your leisure time

5. **Press the down-arrow key once to select the** Standard - Wide **option.**

   This action changes the paper size to 11 by 8½ inches.

6. **Press Enter to lock in the page selection.**

   You return to the Format: Page menu. The Paper Size item should have the new paper-size value listed: 11 by 8½ inches.

7. **Press the Exit key, F7, to return to the document.**

- The wide paper format, 11 by 8 ½, is called the *landscape mode* by WordPerfect's department of naming things. The standard 8 ½-by-11-inch paper is called *portrait mode*. Think of a picture of a person and then of a landscape to help commit these ideas to memory. Or just call them *up-and-down* and *wide modes,* like I do.

- Use the wide format when printing lists and items for which normal paper is too narrow. It also makes the people who look at your handiwork exclaim, "How did you do that?"

- To move to the tippy top of the document, press Home, Home, Home, ↑. To move to the top of a page, press PgUp, PgDn. The Page Size command must be given at the start of a page.

- To create your own paper size, muster up some guts and press A (Add) in the Format: Paper Size/Type menu (in Step 5 of the preceding steps). You see a second menu, from which you can select items that describe the paper's size and so on. This stuff can get complex. I recommend selecting the Standard paper size and pressing the Help key, F3, any chance you get.

- If you're printing an odd-sized piece of paper, remember to load it into the printer before you start printing. Refer to the section on printing envelopes in Chapter 12 for more information.

- You can have several different page-formatting commands in a single document, but it's common to have only one at the document's start. To remove page-size-formatting commands from the document, you must delete the hidden page-size code. Refer to the section on undoing page formatting in Chapter 11 for details.

Centering a Page, Top to Bottom

To put text in the center of a page, you need to do two things: Center the text between the left and right margins and center the text between the top and bottom margins. Centering the text between the left and right margins is covered in the section on centering text in Chapter 9. To center text top to bottom, follow these steps:

1. Move to the top of the page you want centered.

Press Home, Home, Home, ↑ to move to the top of the first page or press PgUp and then PgDn to move to the top of the current page.

2. Press the Format key combination, Shift-F8.

You see the Format menu displayed.

3. **Press P (Page).**

   You see the Format: Page menu displayed. You want the first item, Center Page.

4. **Press C (Center Page).**

   The cursor hops to the column to the right of the `Center Page (top to bottom)` prompt.

5. **Press Y to center the page.**

6. **Press the Exit key, F7, to return to the document.**

   ✔ The Center Page command only works on one page at a time. To center more than one page, repeat these steps for each page in the document.

   ✔ There is no visual feedback on the screen that you've centered a page. Instead, the page looks like one dwarfed page rather than a centered page. Refer to Chapter 12's discussion on the miracle of Print Preview to get a sneak peak at the centered page.

   ✔ All text on the page is centered top to bottom with the Center Page command. It's a good idea to keep as little text on the page as possible: a title, description, and so forth. End the text with a Hard Page command; refer to "Starting a New Page," earlier in this chapter.

   ✔ Refer to the description of undoing page formatting in Chapter 11 for information on uncentering a page, top to bottom.

Deciding Where To Stick the Page Number

If the document is more than one page long, you probably want to number its pages. WordPerfect can do this task for you automatically, so stop putting those forced page numbers in the document and follow these steps:

1. **Move to the tippy top of the document.**

   Press Home, Home, Home,↑. You want to move there because the Page Number command affects all the pages in the document only if it starts at the top of the first page.

2. **Press the reliable Format key combination, Shift-F8.**

   The Format menu appears.

3. **Press P (Page).**

   The Format: Page menu appears. You control page numbering with the sixth item in the list, Page Numbering.

4. Press N (Page Numbering).

You see the interesting Format: Page Numbering menu.

5. Ignore the first three items.

6. Press P (Position).

You see a screen that shows three page layouts. The first is for every page; the other two show page-number positions for odd and even pages.

7. Press the number corresponding with the position on the page at which you want the page numbers to appear.

For example, press 6 to have page numbers appear at the bottom center of each page.

8. Press the Exit key, F7, to return to the document.

You may want to specify a specific page number with which you want WordPerfect to start numbering the document. This is something you may want to do for the second, third, or later chapters in a book. By specifying a starting page number, you can make it appear as though the page numbers in all the chapters are continuous.

To start numbering pages with a specific page number, follow these steps:

1. Press Shift-F8, P, N, 1.

2. Type the page number at which you want the numbering to start.

3. Press Enter.

4. Press the Exit key, F7, to return to the document.

✔ You also can create page numbers by sticking the page number in a header or footer. Refer to "Adding a header" and "Adding a footer," later in this chapter. If you do end up putting the page number in a header or footer, you do need to use the Page Numbering command.

✔ To remove page numbering from a document, refer to the section on undoing page formatting in Chapter 11.

Here are the quick steps for putting a page number at the bottom center of every page in a document:

1. Press Home, Home, Home, ↑, which moves you to the top of the document.

2. Press Shift-F8, P, N, P, 6, which puts the page number at the bottom center of every page.

3. Press F7, which returns you to the document.

Putting Hats and Shoes on a Document

You're almost ready to send your document to that big party the printer is having. But, because you don't want your little darling to look underdressed (or unprofessional), you really should dress it up a bit more. Give the document a header to use as a hat and a footer to use as shoes for each of its pages. Your document will thank you.

Adding a header

 A *header* is not a quickly poured beer. Instead, it's text running along the top of every page in a document. For example, at the top of each page in this book is the part name or chapter name. Those are headers. You can stick headers on your work, complete with a title, your name, the date, the page number, dirty limericks — you name it.

Headers are a document-long thing. The header appears in the document from where you created it to the end of the document. Therefore, to have the same header in an entire document, you need to start at the beginning, the first page. Follow these steps:

1. **Move the cursor to the top of the document or to the top of the first page where you want the header to appear.**

   Press Home, Home, Home, ↑ to move to the top of the document; press PgUp, PgDn to move to the top of the current page. (Check the page number to make sure that you're on the right page.)

2. **Press the Format key combination, Shift-F8.**

   You see the blazing Format menu displayed.

3. **Press P (Page).**

   You see the Format: Page menu. You create a header by using the third item in the list, Headers.

4. **Press H (Headers).**

   The following menu appears across the bottom of the screen:

   ```
   1 Header A; 2 Header B: 0
   ```

5. **Press A (Header A).**

   A second menu appears at the bottom of the screen:

   ```
   1 Discontinue; 2 Every Page; 3 Odd Pages; 4 Even Pages; 5 Edit: 0
   ```

6. Press 2 (Every Page) to have the header appear on every page.

Next you are thrown into the Header Editor, a blank screen where you type the text you want to put in the header.

7. Type the header.

You can change the font, text attributes, and text size; center or flush right the text; or do a number of other interesting things. Try to keep the overall size of the header to less than three lines. Be concise and brief, if at all possible.

If you want to insert the page number in the header, press Ctrl-B. The ^B character that appears will be replaced by the current page number when you print the document.

If you want to insert the current date in the header, press Shift-F5, C. This action inserts an updating date marker in the header, which always displays the current date.

8. Press the Exit key, F7, when you're done entering the header.

This action throws you back to the Format: Page menu.

9. Press F7 again to return to the document.

✔ Guess what? You won't see the header displayed on the screen — not even in bright orange on puce. To see the header, you can edit it (as covered in "Editing a header or footer," later in this chapter), use the Print Preview command (discussed in Chapter 12), or just print the document.

✔ To stick the header on a specific page, use the Go To command: Press Ctrl-Home; at the Go to prompt, type the page number. Press Enter and you're there. (Also refer to the discussion of the Go To command in Chapter 2.)

✔ You can have two headers, an A and a B header, running on different pages. To create this effect, create Header A as described in the preceding steps; in Step 6, however, press 3 (Odd Pages). Then repeat the steps to create Header B: In Step 5, press B and in Step 6, press 4 (Even Pages). Header A then appears only on odd-numbered pages and Header B on even-numbered ones.

✔ To remove a header from a document, refer to the discussion of undoing page formatting in Chapter 11.

✔ WordPerfect makes room for a header at the top of the page. You don't need to leave space for it.

Preventing a header from appearing on the first page

To prevent a header from appearing on the first page of text (which is usually the title page), follow these steps:

1. Press Home, Home, Home, ↑ to move to the first page in the document.

2. Press Shift-F8, P, U, which brings up the Format: Suppress menu.

3. Select what you want to suppress. For example, press 5, Y to suppress Header A for the first page. Or press 1 to suppress everything.

4. Press the Exit key, F7, to return to the document.

These commands suppress the header for the first page of the document — but only the first page. The header appears on all the other pages as ordered.

Adding a footer

A *footer* is text that appears on the bottom of every page. A great footer is *Turn the page, dummy,* although better uses of footers include page numbers, a chapter or document title, or what have you. You create the footer by using steps similar to those for creating the header, described in the preceding section. Here are the steps:

1. **Move the cursor to the beginning of the document or the top of the page where you want the footer to first appear.**

   Press Home, Home, Home, ↑ to move to the top of the document; press PgUp, PgDn to move to the top of the current page (which works sometimes; check the page number to be certain).

   You should really move to the top of the page. Even though you're creating a footer, its code should be placed at the beginning of a page of text.

2. **Press the Format key combination, Shift-F8.**

   WordPerfect presents its Format menu.

3. **Press P (Page).**

   The fourth item in the Format: Page menu, Footers, is the one you want.

4. **Press F (Footers).**

   A menu appears at the bottom of the screen:

```
1 Footer A; 2 Footer B: 0
```

5. Press A (Footer A).

A second menu appears at the bottom of the screen:

```
1 Discontinue; 2 Every Page; 3 Odd Pages; 4 Even Pages; 5 Edit: 0
```

6. Press 2 (Every Page).

This action puts the footer at the bottom of every page. After pressing 2, you are put in the Footer Editor, which is where you type the text of the footer.

7. Type the text you want to see at the bottom of every page.

You can use the character size and attribute commands, center or flush right the text, and so on. Try to keep the size of the footer small — less than two or three lines.

If you want to insert the page number in the footer, press Ctrl-B. The ^B character is replaced with the current page number when you print the document.

8. Press the Exit key, F7, when you're done editing.

The Format: Page menu reappears.

9. Press F7 again to return to the document.

🡒 Just like a header, the footer does not appear in the document. To see it, you can either edit it or print the document. Or refer to the section on Print Preview in Chapter 12.

🡒 If you just want a page number at the bottom of the page, don't bother with creating a footer. Refer to "Deciding Where To Stick the Page Number," earlier in this chapter.

🡒 WordPerfect makes room for a footer at the bottom of the page. You don't need to leave space for it.

🡒 Refer to "Adding a header," earlier in this chapter, for more information about WordPerfect's footers. The same information applies to both headers and footers in a document, but you need to press F (for footer) rather than H (for header) in the commands.

Editing a header or footer

To edit a header or footer you've already created, follow these steps:

1. Press the Format key combination, Shift-F8.

The Format menu appears.

2. Press P (Page).

The Format: Page menu appears.

3. **Press H (Header) or F (Footer), depending on what you want to edit.**

   The following prompt appears at the bottom of the screen:

   ```
   1 Header A; 2 Header B: 0
   ```

   Or it may be this prompt:

   ```
   1 Footer A; 2 Footer B: 0
   ```

4. **Press A or B to edit the appropriate header or footer.**

   For most of us, that's usually going to be A. You see another menu at the bottom of the screen:

   ```
   1 Discontinue; 2 Every Page; 3 Odd Pages; 4 Even Pages; 5 Edit: 0
   ```

5. **Press E (Edit).**

   WordPerfect finds the specified header or footer and then displays a screen that shows you the header's or footer's contents.

6. **Edit the header or footer as you see fit.**

7. **Press the Exit key, F7, when you're done editing.**

8. **Press F7 again to return to the document.**

   ✔ If you want to stop using a particular header or footer, move to the page where you want it to discontinue and then start Step 1. When you get to Step 5, press D (Discontinue). Press F7 to return to the document. The header or footer no longer appears from that page onward.

   ✔ To completely remove the header or footer from the document, refer to the section on undoing page formatting in Chapter 11.

Including Footnotes and Endnotes

I must be in a really good mood today because normally this section would be considered advanced material. Pooh! A lot of people need footnotes or endnotes in their documents. Instead of creating them obtusely, follow these handy steps:

1. **Position the cursor in the document where you want the footnote or endnotes to be referenced.**

   This is the spot that has the tiny number displayed — the spot referring to the footnote or endnote. Here is an example.[1]

---

[1]This is the tiny number.

2. Press the Footnote key combination, Ctrl-F7.

You see the following menu displayed at the bottom of the screen:

```
1 Footnote; 2 Endnote; 3 Endnote Placement: 0
```

3. Decide whether you want a footnote or endnotes.

A *footnote* is a tiny note that appears at the bottom of the current page. *Endnotes* appear after the last line of text on the last page.

4. Press 1 to create a footnote; press 2 to create an endnote.

Either way, the following steps remain the same; it's only a matter of appearance or what your fastidious professor demands of you.

If you press 1 for a footnote, you see the following menu displayed:

```
Footnote: 1 Create; 2 Edit; 3 New Number; 4 Options: 0
```

The same menu appears for an endnote, but the first word changes from *Footnote* to *Endnote*.

5. Press C to create the footnote or endnote.

You are shipped off to Note Editing Land. The footnote/endnote number appears at the top of the page. *Don't delete it!*

6. Start typing the footnote or endnote.

You can use character formatting, attributes, text size, and so on, in the footnote or endnote. But do limit the paragraph formatting: Footnotes don't need to be centered or flushed to the right.

7. Press F7 when you're done entering the footnote or endnote.

You return to the document. The footnote/endnote number appears superscripted in the text.

✔ If you want to edit an existing footnote or endnote, follow the preceding steps; in Step 5, press E (Edit). Then type the number of the footnote or endnote you want to edit. Press F7 when you're done editing.

✔ To change a footnote's number, follow the preceding steps; in Step 5, press N. WordPerfect asks for the new number. Type it and press Enter.

✔ *Footnotes* are at the bottom of the page on which they're referenced. *Endnotes* appear at the end of the document, after the last line of text.

✔ To delete a footnote or an endnote, move the cursor to just before or after the footnote or endnote number in the document. Press the Backspace or Delete key. WordPerfect asks you something like this:

```
Delete [Footnote:2]? No (Yes)
```

Press Y to eliminate the footnote. (The message you see depends on whether you're deleting a footnote or an endnote and which number footnote or endnote it is.)

✔ If you delete or insert a footnote in the middle of a document, the other footnotes are renumbered automatically.

Chapter 11
Cleaning Up
the Crap

• •

In This Chapter

▶ Discovering secret formatting codes in a document

▶ Curing formatitis

▶ Undoing character formatting

▶ Undoing line formatting

▶ Undoing page formatting

• •

I can just hear my grandmother mutter, "My, but that's a filthy title for a chapter. Shush, shush. They'll let you get away with anything these days." Well, at least she's reading the book. And, if she were using WordPerfect, she'd soon realize that there is a lot of c-r-a-p hidden away in each document.

Every time you change the formatting for anything, WordPerfect sticks a secret formatting code into the document. You don't see the code — you may only see a color on the screen — but the code is there, lurking. Because of this, and because stray codes offer you no feedback, a document can quickly be cluttered up with an endless and useless variety of, well, crap.

Discovering Secret Formatting Codes in a Document

You use the Reveal Codes command to peer into the document's inner workings. It enables you to gaze at the many tangled codes and secret instructions WordPerfect buries in the document's soul. To produce such an X ray, press the Alt-F3 key combination; that is, press and hold the Alt key and then press F3. Release both keys. A split screen like the one shown in Figure 11-1 appears.

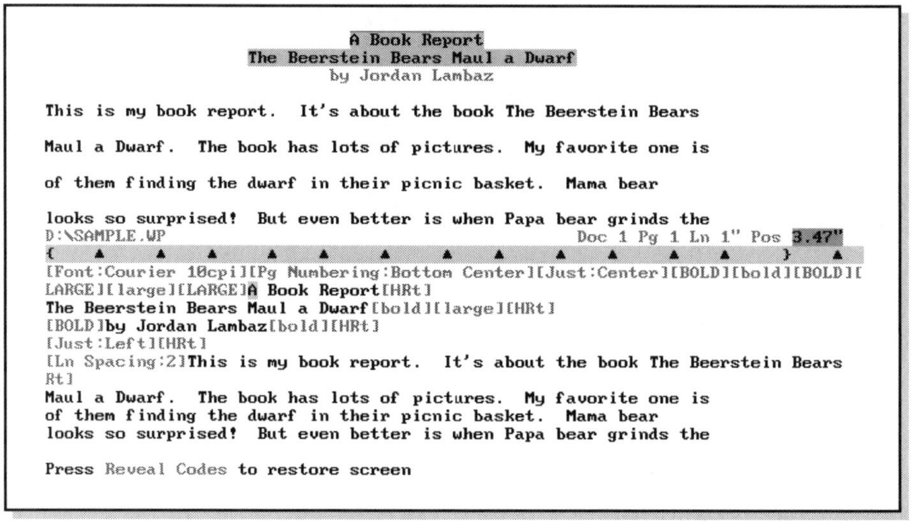

Figure 11-1:
The Reveal Codes command opens an inner eye on the document.

After you press Alt-F3, the screen splits in two. The top part shows a squashed-up version of the document — only 12 lines or so. The bottom part of the screen shows the same portion of the document but also lists all the secret codes. For example, in Figure 11-1, you see font, bold, justify-center, and line-spacing codes.

✔ To restore the document to normal, press Alt-F3 again. You cannot press F1 to cancel the Reveal Codes window.

✔ The bottom half of the screen shows both the document's text and its formatting codes. The formatting codes are displayed in the bold-text color; each code is enclosed in square brackets.

✔ You can edit and create text when the Reveal Codes option is turned on, which can be fun (if there is such a thing in WordPerfect). The WordPerfect pros do this thing all the time, confirming formatting commands that don't show up on the screen.

✔ WordPerfect gets along just fine with stranded codes in a document. However, they can mess up what you see on the screen and impede editing if they get too numerous. The rest of this chapter describes how to snip out the extra and unneeded codes.

✔ On the 101-key Enhanced Keyboard, you can press F11 rather than Alt-F3 to activate the Reveal Codes command, which saves you another claw position.

Curing Formatitis

The reason for the Reveal Codes command is to enable you to clean up the — OK, Grandma, you win — _junk_ in the document. For example, in Figure 11-1 you see the following:

```
[BOLD][bold]
```

The first [BOLD] is the command to turn on the boldface text format. The second one turns it off. Yes, these commands are produced when you press F6, the Boldface key. Any text between them appears in boldface in the document. The problem? No text is between them. This is a stray Bold command, not doing anything in the document.

- ✔ The idea behind showing these codes is to enable you to edit and remove them. For example, you can quickly find and delete occurrences of bold-bold and underline-underline, as well as multiple tab-stop settings, stray page commands, and so on.

- ✔ You also can delete these formatting commands, which is hard to do in the dark without the Reveal Codes command. The next three sections in this chapter explain the details.

- ✔ _Formatitis_ is a different disease from, say, _commaholism_. The commaholic puts too many commas in a sentence. No cure exists other than reading and applying _The Elements of Style,_ by Strunk and White.

- ✔ If you delete a code with the Reveal Codes window turned on, the code just disappears. But, if you try to delete a code when the Reveal Codes window is turned off, you are prompted with the following at the bottom of the screen:

```
Delete [Code]? No (Yes)
```

- ✔ The full array of code names and types is entombed somewhere in the WordPerfect manual. If you really care, look them up there. Otherwise, for the most part, they make sense to anyone who doesn't know what a vowel is.

Undoing Character Formatting

There are two objectives when you undo character formatting: making text normal and looking for stray codes. To make text normal, position the cursor at the spot in the document where the text is definitely not normal. Then press the Reveal Codes key combination, Alt-F3.

Scan for codes in the bottom half of the screen. Anything that's in boldface and in square brackets is suspect. Delete those codes — but only the stray ones — as you delete characters in the document: Position the cursor before or after the code and press the Delete or Backspace key.

The second objective is to remove stray codes from the document. This objective is optional but can be done quite easily. Follow these steps:

1. **Press Alt-F3 to turn on Reveal Codes.**

2. **Move to the top of the document.**

   You do so by pressing Home, Home, Home, ↑.

3. **Press the Search key, F2.**

   The Srch prompt appears at the middle left of the screen, above the white bar.

4. **Enter the double-whammy code you want to search for.**

   For example, to search for double-bold codes, press F6, F6 (the Bold key twice). This action puts the following at the Srch prompt:

   ```
   -> Srch: [BOLD][bold]
   ```

   That's a start and an end bold code with nothing between them — a useless formatting blunder in the middle of the document, and it's unknown because nothing shows up on the screen.

5. **Press F2 to search for the code.**

   If it doesn't exist (and that's rare, at least for a WordPerfect dummy like me), you see * Not Found * displayed. If the code is found, you see it in the Reveal Codes window. Press the Backspace key to delete it. Go back up to Step 2 and search for more codes.

✔ Other codes you may want to search for are as follows (press the key combinations at the far left):

F8, F8	Underline-Underline	[UND][und]
Ctrl-F8, A, I, Ctrl-F8, A, I	Italic-Italic	[ITALC][italc]

✔ To find other codes, look up the proper formatting command sequence in Chapter 8 and then issue those commands twice at the Srch prompt in Step 4 of the preceding instructions.

✔ To undelete the codes, press the Undelete key, F1, and then press 1 to restore.

✔ You can find more information on using the Search command in Chapter 5.

Undoing Line Formatting

You can use the Reveal Codes command as well as the Search command to remove excess line formatting from the document. Although you won't find as many doubled-up line-formatting codes as you do character-formatting codes, you may find excess tab stops or stray text-centering commands. Also, removing the codes directly is often the only way to restore text to normal.

The best way to remove line-formatting codes is to move to the top of the document and then switch on the Reveal Codes command. Press the following keys:

Home, Home, Home, ↑, Alt-F3

Pressing these keys moves you to the top of the document and opens the Reveal Codes window. Here are some things you can scan for:

Double or stray center codes	`[Center][Center]`
Double or stray flush right codes	`[Flsh Rgt][Flsh Rgt]`
Multiple tab-stop settings	`[Tab Set:...]`

You also can remove any excess codes to undo their formatting effects. Locate the codes and then use the Backspace or Delete key to remove them. Here are some common codes you may find and want to delete:

Justification codes	`[Just:Left]`, `[Just:Right]`, `[Just:Center]`, and `[Just:Full]`
Line-spacing codes	`[Ln Spacing:`*n*`]`
Margin codes	`[L/R Mar:`*n*`";`*n*`"]`

✔ Press F1, 1 to immediately undelete any codes you may not have wanted to delete in the first place.

✔ You can search for any code by pressing the Search key, F2, and then issuing the formatting command you want to search for. Refer to Chapter 9 for information on issuing paragraph-formatting commands.

✔ To scan for double center or flush right codes, follow the steps outlined in the preceding section, "Undoing Character Formatting." In Step 4, press Shift-F6 twice to search for stray center codes; press Alt-F6 twice to scan for stray flush right codes:

Shift-F6, Shift-F6	Center-Center	`[Center][Center]`
Alt-F6, Alt-F6	Flush Right-Flush Right	`[Flsh Rgt][Flsh Rgt]`

Undoing Page Formatting

The heinous and stray codes you use for page formatting can also be removed with the assistance of the Reveal Codes command. Often, you may not even know that these codes are lurking in the document until you print. Before you print, scan for the codes by using the Search command, F2, and then pluck them out one at a time.

To scan for and remove stray codes in the document, move the cursor to the absolute start of the document. Do so by pressing the following keys:

Home, Home, Home, ↑

Switch on the Reveal Codes command by pressing Alt-F3.

Following is a list of things to visually scan for. Each of these items affects the text. If you see more than one in a row, or if you see a specific stray one you don't want, position the cursor and delete that code by using the Backspace or Delete key:

Header	`[Header A;Every page;`*text*`...]`
Footer	`[Footer A;Every page;`*text*`...]`
Top/bottom margins	`[T/B Mar:`*n*`";`*n*`"]`
Page centering	`[Center Pg]`
Page size	`[Paper Sz/Typ:11" x 8.5",Standard]`

For example, to uncenter a page, look for the `[Center Pg]` code in the Reveal Codes window. Move the cursor over that code and press the Delete key.

You can use the Search key, F2, to find codes as well. Follow these steps:

1. **Press the Search key, F2.**

   The `Srch` prompt appears at the bottom of the screen (or in the middle of the screen, because the Search Codes window is at the bottom).

2. **Issue the commands used to format the document.**

   Refer to Chapter 10 for the keystrokes you can look for.

   After you press the code's keystrokes (Shift-F8 and so on), the cryptic bracket code for that command appears after the `Srch` prompt.

3. **Press F2 again to find the code.**

   If it's in the document, it is highlighted in the lower, Reveal Codes, window. If it isn't there, you see the `* Not Found *` message displayed. Yippee!

4. Press Backspace to delete the diabolic code and remove its page-formatting sorcery from the document.

✔ Press F1, 1 to immediately undelete any codes you may not have wanted to delete in the first place.

✔ The page-formatting code I most commonly duplicate is the header. I had one document with three headers in a row! By pressing the Reveal Codes key combination, Alt-F3, I was able to quickly delete the first two. I edited the remaining one and kept it in the document. Refer to the section on editing headers and footers in Chapter 10 for additional information.

Part III
Working with Documents

"YES, WE STILL HAVE A FEW BUGS IN THE WORD PROCESSING SOFTWARE. BY THE WAY, HERE'S A MEMO FROM MARKETING."

In this part...

Document sounds so much more important than *that thing I did with my word processor*. It implies a crisp, masterful touch. No, this isn't another dreary report; it's a document. This isn't just a letter complaining to the local cable affiliate; it's a document. It isn't a note to Billy's teacher explaining his rash; it's a document. *Document* sounds professional, so never mind that you had to tie your fingers in knots and print several hundred copies before you got it right. It's a document!

This part of the book explores the thing you use WordPerfect for: making documents. That includes printing documents, working with documents and files on disk, and mail-merging (such an ugly, sordid thing — right up there in mental agony and grief next to paying taxes).

Chapter 12
Printing Stuff

*T*wo guys are riding a bus. One of them, a WordPerfect dummy, says to the other, a typical nondescript dummy, "I'm having trouble sending my document to the printer." And the nondescript dummy says, "Try Quicky-Printy. It's where Marge and I had our Christmas letter done last year." Ba-boom, boom.

The woes of using a computer are so subtle, well, they drive you to create inane jokes. *Sending something to the printer* means nothing until you explain that a *printer* is a device connected to a computer that enables you to print things. Not to mention that if you're really good, the WordPerfect gods smile on you and what you print may actually look something like what you wanted.

Getting the Printer Ready

Before printing, you must make sure that the printer is ready to print. Doing so involves more than flipping on its power switch.

Start by making sure that the printer is plugged in and properly connected to the computer. A cable connects the computer and the printer. The cable should be firmly plugged in on both ends. (The cable needs to be checked only if you're having printer problems.)

The printer should have a decent ribbon. Old, frayed ribbons produce faint text and are actually bad for the printing mechanism. You'll have to spend more later on repair bills if you're trying to save a few bucks now by using a ribbon longer than necessary. Laser printers should have a good toner cartridge installed. If the laser printer's toner-low light is on, replace the toner at once.

You must have paper in the printer to print on. The paper can feed in from the back, come out of a paper tray, or be fed manually one sheet at a time. However the printer eats paper, make sure that you have it set up properly before you print.

Finally, the printer must be *on-line* or *selected* before you can print anything. Somewhere on the printer is a button labeled *on-line* or *select*, and there should be a corresponding light. Press that button to turn on the option (and the light). Even though the printer is plugged in, the power switch is on, and it's doing its warm-up, stretching exercises, it won't print unless it's on-line or selected.

   ✔ Before you can print, you must make sure that the printer is plugged into the wall, is plugged into the computer, is turned on, has paper ready, and is on-line or selected. (Most printers turn themselves on in the on-line or selected mode.)

   ✔ Never plug a printer cable into either a printer or a computer that is on and running. Always turn the printer and computer off whenever you plug anything into them. If you don't, you may damage the internal electronic components.

   ✔ Some special — OK, weird — printers are called *serial printers*. These types of printers plug into the computer's serial port rather than the more logical printer port. I don't need to bore you with details about this stuff. However, if you have a serial printer (and I pity you), some extra setup is involved before you can start printing. Refer to the printer manual or go out and buy *DOS For Dummies,* published by IDG Books Worldwide, and look in Chapter 9.

✔ If you're printing to a network printer — and it makes me shudder to think of it — then someone else is in charge of the printer. It should be set up and ready to print for you. If not, someone you can complain to is usually handy.

✔ Chapter 21 contains additional information on setting up, or *installing,* the printer for use with WordPerfect. That chapter also contains troubleshooting information and a detailed anatomical guide to popular printers, telling you where to shoot the printer for either a quick death or a lingering, slow, and painful one.

Printing a Whole Document

If you think your work is worthy enough to be enshrined on a sheet of paper, follow these steps for printing an entire document, head to toe:

1. **Make sure that the printer is on-line and ready to print.**

2. **Press the Print key combination, Shift-F7.**

   The document disappears (actually, it's just hidden for the moment), and you see the Print menu displayed.

3. **Press 1 (Full Document).**

   The printer warms up and starts to print. You return to the document as WordPerfect continues to print it. You can save that document to disk, start editing another document, create a new document, whip the mouse around in circles, or do whatever amuses you. WordPerfect continues to print in the background. You cannot exit WordPerfect, however, or printing stops.

   ✔ If nothing prints, don't press Shift-F7, 1 again. There's probably something awry, but WordPerfect's muffled voice hasn't alerted you to the problem. Read "Monitoring Printing," later in this chapter, to see what message WordPerfect is trying to send you. Also, check to see whether the printer is on-line or selected.

   ✔ If you have a manual-feed printer, the printer itself begs for paper. The printer says, "*Beep!* Feed me!" You must stand by, line up paper, and shove it into the printer's gaping maw until the document is done printing. Refer to "Printing Envelopes," later in this chapter, to figure this one out.

   ✔ Before you print, consider saving the document to disk and — if we're talking final draft here — doing a spell check. Refer to the section on saving a document to disk in Chapter 13, as well as to the discussion of the spell checker in Chapter 7.

✔ If you try to quit WordPerfect as it's printing, you see the message Cancel print jobs? Press N. Stay in WordPerfect until printing stops.

✔ Here are the keys you press to print an entire document:

Shift-F7, 1

Printing Parts of a Document

OK, fine. You can print an entire document as easily as you can press three keys on the keyboard. But what if you don't want to print all of a 30-page document? Is there a way for you to print parts of a document? You bet.

Printing a specific page

Follow these steps to print only one page of a document:

1. Make sure that the printer is turned on and eager to print something.

2. Move the cursor so that it's sitting somewhere in the page you want to print.

Check the cryptic Pg counter in the lower right corner of the screen to make sure that you're on the page you want.

3. Press Shift-F7, the Print command.

The Print menu appears. The item you want, Page, is number 2 in the list.

4. Press P (Page).

You return to the document as that sole page is printed on the printer.

The single, requested page has a header, a footer, all formatting, and so on — even a page number — just as if you printed it as part of the complete document.

Here are the quickie steps for printing a single page:

1. Move the cursor to the page you want to print.

2. Press Shift-F7, P.

Printing a range of pages

WordPerfect enables you to print a single page, a range of pages, a group of pages, or all odd or all even pages. To print a range or group of pages, follow these steps:

1. **Make sure that the printer is on-line and ready to print.**

2. **Press Shift-F7, the Print command.**

   You see the full-screen Print menu come up. The item you want is the fifth one in the list, Multiple Pages.

3. **Press M (Multiple Pages).**

   You see the following prompt at the bottom of the screen:

   ```
   Page(s):
   ```

4. **Type the pages, range of pages, or secret codes for the pages you want to print.**

   Table 12-1 lists what you can type at this prompt.

5. **Press Enter.**

   The pages you specified — and only those pages — print.

Table 12-1	Acceptable Page-Range Entries
Entry	**Meaning**
x,y,z	Print pages x, y, and z, where each number is a page number separated by commas.
x-y	Print pages x through y. This method specifies a range of pages to print, separated by a hyphen.
0	Print only the odd-numbered pages.
E	Print only the even-numbered pages.

- ✔ If you're printing a document on two sides of sheets of paper, print the odd pages first. Then put the paper back into the printer upside down and print only the even pages.

- ✔ If you're printing odd and even pages, consider setting the *binding offset* to one inch: Press Shift-F7, B, 1, Enter. This key sequence specifies that the odd-numbered pages have an extra inch on the left margins and that even-numbered pages have an extra inch on the right. This extra space allows the pages to be bound without losing any text in the gutter.

Here are the quick steps for printing multiple pages:

1. Press Shift-F7, M.

2. Type the pages or range of pages you want to print.

3. Press Enter.

Printing a block

When a block is marked on the screen, you can press Shift-F7 and WordPerfect asks whether you want to print the block. You see the following prompt:

```
Print block? No (Yes)
```

Check to see whether the printer is turned on and ready to print. Then press Y to print just the selected block. (If you press N, you return to block-marking mode.)

✔ The block prints on the page in the same position it would occupy if you printed the entire document. The page contains any headers, footers, page numbers, and so on, as specified by the document's format (which explains why it may take some time to print a block located at the end of the document).

✔ Chapter 6 explains everything you want to know about blocks (but have forgotten since childhood).

Printing a Document on Disk

Suppose that you've already edited a document and saved it to disk. You don't need to even load that document into WordPerfect to print it (assuming, of course, that it's *perfect*). To print a document that exists on a disk, follow these steps:

1. **Press Shift-F7, the Print command.**

2. **Press D (Document on Disk).**

   The following prompt appears at the bottom of the screen:

   ```
   Document name:
   ```

3. **Type the DOS filename for the document you want to print.**

4. **Press Enter.**

   The document becomes a job in the WordPerfect printing machine. Zip, zip, zip. The document soon comes crawling out of the printer.

> ✔ This is a handy way to print common reports, resumes, and things on disk that don't need editing.
>
> ✔ If the file doesn't exist, or if you mistyped the filename, you see an error message: ERROR: File not found. You have a chance to reenter or edit the filename and press Enter again. Or just give up and press F1.
>
> ✔ To locate a lost file on disk, refer to the section on finding lost files in Chapter 22. Also, check out Chapter 14, which describes how the handy F5 key works.

Printing Several Documents at the Same Time

The best way to print several documents at the same time is to use the List Files key, F5. You mark the files on disk that you want to print and then do a gang print. This procedure is easier than loading each file into WordPerfect, printing it, clearing the file away, and then loading another file. (As I'm fond of saying, "Let the computer do the work.")

To print several files at the same time, follow these steps:

1. Make sure that the printer is turned on and ready to print.

2. Press the List Files key, F5.

You see something like the following at the bottom of the screen:

```
C:\WP\LAUGH\BURP\GIGGLE\*.*
```

What you see varies, but it is undoubtedly just as cryptic. That's a DOS *pathname*. (Quickly run screaming to Chapter 20 if you need help with pathnames.) WordPerfect is telling you, "Me find files in this directory."

3. Most of the time, press Enter here.

However, if the files you want to print are in a different directory, type that directory name and then press Enter. (Again, scream off to Chapter 20 for more information.)

The List Files directory and highly confusing menu appears. Files are listed in the middle of the screen. Just scan for the document filenames you want to print.

4. Use the cursor-control keys to move the highlight to the name of a file you want to print.

If the list of files is long, you can press the down-arrow key to look for additional filenames.

5. Press the asterisk key (∗) to mark a file.

An asterisk appears next to the name of the file. That file is marked and ready for group action.

6. Repeat Steps 4 and 5 to mark any additional filenames you want to print.

7. Press P (Print).

You see the following prompt at the bottom of the screen:

```
Print marked files? No (Yes)
```

8. Press Y (Yes).

You see the following prompt at the bottom of the screen:

```
Page(s): (All)
```

9. Press Enter.

WordPerfect thinks for a minute, and the disk drive churns away. The documents start to print.

10. Press the F7 key to exit from the List Files window.

✔ Do not rename or delete any of the document files you're printing. If you do, WordPerfect won't be capable of finding them and all hell will break loose. You can rename or delete other files — just not those you've marked for printing.

✔ Additional information on using the List Files key, F5, is given in Chapter 14.

Understanding the Miracle of Print Preview

WordPerfect is colorful but not descriptive about what a document will finally look like. So the only way to tell whether that orange on purple blob of text will print the way you want is to print it. But test printing is a pain, and it kills innocent trees. To avoid having homeless-bunny dreams, use the miraculous Print Preview feature.

The Print Preview command enables you to see what the document will look like when printed without printing. This is a great way to see whether headers and footers look OK and to preview text styles and graphics and all the other doodads you toss into a document. To see what you're going to get, follow these steps:

1. Press the Print key combination, Shift-F7.

The screen clears, and the Print menu appears. The item you want is the sixth one down, View Document.

2. Press V (View Document).

The screen clears, and you're placed in graphics mode. You see a graphic depiction of the document on the screen.

3. Use the menu at the bottom of the screen to select several different ways of looking at the document.

Press 1 to see the document at 100 percent, real-life size; press 2 to see a twice-as-big-as-normal view; press 3 to see the whole thing in teeny-tiny mode; and press 4 to display two pages side by side.

Look at the numbers in the right bottom corner of the screen; they tell you which page you're looking at. You can press the PgUp or PgDn key to page through the document. You also can use the cursor-control keys and the Home, cursor-control keys to view parts of the document in the magnified modes.

4. Press F7 to return to the document as displayed on the ugly PC text screen.

✔ Nope, you cannot edit the document in the pretty graphics screen. But you can confirm your font and formatting changes.

✔ Print Preview may not work on older PCs with primitive monochrome graphics. The feature is also unavailable in earlier versions of WordPerfect.

Printing Envelopes

Yes, WordPerfect can print envelopes. No, it's not a snap. Instead of issuing a simple Print Envelope command, you must do several things: Format an envelope page size, set envelope margins, and then print the envelopes. It isn't a Herculean task. It's just involved. Here's what you do:

1. Start by creating a new document in WordPerfect.

Press the Exit key, F7. Save the current document to disk, if necessary. At the Exit WP? prompt, press N. This action starts you off on a clean slate, like sticking a crisp, clean sheet of paper into a comfortable old typewriter.

2. Set the page size to Envelope - Wide.

Press Shift-F8 to activate the Format menu. Then press P (Page) and S (Page Size). Use the cursor-control keys to select Envelope - Wide from the list. When that entry is highlighted, press Enter.

3. At the Format: Page menu, press M (Margins) to set the top and bottom margins.

Set the top margin to 0.5 inch (half an inch). Press Enter. Keep the bottom margin at 1 inch. Press Enter.

4. Press the Cancel key, F1, to exit the Format: Page menu.

You return to the main Format menu.

5. Press L (Line).

You see the Format: Line menu.

6. Press M (Margins).

Set the left margin to 0.5 (one-half inch). Press Enter. Keep the right margin at 1 inch; press Enter.

7. Press F7 to return to the document.

You won't see anything on the screen because WordPerfect's department of strange colors hasn't yet decided on a designer pattern for envelope-page sizes.

8. Type your return address.

If you want to add any fancy fonts here, press Ctrl-F8 and set them. Don't make the return address too big, or you'll offend a miminy-piminy postal-service employee somewhere.

9. Press Enter to move the cursor down the front of the envelope.

Keep an eye on the Ln indicator in the lower right corner of the screen. Stop when it gets to a value greater than 1.75 inches.

10. Reset the left margin to 3.5 inches.

Press the Format key combination, Shift-F8. Press L (Line). You see the Format: Line menu. Press M (Margin) and then type **3.5** (3 ½ inches). Press Enter, Enter. Press F7 to return to the document.

11. Type the destination address.

If you want to make the address larger, press Ctrl-F8, S, L and then type the return address.

These steps create an envelope-formatted document. If you want to preview it with the Print Preview command, press Shift-F7, V. Say to yourself, "Hey! It looks like an envelope!" Refer to Figure 12-1 for an example. Make sure that everything is lined up properly.

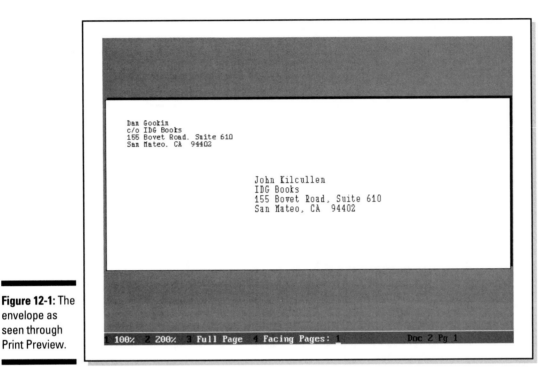

Figure 12-1: The envelope as seen through Print Preview.

Print the envelope as you do any document: Press Shift-F7, 1 (or follow the steps presented in "Printing a Whole Document," earlier in this chapter). However, the envelope page-size format has a special manual-feed command in it. After you press Shift-F7, 1, the computer beeps at you. WordPerfect is waiting for you to manually insert the envelope in the printer. You may see the following message displayed at the bottom of the screen:

```
Press Shift F7,4 to resume printing
```

Proclaim out loud, "What now?" Press Shift-F7 to see the Print menu. Then press C to select Control Printer. You see the Print: Control Printer menu displayed. Near the middle of the screen, by the Action prompt, you see the following message:

```
Insert paper
Press "G" to continue
```

Make sure that the envelope is ready to be eaten by the printer. Press G and it prints.

Now, if WordPerfect only had a stamp-licking function. . . .

✔ This is one of the most irritating things WordPerfect does: Press Shift-F7, 1 to print. Fine. It dumps you back into the document. *Beep!* Press Shift-F7 again and then C. Why the repetitive steps? I mean, it knows you need to press Shift-F7 again, so why not just present a `Press "G" to continue` prompt at the bottom of the screen? And while I'm at it, the schools are terrible, hospital food is awful, and our taxes are too dang high!

✔ Envelopes go into a laser printer face up with the top part pointing to the left as you stand in front of the manual feeder. For a top-feeding dot-matrix printer, stick the envelope in upside down facing away from you. Be sure to line up its left edge against the zero-inch mark (which should be somewhere unobvious and too tiny to see). Some printers have handy envelope feeders; pray that yours is one of them.

✔ You can save envelope files to disk — especially if they have addresses you use often. But, for just printing an occasional envelope, consider creating a generic ENVELOPE file as explained in the next tip. For example, my ENVELOPE file contains all the proper envelope-formatting codes, plus my name, street, and city in the return-address position. When I want to print an envelope, I load ENVELOPE, fill in the destination address, and print.

✔ To create a generic ENVELOPE file on disk, follow the steps in this section. But, at Step 11, type **Sample** rather than a destination address. At that point, save the document to disk as ENVELOPE. Retrieve the document later, replace *Sample* with a real destination address, and then print a quick envelope.

Monitoring Printing

WordPerfect lets you go off and do other things while it's printing. For example, you can print a document, save it, and then start over with something new. WordPerfect continues to print. If you're printing a jillion documents, WordPerfect keeps track of them all and prints each of them, one after the other. You never need to sit and wait. Of course, you can't quit WordPerfect, so you're often left twiddling your thumbs.

Instead of burning excess calories exercising your phalanges, you can become
a passive participant in the printing process. It's like watching Congress on
C-SPAN but without the oratories, smiling, and back pats. Here's what you do:

1. **Press Shift-F7, the Print command.**

   You see the Print menu displayed.

2. **Press C (Control Printer).**

   This action brings up an interesting screen that controls what WordPerfect
   calls *printer jobs*. Printer jobs are all the documents you have lined up to
   print (see Figure 12-2).

There's really nothing for you to do in the Print: Control Printer screen except
for cancel a print job, as explained in the next section. But you can observe
several interesting things about the documents being printed and even discover
why some documents aren't printing. This screen also gives you an idea of how
much more printing you have to do.

✔ Press F7 to exit the Control Printer screen and return to the document.
   Everything continues to print — even when you're not watching.

✔ Each file WordPerfect prints is called a *printer job*. The jobs are numbered
   from 1 to 99, and then they start over again at 1. The numbers get higher
   the more you print and the longer you stay in WordPerfect.

✔ When you print a document on disk, its filename appears by the printer
   job number (in the Document column). When you print a document you're
   currently working on, the document name is (Screen).

```
Print: Control Printer

Current Job

Job Number: None                          Page Number:  None
Status:     No print jobs                 Current Copy: None
Message:    None
Paper:      None
Location:   None
Action:     None


Job List

Job  Document                Destination        Print Options




Additional Jobs Not Shown: 0


1 Cancel Job(s); 2 Rush Job; 3 Display Jobs; 4 Go (start printer); 5 Stop: 0
```

Figure 12-2: The
Print: Control
Printer screen
monitors printer
jobs.

✔ If you quit WordPerfect before printing is done, all printing stops. A warning message appears, alerting you to this catastrophe. Press N if that happens.

✔ The Message and Action prompts near the top of the Control Printer screen often tell you what's going on and how to cure common problems. For example, if the printer isn't turned on and you're trying to print, the Message prompt may be Printer not accepting data. Next to the Action prompt is a suggested course of action: Check cable, make sure printer is turned ON; Press Help for additional information. (In other words, turn on the printer.)

✔ The Print: Control Printer screen is a great, busy screen you can keep on the screen to convince the boss that you're really working hard. Consider putting a sticky note on the monitor: "Spooling, be right back." It's very effective.

Canceling a Print Job

Sometimes you'll print something and then change your mind. This situation happens all the time. (Rumor has it Gutenberg originally wanted to print a hanging, floral wall calendar.) Or maybe the printer is slow, you pressed Shift-F7, 1 too many times, and now you find that you're accidentally printing several dozen copies of the same document. Ugh.

Because WordPerfect prints in the background, pressing the F1 key won't cancel printing. Instead, follow these steps to cancel a print job:

1. Press Shift-F7, the Print key combination.

You see the Print menu displayed.

2. Press C to wiggle yourself into the Control Printer screen.

You see a list of printer jobs on the screen. Look for the one you want to cancel. If you're printing a lot of documents, press D (Display Jobs) to list all the printing jobs. Most of the time, the job you want to cancel is sitting right on top of the list.

3. Note the job number.

Be observant! It isn't always number 1. And pay attention to the name: Filenames are listed, but stuff you're working on right now appears as (Screen).

4. **Press C, which selects the Cancel Job item from the menu at the bottom of the screen.**

   You see the following prompt displayed:

   ```
   Cancel which job? (*=All Jobs) n
   ```

5. **Type the number of the print job you want to cancel or press Enter if the proper number is displayed.**

   WordPerfect makes an attempt to stop printing. This is about as effective as a four-year-old's attempt to clean his or her room. While WordPerfect is trying to stop, you see a string of "I'm trying to stop, really" messages. Just be patient and let WordPerfect clear its mind.

   After the havoc has been wrought, you may see a Press "G" to continue message.

6. **Press G and then press F7 to exit from the Print menu and return to the document.**

   If you want to cancel more jobs, skip back to Step 3 and cancel them as well.

   ✔ Only when you see the status message No print jobs is WordPerfect really done printing.

   ✔ Canceling a print job is not an immediate thing. After the Control Printer screen clears up and WordPerfect calms down, you may still have a few pages printing in the printer. Relax. Think of calm blue waters. Wait. Then pick up the pieces and start over.

Chapter 13
Working with More Than a File — a Document

A document is what you see on the screen in WordPerfect. It's the *text* you create and edit, the *formatting* you apply, and the *end result* that's printed. But a document is also a file you store on disk for later retrieval, editing, or printing. This is where things get rough because big bully DOS horns in on the action. To work with documents on disk, you need to wrestle with DOS filenames. Personally, I'd rather exist on a diet of bird seed and vending machine food, but we're all stuck with DOS so let's try to make the best of things.

Working on Two Documents at the Same Time

This is weird — and handy: WordPerfect enables you to work on two documents at once. Two, yes, two. You don't have to save one to disk and start over; just use the handy Switch key combination, Shift-F3.

To switch to the second document, cleverly called *Doc 2,* press Shift-F3. If a document is on the screen, the document called *Doc 1,* it goes away and you are presented with a new blank page. Welcome to Document 2! You can switch back to Document 1 by pressing Shift-F3 a second time.

The clue about whether you're in Document 1 or Document 2 is in the scribbling at the lower right corner of the screen. Doc 1 means you're working on Document 1. Doc 2 means you're in Document 2. The goings on of one document are independent of the other. Printing, spell-checking, formatting, and so on, only affect the document currently visible on the screen.

✔ When a block is marked on the screen and you press Shift-F3, the block converts to all uppercase or all lowercase letters. Refer to the section on uppercase and lowercase conversion in Chapter 8.

✔ You can copy a block from one document to the other. Just press Shift-F3 when you see the `Move cursor, press Enter to retrieve` prompt at the bottom of the screen. Press Enter when you're ready to paste the cut or copied block into the other document. Refer to Chapter 6 for detailed block action.

✔ Suppose that you have something in both Doc 1 and Doc 2, and you're working on Doc 1. When you press the Exit key, F7, to quit WordPerfect, you see the message `Exit Doc 1?` rather than `Exit WP?` If you press Y, you are thrown over into Doc 2. If you press N, you stay in Doc 1 and start over with a new slate.

A strange, esoteric aspect of WordPerfect's windows that you don't need to read about

The two documents, Doc 1 and Doc 2, are actually two *windows*. This feature was touted as an amazing productivity boost when it was introduced in the early '80s: Work on two different windows at once. Amazing. But it never really caught on (probably because Microsoft Word let you work with eight documents in eight windows at once).

When you start WordPerfect, the Doc 1 and Doc 2 windows are full size, but you can split the screen to view both. You do so with the screen-splitting command, Ctrl-F3, W.

This key sequence brings up the `Window` prompt, which enables you to set the number of lines in a window. Type the number **12** and press Enter. The screen splits, and you see both Doc 1 and Doc 2. Cool! Who'd have thought of it?

You can switch between the windows with the Shift-F3 key combination. The document currently active is pointed at by the row of triangles found in the bar in the middle of the screen. If you want to use WordPerfect in full-screen mode, press Ctrl-F3, W again and type **24** for the window size.

Few people use the Window command to split the screen. It's just too hard to be productive when so little is displayed at once. What would be better is having access to more than two documents. This feature is available with WordPerfect for Windows, and it can come in handy when you're busy with several irons in the fire.

Saving Documents

You don't save a document to disk only when you're done with it. In fact, you should save almost *immediately* — as soon as you have a few sentences or paragraphs. Save! Save! Save!

After you've saved a file to disk once, you're not off the hook. You should save the file again (and again) while you're working on it. Why? Because it's smart!

And when you're done for the day? Yes, you really should save (save, *save*) again.

Saving a document to disk (for the first time)

To save a document that hasn't already been saved to disk, follow these steps (if you've already saved the file, skip to the next section):

1. **Press the Save key, F10.**

   You see the following prompt at the bottom left corner of the screen:

   ```
   Document to be saved:
   ```

2. **Type a DOS filename for the document.**

   This is the tricky part. DOS filenames can only contain letters and numbers and can be no more than eight characters long. You must be brief and descriptive (which rules out most lawyers from effectively naming files).

3. **Press Enter.**

   If everything goes right, the disk drive churns for a few seconds and eventually you see the filename — plus a few cryptic DOS characters — at the lower left corner of the screen. The file has been saved.

If there is a problem, you likely see one of three error messages. One of the messages is

```
Replace filename? No (Yes)
```

This message means that the disk already contains a file with the name that appears in place of *filename*. Press N, skip back to Step 2, and type another name. If you press Y, the current file replaces the other file on disk, which is probably not what you want to do.

The other two messages are

```
ERROR: Invalid drive/path description

ERROR: Invalid filename
```

These two error messages mean that you tried to save a file to disk and there was a problem. Most likely, you used a naughty symbol in the filename. Try again at Step 2 and use only letters and numbers in the filename.

- ✔ You can find additional rules about naming files in Chapter 14, in the section on naming files.

- ✔ You should organize your files, storing them in special places on the disk called *subdirectories*. This subject is covered in the discussion on finding a place for your work in Chapter 14. Technical mumbo-jumbo on subdirectories is hidden away in Chapter 20.

Saving a document to disk (after that)

You should save the file to disk every so often — usually after you write something either so brilliant or so complex that you don't want to retype it again. (If you haven't yet saved the document to disk, refer to the preceding section.)

Saving the document to disk a second time updates the file on disk. This procedure is painless and quick:

1. **Press the Save key, F10.**

   You see the following prompt at the bottom left corner of the screen:

   ```
   Document to be saved: filename
   ```

   The filename that replaces the word *filename* in this prompt is the name of the document. Often it contains special symbols and doodads, reminiscent of a DOS filename. That's OK; it's what you want.

2. **Press Enter.**

   You see a second prompt:

   ```
   Replace filename? No (Yes)
   ```

   WordPerfect is telling you that the file already exists. That's great; you're updating that file on disk.

3. **Press Y.**

   The old document on disk is overwritten with the new, updated one you
   have on the screen, which is exactly what you want.

4. **Continue working.**

   I recommend going back and repeating these steps every so often as you
   continue to toss words down on the page.

If you've already saved a file to disk, its name appears at the bottom left corner
of the screen. If no name appears there when you press F10, refer to the
preceding section for instructions on saving a file for the first time.

Here are the keys you press to update a document file on disk:

F10, Enter, Y

Saving a document to disk and quitting

You're done for the day. Your fingers are sore, and your eyes are glazing over.
Everywhere you look, you see Doc 1 Pg 4 Ln 9.49" Pos 3.53" off to your
lower right. You blink, rub your eyes, and stretch out your back. Ah, it's Miller
time. But, before you slap your buddies on the back and walk into the sunset,
you need to save the document and quit for the day:

1. **Press the Exit key, F7.**

   The following prompt appears at the bottom of the screen:

   ```
   Save document? Yes (No)
   ```

2. **Press Y to save the document.**

   You see the following prompt:

   ```
   Document to be saved: filename
   ```

   The filename that replaces the word *filename* in this prompt is the name of
   the document. If you don't see a filename displayed, enter a filename.
   (Refer to "Saving a document to disk (for the first time)," earlier in this
   chapter, for information on saving a file for the first time.)

3. **Press Enter.**

   You see a second prompt:

   ```
   Replace filename? No (Yes)
   ```

This prompt tells you that the file already exists on disk. It's OK to replace it because you're updating your work before you quit WordPerfect.

4. Press Y.

The document is saved to disk. Next comes the final question:

```
Exit WP? No (Yes)
```

If you change your mind here — and want to go back and edit the file you just saved — press F1. Otherwise, you're ready to quit WordPerfect: Continue with Step 5.

If you have opened a second document in WordPerfect, you see the following message:

```
Exit Doc n? No (Yes)
```

Press Y to quit Doc 1 or Doc 2, the other document still in memory. If you still want to quit WordPerfect, repeat steps 1 through 4 for the other document.

5. Press Y to quit WordPerfect.

You soon find yourself at the DOS prompt. Once there, you can start another program or turn off the PC for the day.

Always quit WordPerfect by using the F7 key. Never turn off the PC or reset it when WordPerfect is on the screen.

Here are the quickie keys for saving a document and quitting WordPerfect (assuming that you've already saved the file to disk):

F7, Enter, Enter, Y, Y

Saving and starting over with a clean slate

When you want to save a document, clear it off the screen, and start over with a clean slate, follow the same steps outlined in the preceding section. In Step 5, however, press N in response to the Exit WP? prompt. As a matter of fact, press N when you see either of these prompts:

```
Exit WP? No (Yes)
Exit Doc n? No (Yes)
```

These actions keep you in WordPerfect, starting over fresh with a new document.

> ✔ If you haven't yet saved the document to disk, refer to "Saving a document to disk (for the first time)," earlier in this chapter. Always save the document right after you start writing something.
>
> ✔ There is no need for you to quit WordPerfect and start it over to begin working with a blank slate.

QUICK STEPS

Here are the quickie keys for saving a document and starting over again with a clean slate (assuming that you've already saved the document to disk):

F7, Enter, Enter, Y, N

Pulling Files into WordPerfect

After you have saved files from destruction by supplying them with filenames, you can pull them back into WordPerfect at any time. Not only can you retrieve WordPerfect files into a full-screen WordPerfect editing session, but you also can dump a new file into a document you're currently editing or even pull up a DOS text file into WordPerfect.

Retrieving a document from disk

When you first start WordPerfect, or after you clear away one document and start over again with a clean slate, you can retrieve a previously saved document from disk into WordPerfect for editing.

To grab a file from disk — that is, to *retrieve it* — follow these steps:

1. Press Shift-F10, the Retrieve command.

You see the following prompt at the bottom of the screen:

```
Document to be retrieved:
```

2. Type the name of the document stored on disk.

3. Press Enter.

WordPerfect finds the document and loads it on the screen for editing. You may see the message Converting for default printer or Converting DOS text file. That's OK; the document file on disk is being made kosher for WordPerfect.

4. Go!

✔ If the document isn't found, you see an error message and are given the chance to try again. Edit the document filename if you want by using the ← and → and the Delete and Backspace keys, or type a new filename. If you still get an error message, refer to the section on finding lost files in Chapter 22.

✔ You also can use the miraculous F5 key to hunt down a file on disk and load it into WordPerfect. Refer to Chapter 14.

✔ Argh! If the screen fills with scary-looking stuff, then what you tried to load from disk probably wasn't a WordPerfect file. Press these keys to get rid of it: F7, N, N.

✔ If you want to load a document when WordPerfect first starts, type that document's filename after you type **WP** (and a space) at the DOS prompt. Refer to the section on editing a document on disk in Chapter 1.

Loading one document into another document

If you press Shift-F10, the Retrieve command, after a document is already on the screen, you load one document into another. There's no problem with doing so, provided that it's what you want in the first place.

To load one document into another, follow these steps:

1. **Position the cursor in the current document where you want the other document's text to appear.**

2. **Press Shift-F10, the Retrieve command.**

3. **At the prompt, type the name of the file you want to paste into the current document.**

4. **Press Enter.**

The text of the new document appears right where the cursor is.

✔ Refer to the preceding section, "Retrieving a document from disk," for additional details about the Retrieve command.

✔ You can't use the F1 key to undo what you've done, *so be careful.* Especially be careful that you're loading a WordPerfect document or text file and not some weirdo cryptic file that will take years to delete from the document.

✔ The resulting, combined document has the same name as the original document; save it with that name if the combination of files is what you want.

✔ You can retrieve any number of files into a document. There is no limit, but you should avoid creating a huge hulking cow of a document if possible.

✔ These steps enable you to retrieve a file saved on disk and stick it into another document. This procedure is often called *boilerplating,* where a commonly used piece of text is slapped into several documents. It's also the way cheap romance novels are written.

Loading a DOS text file

A *DOS text file* is a special, nondocument file that you can load into WordPerfect for editing. It's a nondocument file because it contains no formatting, boldfacing, underlining, centering, headers, or footers. It's just plain old text.

Loading a DOS text file is no big deal. WordPerfect eats DOS text files and automatically converts them into documents. If you save the file to disk again, it becomes a WordPerfect document, complete with any formatting changes you may have added. However, most of the time you work with a DOS text file, you are directed to save the file back to disk as a DOS text file. This procedure is covered in the next section.

✔ DOS text files are also called *ASCII files.* ASCII is an acronym that basically means a DOS text file. You pronounce it *ASK-ee.*

✔ To retrieve a DOS text file, follow the steps outlined in either "Retrieving a document from disk" or "Loading one document into another document," earlier in this chapter.

✔ The only critical thing you should know about dealing with a DOS text file is that you're often required to save the file back to disk in the DOS text format — not as a WordPerfect document. These steps are outlined in the next section.

Saving a DOS Text File

WordPerfect always saves documents to disk as WordPerfect document files. This feature keeps all the formatting and special stuff intact for the next time you work on the document. But WordPerfect is also capable of saving files in the DOS text format, also known as *saving a file in ASCII format.*

To save a document in the DOS text or ASCII format, follow these steps:

1. Press Ctrl-F5, the Text In and Out key combination.

You see the following menu displayed at the bottom of the screen:

```
1 DOS Text; 2 Password; 3 Save As; 4 Comment; 5 Spreadsheet: 0
```

2. Press T (DOS Text).

This action tells WordPerfect that you want to do something in the DOS text (ASCII) format. You see the following prompt displayed:

```
1 Save; 2 Retrieve (CR/LF to [HRt]); 3 Retrieve (CR/LF to [SRt] in HZone): 0
```

3. Press S (Save).

You are prompted to enter a filename:

```
Document to be saved (DOS Text):
```

4. Type a filename for the DOS text file.

5. Press Enter to save the file to disk.

If the file already exists, you are asked whether you want to replace it; press Y to replace it or N to try another name. The name in the lower right corner of the screen reflects the name of the text file you just saved.

To resave the document by using a WordPerfect filename, use the Save command as described in "Saving a document to disk (for the first time)," earlier in this chapter.

✔ Saving a DOS text file may be a requirement in some instances (for example, if you're ever asked to edit the special CONFIG.SYS or AUTOEXEC.BAT files). You can load those files into WordPerfect as you do any WordPerfect document, but you must save them back to disk as DOS text files.

✔ You can save a document as both a DOS text file and a WordPerfect document file. First, save the file to disk as a WordPerfect document. Then save the file to disk as a DOS text file, using a different name. (Some users put the extension TXT on a DOS text file.) The reason for doing this is so that you have both a DOS text file, which is what DOS wants, and a WordPerfect file, which contains secret codes and prints out really purty.

Here are the quick steps for saving a document as a DOS text file:

1. Press Ctrl-F5, T, S.

2. Type the text filename.

3. Press Enter.

TECHNICAL STUFF

Saving WordPerfect files for other word processors

If you're saving to disk a document that must be read by another, alien word processor, use the Save As Generic option. Saving a file with this option still saves the document as a DOS text file but in a format more easily digested by other word processors. Here are the steps:

1. Press Ctrl-F5, A, G.

2. Type the text filename.

3. Press Enter.

Other than the generic format, all the rules, warnings, and whatnots about saving DOS text files still apply.

The 5th Wave   By Rich Tennant

"THE MANUFACTURERS OF A DATA ENCRYPTION PROGRAM THAT SCRAMBLES MESSAGES INTO A BRAINLESS MORASS OF INDECIPHERABLE CODE, HAS JUST FILED A 'LOOK AND FEEL' COPYRIGHT SUIT AGAINST OUR WORD PROCESSING PROGRAM."

Chapter 14
Managing Files

• •

In This Chapter

▶ Naming files

▶ Finding a place for your work

▶ Using a new directory

▶ Using the marvelous F5 key

▶ Looking at documents on disk

▶ Copying files

▶ Deleting files

▶ Renaming files

▶ Finding text in files

• •

The more you work in WordPerfect, the more documents you create; because you always save those documents to disk, the more files you make. This is how a hard drive gets full of stuff; you create it. In a way, your hard drive is like your closet. It's full of stuff. And, unless you have a handy closet organizer — like the one on TV I bought for three low, low payments of $29.95 — things are going to get messy. This chapter tackles the subject of files — using and organizing them. (I'd carelessly toss in a joke about women's shoes in closets here, but my wife would hit me.)

Naming Files

When you save your precious work to disk (which is always a good idea), you need to give it a filename. But naming files isn't all that much fun, which has nothing to do with WordPerfect; point your fingers of blame at DOS.

DOS is the one that has such restrictive filenames!

DOS is the one that limits you to eight measly characters!

DOS is the one that lets you use only numbers and letters!

DOS is the scourge on which . . . OK. Let's not get carried away.

To save a document to disk, you need to use a DOS filename. Here are the rules:

✔ A DOS filename can be no more than eight characters long. It can be less, sure. A one-character filename is OK but not very descriptive.

✔ You can use any combination of letters or numbers to name a file. Extra points are awarded for being clever. Uppercase and lowercase letters are the same to DOS.

✔ A DOS filename can start with a number. In fact, the name of this file, the document that contains the text for this chapter, is 14 (a one and a four). That's a perfectly legit DOS filename — and descriptive too because it tells me what this file contains. (A filename like CHAP14 is more descriptive and also legit; CHAP14.WP is even more so.)

✔ A DOS filename cannot contain spaces.

✔ A DOS filename cannot contain symbols. OK, that's a half truth. But why clutter your brain with the symbols it can and cannot have? It's just better to name files by using letters and numbers.

✔ A DOS filename can have an optional filename extension. An *extension* follows the filename and can contain one, two, or three characters. A period separates the filename from the extension, and that's the only time you see a filename with a period in it. Filenames do not end in periods.

✔ Sometimes filenames are displayed with spaces in them. Ignore the spaces. The spaces are used for lining up the filenames and extensions on the screen. You do not need to type the spaces to enter a filename.

✔ A *pathname* is a super-long filename, describing exactly where a file is on a disk drive. The pathname contains a colon, letters, numbers, and backslash characters. For more information, refer to the next section.

✔ Examples of good and bad filenames are provided in Chapter 1, in the section on saving your stuff.

Finding a Place for Your Work

A hard drive can be a rugged and unforgiving place — like the parking lot at Nordstroms during a shoe sale. Trouble looms like it does when the last pair of off-white pumps is priced under $10. Unless there is some semblance of organization, chaos rules.

To work the hard drive right, you need organization. It's a big deal: organization. Special places called *directories* are on the hard drive; sometimes the nautical term *subdirectories* is used instead. These places are like holding bins for files. All files of a certain type can be stored in — and retrieved from — their own directories.

The organization and setup of directories are covered in Chapter 20. Your guru or the person responsible for setting up your computer should have built some of these directories and arranged them for your use. (If not, you can create directories as needed; refer to Chapter 20.)

Each directory is known by a specific name. That name is called a *pathname*. The pathname includes the disk-drive letter, a colon, a backslash, and then a directory name. If you have a directory within another directory (a subdirectory), its name is also included in the pathname, along with extra backslash characters to make it all look confusing.

Table 14-1 lists some common pathnames. Please write in any additional pathnames you use, along with their purposes. If all this stuff has you shaking your head, have your guru fill in the pathnames for you.

Table 14-1	Some Common Pathnames
Pathname	**Contents/Description**
C:\	Drive C, main root directory
A:\	Drive A, main root directory
C:\WP	WordPerfect's directory (may also be WP51)
C:\DOS	DOS's directory

✔ You can use pathnames with the List Files key, F5. Directing WordPerfect to use a specific directory is covered in the next section.

✔ You can combine a pathname with a filename for use with the Save (F10) and Retrieve (Shift-F10) commands. This is a long and complex thing to do, however, and has great potential for typos. I recommend that instead of typing a pathname, you use the F5 key to change directories. (Only those well versed in DOS-talk usually mess with pathnames anyway.)

✔ Yes, the complete pathname for a document is what you see in the lower left corner of the screen after you save a file. If you can read it, great. Otherwise, consider it similar to those meaningless numbers and letters that appear on an airplane ticket.

Using a New Directory

To use a specific directory on the hard drive with WordPerfect, follow these steps:

1. Press F5, the List Files key.

The current directory that WordPerfect is using is displayed at the bottom left corner of the screen:

```
Dir C:\WP\*.*
```

This cryptogram says that WordPerfect is using the \WP directory on drive C. The *.* is a reference to all the files in that directory; ignore it.

2. Press the equal (=) key.

This action tells WordPerfect to switch to a new directory so that you can use the files in that directory. You see something like the following:

```
New directory = C:\WP
```

3. Type the name of the new directory you want to use.

For example, suppose that you want to use files in the C:\WP\WORK directory. You type that exactly as follows:

C:\WP\WORK

That is, press C and type a colon (:) to specify drive C. Then type **\WP** to specify the \WP directory. Then type **\WORK** to specify the WORK subdirectory under the \WP directory.

Don't put any spaces in there and don't end the line with a period. Also, do not type any filenames; this is a directory-only command. (Filenames work with the Save and Retrieve commands.)

4. Press Enter.

This action causes WordPerfect to switch over to the new directory.

✔ After you switch to the new directory, you can use WordPerfect's Save (F10) and Retrieve (Shift-F10) commands to save and retrieve files only to and from that directory.

✔ If you type the name of a directory that doesn't exist, WordPerfect asks whether you want to create it. Press N if you meant another directory. (If you want to create a directory, refer to Chapter 20.)

✔ If you don't use the F5 key to switch to another directory, you stick all the files into the same, cluttered closet-like directory. It's best to put files into properly divided directories to keep your work organized.

Using the Marvelous F5 Key

The F5 key has a powerful and interesting command attached to it: List Files. This is as close to DOS as you dare come while using WordPerfect. Indeed, you can skip DOS altogether if you become dexterous with the F5 key. Here's how it works:

Press the F5 key. You see a prompt at the lower left corner of the screen that looks something like this:

```
Dir C:\WP
```

Dir means *directory.* It's followed by the DOS pathname of the directory WordPerfect is currently using to store files. (This murky subject is hammered out in Chapter 20.)

You're given the opportunity at the Dir prompt to look at the current directory or another directory on disk, or to change WordPerfect's directory. Changing the directory is covered in the preceding section. Because this is just a look-see exercise, press Enter to see the current directory. You see a crowded display, similar to the one shown in Figure 14-1. Busy, busy, busy! I could take all day telling you what's going on. Instead, look at the following list for the high points:

✔ Say, isn't that the current date and time in the upper left corner of the screen? Too bad it isn't updated every minute.

✔ All the files, WordPerfect documents, and such are listed in two columns in the center of the screen. The display has the filename and optional extension lined up in columns. Keep in mind that there are no spaces in the filenames; the spaces in the filenames are there just for show.

✔ Look at the bottom of the screen. It's a menu!

The rest of the sections in this chapter examine how the commands in the List Files menu/window/contraption work.

✔ Press F7 to exit the List Files crowded-and-overdone screen.

✔ Use the cursor-control keys (the up and down arrows, anyway) to move the highlight bar on the screen. More files may be available; keep pressing the down-arrow key to check for them. The commands in the menu at the bottom of the screen affect the currently highlighted file.

✔ Mark several files and treat them as a single unit. Mark files by highlighting one and then pressing the asterisk (*) key. Highlight another file and press the asterisk again. Mark all the files you want this way. After a group of files is marked, you can copy, delete, rename, or print the group by selecting the appropriate command from the menu at the bottom of the screen.

```
08-04-92  05:28p             Directory C:\PROJECTS\WINDOWS\*.*
Document size:        0   Free: 33,656,832 Used:      828,647    Files:       17

      .   Current   <Dir>                      ..    Parent    <Dir>
    NOTES     .     <Dir>   05-04-92 09:13a    APPXA    .DOC    14,459   06-07-92 04:38p
    APPXB    .DOC    4,524  06-05-92 03:38p    BACK     .BAT        81   06-11-92 09:41p
    CHAP01   .DOC   63,421  06-07-92 12:03p    CHAP02   .DOC    78,951   06-06-92 10:05p
    CHAP03   .DOC   79,777  06-06-92 10:51p    CHAP04   .DOC    88,821   06-07-92 09:27a
    CHAP05   .DOC   41,346  06-07-92 11:41a    CHAP06   .DOC    82,985   06-07-92 12:58p
    CHAP07   .DOC   48,142  06-07-92 03:13p    CHAP08   .DOC    72,397   06-07-92 03:59p
    CHAP09   .DOC   37,385  06-07-92 04:30p    FIGURES  .ZIP   189,153   06-07-92 06:11p
    INTRO    .DOC   11,983  06-07-92 05:54p    JONK     .DOC     2,846   06-08-92 01:20p
    LETTER   .DOC    3,584  06-07-92 10:40p    TOC      .DOC     8,792   06-07-92 04:39p




    1 Retrieve; 2 Delete; 3 Move/Rename; 4 Print; 5 Short/Long Display;
    6 Look; 7 Other Directory; 8 Copy; 9 Find; N Name Search: 6
```

Figure 14-1:
WordPerfect's garish List Files menu/screen/ display/salad bar.

✔ To unmark files marked with asterisks, press Home, Home, ↑, Enter, Enter.

✔ To load a file from disk, highlight the filename and press R (Retrieve). The result is the same as using the Shift-F10 key combination in WordPerfect, but with the List Files screen you can peruse several files — even peek into them to see what golden nuggets they contain. Refer to "Looking at documents on disk," later in this chapter.

✔ If you already have a document loaded in WordPerfect and you highlight a file and press R to retrieve it, you see a prompt at the bottom of the screen:

```
Retrieve into current document? No (Yes)
```

Press Y if you want to stick the highlighted document into the document you are currently editing at the cursor position. If this isn't what you want to do, press N.

✔ Near the top left of the List Files window/menu/clutter are the words Document size followed by the size of the current document in characters. If the size is 0, you don't have a document loaded in WordPerfect.

✔ The current directory name is displayed at the top of the screen. This is the directory WordPerfect is currently using. To switch directories, refer to "Using a New Directory," earlier in this chapter. After you switch directories, use the List Files command to take a look at the files in that directory.

Looking at documents on disk

Wouldn't it be nice if you could look into a document before you loaded it, like getting a sneak preview? Doing so is entirely possible with the List Files key, F5.

Press the F5 key and then press Enter. You see the List Files screen/window/stock-quotes thing on the screen. A list of files appears in the middle of the screen.

Use the cursor-control keys to highlight a filename. When the filename for which you want a sneak preview is highlighted, press the Enter key. This action activates the Look command, which enables you to examine a file — to x-ray it.

✔ Use the ↑ and ↓ keys to peruse the file or use the numeric keypad's plus and minus keys.

✔ Press F1 when you're done looking at a file.

✔ If the file is a WordPerfect document, you see it in color, just as you do in WordPerfect. Other files may show up as text only. Weird files (those consisting of cryptic computer instructions and gunk) show up equally weird on the screen.

✔ Do not try to load any of the weird files into WordPerfect. Although WordPerfect will choke, it won't die. If you do load a weird file (and I don't know why, seeing how I just warned you), press F7, N, N to clear it away and start over.

Copying files

You can use the List Files screen/menu/whatever to copy files to and from directories in the system. After you have the List Files screen in front of you (press the List Files key, F5, and then press Enter), follow these steps to copy files:

1. Select the file you want to copy.

Move the highlight bar to the file. If you want to do a gang copy, move the highlight bar by using the cursor-control keys and press the asterisk key to mark files.

2. Press C to activate the Copy command.

If only one file is highlighted, you see the following at the bottom of the screen:

```
Copy this file to:
```

Skip to Step 3.

If you marked a group of files, you see the following at the bottom of the screen:

```
Copy marked files? No (Yes)
```

Press Y (Yes). You then see the prompt `Copy all marked files to:`.

Continue with Step 3.

3. Enter the *destination*, the place where you want to copy the file or files.

For example, if you want to copy the marked file or files to a floppy disk in drive A, type **A:** (that's the letter A and a colon). If you want to copy the file or files to another directory, type the complete pathname.

4. Press Enter.

The file or files are copied to the specified destination.

- ✔ Press F7 when you want to exit the List Files screen/menu/scrambled eggs on brain.

- ✔ Make sure that you have a formatted disk in drive A or drive B before you copy files there. Refer to the section on formatting disks in Chapter 20 for more information.

- ✔ If a file by the same name already exists at the destination, you are asked whether you want to replace it. My advice is to press N unless you're absolutely certain that you're not overwriting something important. Try the Copy command again, this time using a different destination or another disk.

- ✔ For help copying files, specifying destinations, and such, refer to *DOS For Dummies,* published by IDG Books Worldwide. The information provided in that book's Chapter 3 on file fitness applies to WordPerfect's Copy command as well.

Deleting files

You can use the List Files menu/screen/atrocity of organization to pluck unworthy files from the hard drive. Before you begin your act of utter destruction and lay the files at peace, here's a warning: *Don't delete anything you need.* However, deleting older copies of files, backups, or just plain old junk (junk files happen) is OK.

Start with the List Files screen in front of you. When you're ready to destroy, follow these steps:

1. **Select a file to blow away.**

   Move the highlight bar to that file. If you're feeling particularly feisty, use the cursor-control keys to move the highlight bar and press the asterisk key to mark one or more files.

2. **Press D (Destroy).**

   OK, the D stands for the Delete command. If you are deleting a single file, you see the following at the bottom of the screen:

   ```
   Delete filename? No (Yes)
   ```

   Skip to Step 3.

   If you marked a group of files for slaughter, you see the following at the bottom of the screen:

   ```
   Delete marked files? No (Yes)
   ```

   Press Y (Yes). You see the message `Marked files will be deleted. Continue?`

   Go to Step 3.

3. **Press Y.**

   The file or files are no more. Gone! Gone! Gone! Purge dem files!

   ✔ Press F7 when you want to exit the List Files menu/screen/host of atrocities.

   ✔ Oops! If you want to undelete a deleted file, refer to Chapter 22.

   ✔ *Die Lust der Zerstörung ist zugleich eine schaffende Lust!* (M. Bakunin)

Renaming files

The List Files command also comes in handy if you want to rename files on disk. Although you can rename a group of files, I recommend doing it one file at a time; dealing with groups here can get complicated fast.

With the List Files menu/screen/happening displayed (press F5 and then the Enter key), follow these steps to slap a new name on a file:

1. **Select the file you want to rename.**

   Use the cursor-control keys to move the highlight bar until it highlights the file you want to rename.

2. **Press 3 (Move/Rename).**

   You see the following prompt displayed at the bottom of the screen:

   ```
   New name: filename
   ```

3. **Type a new name.**

   You can use the ← and → or Backspace and Delete keys to edit the filename displayed.

4. **Press Enter when you've entered a new name for the file.**

- ✔ Changing a file's name does not change its contents.

- ✔ You cannot give a file a name used by another file; no two files can have the same name. If you try to give a file an existing filename, you see a `Replace filename?` prompt. Press N and then start over with Step 1, choosing another name.

- ✔ You must follow the proper rules for naming a file when you use the Rename command. Refer to "Naming Files," earlier in this chapter. If you use a forbidden character in the filename or commit some other DOS sin, you see the error message `Can't rename file`. Try again.

- ✔ Never rename a file that has the extension COM, EXE, BAT, or SYS.

Finding text in files

At last, something most excellent with which to end this chapter. You can use the List Files command to locate text in WordPerfect documents. This is a great feature for document fishing — those times when you have forgotten a document's name but don't want to tediously load a bunch of files individually to scan for text. Instead, follow these steps to search for specific text in files:

1. **Press F5, the List Files key.**

2. **Press F (Find).**

   You see a list of options displayed at the bottom of the screen:

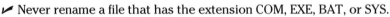

```
Find: 1 Name; 2 Doc Summary; 3 First Pg; 4 Entire Doc; 5 Conditions; 6 Undo: 0
```

3. **Press E (Entire Document).**

   This action directs WordPerfect to scan from top to bottom all the files in the current directory for the text you're about to type. You see the following prompt:

   ```
   Word pattern:
   ```

4. Type the text you want to scan for.

Be specific and be brief. For example, scan for a name or a key word —
something particular to the document you're hunting down.

5. Press Enter.

WordPerfect scans all the files, looking for the specified text. As it's looking
through the files listed on the List Files screen, WordPerfect displays the
following message:

```
Searching file xx, of xx
```

When the search is done, WordPerfect displays in the List Files window/
thing only those files that contain text matching the text you specified.

To narrow the number of files down even further, you can search this
abbreviated list of files by using a different word. If you are lucky, only one
file is displayed — the file you want.

✔ This feature isn't available in earlier versions of WordPerfect.

✔ To search another directory, press F5, type that directory's pathname, and
then press Enter. WordPerfect displays the files found in that directory
and subsequently searches only those files.

✔ To retrieve a found document, highlight it by using the cursor-control keys
and press R (Retrieve).

Chapter 15

Mail-Merging
(Mind-Blowing Stuff)

• •

In This Chapter

▶ Getting an overview of mail merge

▶ Preparing the primary document

▶ Preparing the secondary document

▶ Merge mania!

• •

*M*ail merge: ugh. What it is: a way of producing several customized documents without having to individually edit each one. We're talking form letters here — but sneaky form letters that you can't really tell are form letters.

Mail merge: ugh. What it isn't: easy. In fact, the Mail Merge key, F9, isn't even marked on the *WordPerfect For Dummies* keyboard template. The reason is that you have to look in the manual anyway, so why bother? But, instead of picking up the manual (and I don't want anyone injuring his or her spine), read this chapter, which contains the basic, need-to-know steps for mail-merging.

Getting an Overview of Mail Merge

There are two ways for you to handle WordPerfect's Mail Merge feature:

1. Read this chapter.

2. Start drinking heavily.

I'll outline the first approach here. The second approach you can attempt on your own. (If you've been through this before, skip to "Preparing the Primary Document.")

Mail merge is the process of taking a single form letter, stirring in a list of names and information, and then merging both to create several documents. Each of the documents is customized with a list of names and information you provide.

The file that contains the names and other information is called the *secondary document.* The file that contains the form letter is referred to as the *primary document.*

You start by creating the primary document in WordPerfect. Create it as you do any other document, complete with formatting and other mumbo-jumbo. But, where you would put *Dear Mr. Blather,* you put a fill-in-the-blanks special code, called a *field.*

Continue creating the primary document, putting in fields where you later want customized information. This procedure is similar to working Mad Libs, but in WordPerfect you usually provide fields for nouns instead of writing in verbs, adverbs, and adjectives. When you're done, you save the primary document to disk.

The secondary document contains the names, addresses, and other information you want to merge into the primary document. But unlike the primary document, the secondary document is created with a special format. It's almost like filling in information in a database program. (In fact, that's exactly what it is.)

Each of the names, addresses, and other information in the secondary document composes what's called a *record.* WordPerfect creates a custom letter by using the primary file as a skeleton and fills in the meat by using a record from the secondary file. I know — totally gross. But nothing else I can think of now describes it as well.

Because no sane person commits this routine to memory (and for good reason), the following sections provide outlines to follow so that you can create a mail-merge document by using primary and secondary document files. Cross your fingers and check on the kids; we're goin' mail-mergin'.

Preparing the Primary Document

The primary document is the fill-in-the-blanks document. Create it as you do any document. Type away, inserting formatting and such as necessary. Only leave certain key items blank. Actually, you don't leave them blank; instead you type *fields.*

Fields represent information to be read from the secondary document and plugged into the primary document. Here's how to create a field:

1. Position the cursor where you want the field.

Position the cursor just as you'd position it before typing a name, an address, or another key element in a document.

2. Press Shift-F9.

The following menu appears at the bottom of the screen:

```
1 Field; 2 End Record; 3 Input; 4 Page Off; 5 Next Record; 6 More: 0
```

3. Press F (Field).

You see the following prompt:

```
Enter Field:
```

4. Type the name of the field.

The field is the fill-in-the-blanks part of the document. Each field (or blank) must have a unique name. Be brief and specific. Use lowercase letters.

Examples of field names include *name, company, address1, address2, product, activity, feeling1,* and so on.

5. Press Enter.

The field name is inserted into the document in the following format:

```
{FIELD}name~
```

Look at that cryptic code as a blank to be filled in later. Do not delete the {FIELD}, the tilde (~), or any part of the field name unless you want to remove the code from the document.

6. After creating a field, continue typing.

Press Enter to start a new line, type a comma or a period — do anything you have to in order to make the field fit in. To create additional fields, repeat steps 1 through 6.

7. When you're done creating the primary document, save it to disk.

So that you have an idea of what's going on, look at Figure 15-1, which shows a sample primary document. The fields have been highlighted so that you can see them. On the screen, the fields appear in the regular text color or whichever color is associated with the text formatting you applied.

```
August 4, 1992

{FIELD}name~
{FIELD}company~
{FIELD}address1~
{FIELD}address2~

Dear {FIELD}name~

     I love your {FIELD}product~, it's really changed my life.  I use it
every {FIELD}day~ right after I {FIELD}activity~.  It makes me feel
{FIELD}feeling1~, {FIELD}feeling2~, and {FIELD}feeling3~.  In fact my wife,
{FIELD}spouse~ uses {FIELD}product~ too, and she says it makes her
{FIELD}emotion~ to do her {FIELD}chore~.

     We don't know what we'd do without {FIELD}product~ from such a fine
company as {FIELD}company~.  Thank you again!

Sincerely,


Dan Gookin


D:\PRIMARY                                    Doc 1 Pg 1 Ln 3.67" Pos 4.8"
```

Figure 15-1:
A sample primary document with many fields in place.

▸ Remember the field names. Print the primary document and highlight the names or jot them down on a piece of paper. You need to know the names when you create the secondary document.

▸ Type the field names in lowercase letters. You can use numbers in the field names if you like — for example, *address1* and *address2.*

▸ You can use the same field name in a number of places in the document. Just follow these steps and insert the field again, just as you would a name, an address, a company name, and so on, into a document.

Here are the quick steps for entering a field into a primary document:

1. Press Shift-F9, F.

2. Type the field name.

3. Press Enter.

Preparing the Secondary Document

The secondary document is a database file of sorts — not a traditional Word-Perfect document. It starts with the list of fields — the names of the blanks in the primary document that need to be filled in. The secondary document also contains several lists, or records, of information that WordPerfect will merge into those fields.

Start the secondary document as a blank slate. Switch over to Doc 2 or save and clear away the primary document. (Refer to the sections in Chapter 13 about working on two documents at once and saving and starting over with a clean slate.)

To create a secondary document, follow these steps:

1. **Press Shift-F9**.

   This action displays the cryptic Merge Mania menu at the bottom of the screen.

2. **Press M (More).**

   You see a box full o' stuff displayed over the upper right corner of the document. Look through the list for the item entitled FIELD NAMES.

3. **Press F.**

   This action should bring the highlight bar in the box to the word *FIELD*.

4. **Press the ↓ key to highlight** {FIELD NAMES}.

5. **Press Enter.**

   You see a prompt at the bottom of the screen:

   ```
   Enter Field 1:
   ```

6. **Type the field names you used in the primary document.**

   You can type the field names in the same order that they appear in the primary document. Type a field name and then press Enter. For example, you may type the following, pressing Enter after each:

   name

   company

   address1

   address2

   Type each of the field names you jotted down in the preceding section. Type them exactly as they were entered into the primary document, including any numbers.

7. **After you enter the last field name, press F7.**

   You return to the secondary document.

The field names are placed at the top of the screen. Note the following things about the field names that are now in the secondary document:

   ✔ The field names start with a {FIELD NAMES} doohickey.

   ✔ Each field name is tailed by a tilde character (~).

- ✔ The last field name has a double tilde following it.
- ✔ The field names end with an {END RECORD} doohickey and a hard-page break (a row of equal signs).

At the bottom of the screen is the message Field 1. WordPerfect is waiting for you to put information into the various fields — the items that will fill in the related blanks in the primary document. WordPerfect is waiting for you to create a record.

Each group of fields is called a record. For each record, you must fill in the various fields. This procedure is like filling in a response card or one of those endless forms at a government bureaucracy. Here's how that works:

1. **Type the text you want to fill in for the first field.**

   The field name appears at the bottom of the screen. Here is an example:

   ```
   Field: name
   ```

   Type a name or the proper data you want for that field.

2. **Press the F9 key.**

   Do not press Enter unless you want the Enter key as part of the field.

   Pressing F9 displays {END FIELD} on the screen and drops you down to the next line (the next field in the record). Notice the new field name at the bottom left corner of the screen.

3. **Repeat steps 1 and 2 for each field in the primary document.**

   When you get to the last field, don't press F9. Instead, go to Step 4.

   A clue that you're at the last field is that the Field prompt at the bottom of the screen changes from showing a field name to showing a number. If you carelessly reach that point, press Backspace to erase the last {END FIELD} marker and then go to Step 4.

4. **Press Shift-F9, E.**

   After the last field, you don't press the F9 key. (If you did, press Backspace to erase it.) Pressing Shift-F9, E inserts the {END RECORD} thingamabob plus a row of equal signs into the document. You're now ready to type the next record and all its fields.

5. **Repeat steps 1 through 4 for the next record of information you want plugged into the primary document.**

   Keep doing these steps for all the information you have, entering data for all the people to whom you'll be mailing letters, resumes, reports, eviction notices, and so on.

6. **When you're done entering fields and records, save the secondary document to disk.**

✔ The {FIELD NAMES} item should be the first record in the secondary document. That's how WordPerfect matches up the names and other information you have entered into the secondary document to the correct spaces in the primary document. Do not edit or alter the first record in any way. If you mess it up, start over again with a new document.

✔ Remember to press F9 to end each field. *Do not press Enter.* If you do press Enter, press Backspace to delete the [HRt] code and then press F9 instead.

✔ Press Shift-F9, E after the last field to end the record and start a new record.

Here are the quick steps you follow to create the first record — the field names — at the top of the secondary document:

1. Press Shift-F9, M, F.

2. Highlight {FIELD NAMES} in the list and press Enter.

3. Type each of the field names, pressing Enter after each.

4. Press F7 when you're done.

Here are the quick steps you follow to enter each record into the secondary document:

1. Type the information for each field. (The field name appears at the bottom of the screen.)

2. Press F9 when you're done typing the information for a field. Do not press the Enter key.

3. After the last field in the record, press Shift-F9, E.

Merge Mania!

After creating the primary and secondary documents, you're ready to merge away. Ensure that both primary and secondary documents have been saved to disk. Doing so is very important.

Start with a blank slate. Refer to the section on saving and starting over with a blank slate in Chapter 13 if you need instructions. Then follow these steps:

1. **Press the Merge Mania key combination, Ctrl-F9.**

   You see the following menu displayed at the bottom of the screen:

   ```
   1 Merge; 2 Sort; 3 Convert Old Merge Codes: 0
   ```

2. **Press M (Merge).**

   You are prompted to enter the name of the primary document:

   ```
   Primary file:
   ```

3. **Type the name of the primary document.**

4. **Press Enter.**

   WordPerfect prompts you for the name of the secondary document:

   ```
   Secondary file:
   ```

5. **Type the name of the secondary document.**

6. **Press Enter.**

   WordPerfect displays the message * Merging * as it works.

After a few moments — or longer, depending on how detailed the merge is and how many records you have — you have a complete, merged document.

The primary file appears several times on the screen, with information from the secondary file plugged into each copy. All the files are separated by hard-page breaks (a row of equal signs).

- ✔ Always examine the results of the merge. Some things may not have fit properly, and doubtlessly some editing is involved.

- ✔ Save the completely merged files as a document on disk. WordPerfect doesn't do this task automatically. In the end, you have the primary file, the secondary file, and the resulting merged files — three files on disk.

- ✔ You can print right from the merged file to get those custom, uniquely crafted documents out to the foolhardy who actually think you took the time to compose a personal letter. Ha! Isn't mail merge great?

Part IV
Making WordPerfect Less Than Ugly

The 5th Wave

"HE SAID 'WHY BUY JUST A WORD PROCESSOR WHEN YOU CAN GET ONE WITH A MATH AND GRAPHICS LINK CAPABLE OF DOING SCHEMATICS OF AN F100 AIRCRAFT ENGINE?' AND I THOUGHT, WELL, WE NEVER BUY 'TOASTEMS' WITHOUT BRAN,..."

In this part...

WordPerfect is really an ugly stepsister of a program. Yikes! The things it does on the screen can be incredibly confusing and chaotic. Every time I print, it amazes me how nice the documents look. On the screen — hurl!

This part of the book attempts to trowel over the rough spots on WordPerfect's ugly face. Ways are available for making WordPerfect better looking. And, unlike when you're meeting Ludmilla, your blind date from hell, these methods do not involve the consumption of alcohol.

Chapter 16
Showing Text on the Screen

. . . .

In This Chapter

▶ Changing text colors from hell
▶ Putting more characters on the screen
▶ Seeing real underlines
▶ Seeing real italics
▶ Seeing real small caps

. . . .

*W*ordPerfect has a tough time conveying what text will look like. It only has the PC's text characters to deal with, and they're all the same. So, to display underlined or very large text, WordPerfect resorts to strange colors. This feature takes some getting used to, but you'll manage. What's weirder is working on someone else's PC that has a different set of colors for boldface, underline, or italics. Yes, the colors can be changed if you like. What's weirder still is that WordPerfect is capable of showing you underlined or italic text on the screen. Honest! These are the secrets divulged in this chapter.

Changing Text Colors from Hell

If you're fed up with the colors WordPerfect uses to display information on the screen, take heart. You can change those colors. Blue, green, red, cyan, magenta, brown, white, black, yellow — you can use up to 16 colors on 8 colorful backgrounds to decorate the screen. Have WordPerfect match your wallpaper! Welcome to Interior Design for the PC 101.

For reasons WordPerfect scientists are busily researching, some people prefer their own custom colors to those offered by default. Mentally, some WordPerfect users may associate purple with underlining more readily than the blue-on-white text WordPerfect uses for underlining. Or maybe they just want to be different and see white-on-black text rather than white-on-blue text. Whatever the reason, you can join the be-different crowd and change the colors on the screen.

```
Setup: Colors          A B C D E F G H I J K L M N O P
                       A B C D E F G H I J K L M N O P
      Attribute        Foreground  Background   Sample
      Normal               H           B        Sample
      Blocked              H           E        Sample
      Underline            B           H        Sample
      Strikeout            A           D        Sample
      Bold                 P           B
      Double Underline     B           D        Sample
      Redline              E           H        Sample
      Shadow               B           H        Sample
      Italics              O           B        Sample
      Small Caps           E           D        Sample
      Outline              F           D        Sample
      Subscript            E           H        Sample
      Superscript          F           H        Sample
      Fine Print           A           F        Sample
      Small Print          H           F        Sample
      Large Print          E           A        Sample
      Very Large Print     D           A        Sample
      Extra Large Print    H           A        Sample
      Bold & Underline     P           H        Sample
      Other Combinations   A           G

      Switch documents; Move to copy settings    Doc 1
```

Figure 16-1:
The Setup:
Colors menu
in all its
glory
(although
you see it in
color on the
screen).

To see WordPerfect's text-color menu, press the following keys:

Shift-F1, D, C, 1

This key sequence activates WordPerfect's Setup: Colors menu. The menu is shown in Figure 16-1, but the figure lacks the colors you see on the screen.

The column at the far left lists the various attributes to which WordPerfect assigns colors. There are two things to color: the foreground and the background. Letters indicating the colors assigned to each attribute are shown in the next two columns; the third column shows you how that text will look on the screen.

The one or two rows of letters at the top of the screen, showing the letters A through P or the letters A through H, represent colors you can pick. For example, normal text has a foreground color of H (white) and a background color of B (blue). If this setup disgusts you, use the cursor-control keys to select a different color-letter and change the attribute's screen color to something else. Press the letter key associated with the color you want.

- ✔ The most common text attributes are Normal, Blocked, Underline, Bold, Italics, Small Caps, Superscript, and Bold & Underline. Try to make these items unique so that they stand out on the screen. The Other Combinations option is used whenever you combine two or more styles.

- ✔ If you dabble around on this screen and change your mind, press F1 to cancel. Otherwise, press F7 to set the new colors. Press F7 again to return to the document.

✔ The colors you set affect only one of WordPerfect's two documents. To use the same colors for the other document, press Ctrl-F4, Y. If you want each document to use its own color set, press Shift-F3 to modify the colors in the second document. (Refer to the section on working on two documents at once in Chapter 13 for additional information.)

Putting More Characters on the Screen

WordPerfect displays text on a screen 80 columns wide by 25 rows deep. The bottom row is used for displaying menus and other information. This is a good-sized area of text, but it only shows you a fraction of a page.

It's a lie! It's a lie! WordPerfect isn't limited to showing you only an 80-by-25 cut of a document. Provided that you have the graphics hardware in your PC, you can view larger and larger sections of text. Press these keys to start the change:

Shift-F1, D, T

This key sequence brings up the Setup: Text Screen Driver menu. You see a list of *screen drivers,* special programs WordPerfect uses to display information on the screen.

The screen driver WordPerfect is currently using has an asterisk by it. For most of us, it is the IBM VGA (& compatibles) selection. If this isn't the option selected, the screen driver with the asterisk by it is the one customized to your particular computer's hardware.

Press Enter. You see a list of display options. The one currently in use, probably (80x25), has an asterisk by it. Any additional options are displayed as well. For the IBM VGA (and compatibles) driver, the following options are displayed:

```
80x25  16 Color
80x28  16 Color  Save Font
80x43  16 Color  Save Font
80x50  16 Color
80x50  16 Color  Save Font
```

You may not see all these options, but what you do see represents the various screen resolutions (what tech-weenies call the *aspect ratios*) available for use by WordPerfect. They all show 80 columns of text, but each one down the list shows more and more rows of text. The final values, 80x50, show almost a complete page of text on the screen at once.

To select another screen resolution, use the ↑ or ↓ key to highlight the option you want; press Enter to select it. Press F7 twice to lock in the change and return to the document. If you like the current screen resolution, keep pressing F1 to cancel and return to the document.

- ✔ Not all PCs can switch to a higher resolution screen.

- ✔ If you change to a higher resolution screen, you won't be able to see underline, italics, or small caps as described in the later sections of this chapter. You still have the tasteless formatting screen colors, however, as a booby prize.

- ✔ Ignore the Save Font stuff next to some of the option names. If you're curious about what it means, highlight a Save Font item and press the Help key, F3. After you read the description, you may still not know what Save Font means. I've yet to figure it out myself.

- ✔ You can use other screen drivers with WordPerfect to wring out even more characters on the screen. My PC's video system came with a special program that lets me see 132 characters across by 52 down — nearly an entire page of teeny-tiny text. Unfortunately, it's barely readable. Your PC may come with similar programs. Force your PC guru to set up the driver files for you if you want to experiment.

Seeing Real Underlines

If Word for Windows owners taunt you and dance around singing, "You ain't got no underline!" stick your nose in the air and ignore them. Yes, indeed, WordPerfect is entirely capable of displaying underlined text on the screen. You don't even need a monochrome monitor to pull off this stunt.

To actually see real underlines on the screen, press these keys:

Shift-F1, D, C

You see the Setup: Color/Fonts menu. If item 3 says Underline Font, 8 Foreground Colors, you're in business.

Press U to activate the underline font. Press the F7 key to return to the document.

Oh, happy day; you can now see underlines on the screen. Real underlines. Cool. Rub your hands together and grin like a fool.

✔ The underline font may not be available on all PCs.

✔ When you use the special underline font, you lose the variety of text colors on the screen. And, if you've redone the text colors, they go away as well. This is but a small price to pay for real underlines, don't you agree?

✔ To adjust the screen colors when the underline font is on, press Shift-F1, D, C, 1. You see an abbreviated Colors menu, but you can still change some of the colors on the screen.

✔ To change back to the more colorful text font, press Shift-F1, D, C, N. Press the F7 key to return to the document.

Seeing Real Italics

More exciting than seeing real underlines on the screen is seeing real italics. To switch over to the italics font, press these keys:

Shift-F1, D, C

In the Setup: Color/Fonts menu, look at the second item, Italics Font, 8 Fore-ground Colors. Press I to activate the italics font and then press the F7 key to return to the document.

✔ Italics is much more cool on the screen than florescent text, don't you agree?

✔ As with the underline font, your PC may not have the italics font available. Other restrictions apply; refer to the preceding section for the caveats about using a different font on the screen.

Seeing Real Small Caps

I use italics more than anything and enjoy seeing it on the screen. Underline? Hey, all the WordPerfect users in the department of urban whatever are probably eating an extra doughnut for the privilege of seeing real underlines on the screen. Small caps? You can have them, too, if you want 'em. Press these keys:

Shift-F1, D, C, C

I'm not going to bother explaining what each key does again; refer to "Seeing Real Underlines" earlier in this chapter for a blow-by-blow account. Press the F7 key to return to the document and enjoy all those small caps.

✔ Not every PC can do small caps. But of the three different text styles you can see on the screen, I'll admit that small caps look the coolest (although they're not really the most useful).

✔ Refer to the preceding two sections for additional notes on using weird fonts in WeirdPerfect.

Chapter 17
Using WordPerfect's Menu Thing

● ●

In This Chapter

▶ Looking at the menu thing

▶ Using the menu thing

● ●

*S*triving to make WordPerfect easier to use, the folks at WordPerfect World Headquarters decided to let you use a mouse. Yeah! And then they added a happy, friendly, pull-down menu system, complete with menu items that are clearly visible. Huh? This addition ended WordPerfect's manual-transmission system of not knowing what to type and replaced it with an automatic-transmission system. Too bad no one ever uses it.

This chapter chews slowly on WordPerfect's menu thing, which I bet you didn't even know existed. You don't need a mouse to use the menu thing. In fact, you just need to remember it's there. Personally, I don't use the menu thing. But you may find it handy or at least something fun to play with while you wait for documents to print.

Looking at the Menu Thing

The menu thing is hidden at the top line of the screen. To see it, press Alt-= (equal-sign key). Press and hold the Alt key and press the equal-sign key (=). Release both keys. The menu thing appears at the top of the screen.

✔ To make the menu thing go away, press the Cancel key, F1.

✔ You can activate the menu thing by pressing the right mouse button. Select menu items by clicking the left mouse button. Click the right mouse button again to make the menu thing go away.

Using the Menu Thing

All of WordPerfect's commands have been shuffled into categories and placed into the menu thing. You select items by using the cursor-control keys to move the highlight and then pressing Enter. From that point on, the commands perform just as they do if you had pressed the proper keys on the keyboard.

For example, if you want to print a document, do the following:

1. **Press Alt-= to make the menu thing visible.**

2. **Press F to activate the File menu, or press the ↓ key or Enter.**

3. **Press ↓ some more to highlight the Print menu item.**

4. **Press Enter to select Print.**

   You see the Print menu just as if you had been quick enough to press Shift-F7.

✔ Personally, I prefer pressing Shift-F7 to doing four steps to use the menu thing.

✔ All of WordPerfect's commands are hidden in the various menu items. I could run on for pages and pages explaining everything, but you get the idea. Actually, in my opinion, the *WordPerfect For Dummies* keyboard template is a better tool than the menu thing.

✔ If you have a mouse, the menu thing makes for a handy, mouse-happy way of selecting WordPerfect commands. Mouse-aholics should love it. The rest of us will use the keyboard, thank you.

✔ What more can I say? I don't know.

Chapter 18
Using WordPerfect in Windows

*T*his chapter is about using WordPerfect *in* Windows. It's not about using WordPerfect *for* Windows, which is an entirely different program that is laughed at, er — *covered* — in the next chapter. This chapter offers soothing words of advice to that handful of readers who use the product the folks in Utah call WordPerfect for DOS under an operating system called Windows. It happens all the time. In fact, I'm running WordPerfect for DOS in Windows as I type these words. It's livable. Not ideal, but livable.

If you don't have Windows, or don't use WordPerfect in Windows, you can freely skip this chapter. (It's not like there's going to be a test on it or anything.) There are lots of Windows sayings and conventions used in this chapter. If you really need help with Windows, consider reading *Windows For Dummies,* published by IDG Books Worldwide.

Setting Up WordPerfect in the Program Manager

You can't just walk into Windows and work with WordPerfect. Windows is as ignorant of WordPerfect as WordPerfect is ignorant of Windows. You must deliberately set up a Windows computer to run WordPerfect. Here's my advice:

Have someone else do this stuff. Seriously. There are plenty of Windows wizards out there who will gladly configure your PC to have WordPerfect ready and available as an icon in Windows.

If you fail to find someone to do it for you, do the following steps. Note that I'm assuming that you know how to use a mouse in Windows and that you know what the Program Manager is and that you really want to go through 12 steps to use WordPerfect in Windows. Take a deep breath and begin:

1. **Activate the Program Manager.**

   Click somewhere on its window to bring that window to the top.

2. **Select the Run item from the Program Manager's File menu.**

   Click on the File menu with the mouse and then click on the Run item. You see the Run dialog box displayed.

3. **Type the following:**

   SETUP

   That is, type **SETUP** as one word; nothing else is required.

4. **Click on the OK button.**

   This action starts the Windows Setup program, the best way to add WordPerfect to Windows. (Ignore what anyone else says; this is it.)

   The Windows Setup program appears. It ain't much to look at, but it's a worthy piece of programming.

5. **Select the Set Up Applications item from the Options menu.**

   Click on the Options menu and then click on the Set Up Applications item. You see the Setup Applications dialog box displayed.

6. **Take a minute to read the dialog box.**

   On second thought, don't bother. Instead, click on the little o button by the item that reads `Ask you to specify an application`. Ensure that the o button is filled in with all black.

7. **Click on the OK button.**

   You see yet another dialog box, the Setup Applications dialog box. (Keep thinking to yourself, "Windows is easy, Windows is easy. . . .")

8. **Type the full pathname for WordPerfect.**

   Here's where things get rough — as if they weren't rough already. For most of us, that means type the following:

   C:\WP51\WP.EXE

If you don't have WordPerfect on drive C or in the WP51 directory, ask your guru where the WordPerfect files are located or make the guru set things up for you. Alternatively, if you're familiar with Windows, use the Browse button to locate the file WP.EXE.

9. Press Enter after typing the pathname.

If you see an error message here, it's probably telling you that the Setup program couldn't find WordPerfect. You may have typed the wrong subdirectory or pathname. Try again at Step 8 or use the Browse button to look for WP.EXE. (It helps if you're familiar with the way the Windows Browse button works.)

10. Look.

If you lucked out, you are looking at another dialog box (Windows is full of them) that displays some text and whatnot. But more importantly, you see a list of items in which WordPerfect is highlighted. Nirvana!

11. Click on the OK button. ·

In a flash, the WordPerfect program is added to the Program Manager's repertoire.

If you see another dialog box here, it may be asking you a question about PIF the magic dragon or something. Read the instructions and let your instinct tell you which button to click.

12. Select Exit from the Options menu to quit the Setup program.

✔ Isn't Windows easy to use? No, seriously, if you use the PC only for WordPerfect, dispense with Windows. Just run WordPerfect from DOS when the computer starts.

✔ Here is the shortcut step for setting up WordPerfect in Windows: Consider having someone else set up WordPerfect to run under Windows.

Starting WordPerfect in Windows

When WordPerfect is squared away and sitting as an icon in the Program Manager, you're ready to run it. Here's how that works in Windows:

1. Find the WordPerfect icon in the Program Manager.

It is probably a plain old ugly MS-DOS icon with *WordPerfect* displayed underneath it.

If you can't readily find the WordPerfect icon, look for the group named Applications. Or look in the Main group. Double-click on a group to open it and examine its iconic contents.

2. Double-click on the WordPerfect icon.

This action runs WordPerfect on the screen as you're used to it: all text, ugly colors — the whole nine yards.

✔ Use WordPerfect in Windows just as you do in DOS. The program appears in text mode on the screen, just as you're used to seeing it. Feel free to wipe those droplets of sweat from your furrowed brow.

✔ To use WordPerfect in graphics mode in Windows, refer to the next section, "Switching to Graphics Mode."

✔ When you're done using WordPerfect, press the F7 key as you normally do to quit. When WordPerfect vanishes from the screen, you return to Windows' blazing, graphics interfaceological glory.

Switching to Graphics Mode

Windows is a pretty, young, graphical program going to school in Southern California. WordPerfect is an ugly zit on the face of Windows.

What kind of valley girl or guy wants an ugly zit? Not me, no way. But you can add a dollop of Clearasil to WordPerfect's acne-ravaged look in Windows by running WordPerfect in a graphical window.

You can only pull off the graphical-window trick on computers that run Windows in enhanced mode. To see if yours is such a machine, start WordPerfect in Windows and then press the following key combination:

Alt-Enter

If your screen suddenly snaps into graphics mode, and you can see the rest of Windows as well, you're in enhanced mode. If it does nothing, sob quietly and turn bitter.

✔ Alt-Enter is a Windows key command. It doesn't belong to WordPerfect. Alt-Enter enables you to run a DOS program in a graphical text window on the screen. This setup makes WordPerfect fit in better with the Windows motif.

✔ You can continue to use WordPerfect in graphics mode as long as you like. To switch back to text mode, press Alt-Enter again.

✔ If you accidentally press Alt-spacebar, you are switched to graphics mode instantly. Press Alt-Enter to return to text mode or just press the Esc key to get rid of the "control menu."

✔ If the WordPerfect window is too small or too large, you can change its size as you do any window's size. You also can change the font used to display characters. Press Alt-spacebar, F. Then select a new font size from the list displayed in the Font Selection dialog box.

TECHNICAL STUFF

No need to bother with this information on creating a WordPerfect PIF file

You don't really have a need for a WordPerfect PIF file under Windows. I use one because I like WordPerfect to come up in a graphical window on the screen. If you do, too, create a WordPerfect PIF file for Windows. Start the PIF Editor application and enter the full pathname to WP.EXE as the Program Filename.

Select High Graphics for the Video Memory item. Do so because WordPerfect has Print Preview. If you don't select High Graphics, you can still use the Print Preview feature, but if memory in Windows gets low, the feature may become unavailable.

Check the Windowed radio button if you want WordPerfect to appear in a graphical window on the screen. Also, if you want WordPerfect to continue to print in the background while you're off doing something else, click on the Background check box. Other than these changes, leave the rest of the PIF settings the same.

Save the PIF file to disk as WP.PIF. Then update the WordPerfect icon in the Program Manager: Highlight it and press Alt-Enter to bring up its Program Item Properties dialog box. Type **WP.PIF** at the Command Line prompt and click on OK. You're in business.

Temporarily Getting Out of WordPerfect

Unlike with DOS, when you use Windows you can do several things at once. If you just need to break away and play a game — er, do some financing — you can temporarily exit WordPerfect by pressing one of the following key combinations:

Ctrl-Esc Pressing this key combination brings up the Task List dialog box. You see a list of the programs Windows is running — all at once. Double-click on the program in the list that you want to run next. For example, if you were running another program, double-click on the WordPerfect item when you want to return to it.

Alt-Esc This is the task-switching key combination. When you press Alt-Esc, you switch to another program running in Windows. It's anyone's guess which program this is, which is why I recommend pressing Ctrl-Esc.

Alt-Tab Press and hold the Alt key and press the Tab key. *Do not release the Alt key.* This key combination clears the screen and displays the name of another program running in Windows. You can continue to press the Tab key to see every program's name. Only when you release the Alt key are you zapped into another program.

✔ Even though you leave WordPerfect to do something else, you haven't quit the program. WordPerfect is still running; it's just not up on the screen. To return to WordPerfect, use one of the three key combinations listed and select WordPerfect as the program you want to run.

✔ If WordPerfect is already running and you try to run it again, you see the message Are other copies of WordPerfect currently running? If you see this message, or anything similar, press F1 to immediately cancel. Then use one of the three key combinations listed here to locate the already-running copy of WordPerfect.

Associating Files in the File Manager

A handy way to run programs in Windows is to associate them with their files in the File Manager, which means that you tag a certain type of file as belonging to a program. For example, you can earmark all files with the extension WP as documents that belong to WordPerfect.

Why associate WP files with WordPerfect? So that you can use the File Manager to locate documents and then double-click on them to both start WordPerfect *and* load said document. At times this stuff actually works in Windows. Follow these steps to associate files with the WordPerfect program:

1. **Use the File Manager to locate a WordPerfect document on disk.**

   The document file must have the extension WP or some other extension common to all (or most of) your document files.

2. **Click once on the filename to highlight it.**

3. **Select the Associate item from the File menu.**

4. **In the Associate dialog box, type the full pathname of the WordPerfect program.**

   For most of us, that means type the following:

   C:\WP51\WP.EXE

   This is the same pathname specified in "Setting Up WordPerfect in the Program Manager," earlier in this chapter. Normally, the pathname is typed exactly as shown here. If you have WordPerfect's WP.EXE file on another drive or in another subdirectory, adjust the pathname accordingly.

5. **Click on the OK button.**

   All files with the WP extension, or those matching the extension on the file you selected, are now associated with WordPerfect.

To automatically run WordPerfect and load one of those files, select an associated file in the File Manager and double-click on it.

- ✔ Associated files appear in the File Manager with teeny horizontal lines on their icons. Unassociated files appear by blank icons.

- ✔ Associating files isn't magic. It only works by file extension. So if you, like me, don't always give files a WP extension, the association doesn't work. Gee, isn't Windows easy?

- ✔ If you double-click on an associated file and see the message `Are other copies of WordPerfect currently running?` when WordPerfect starts, press the F1 key. You already have a copy of WordPerfect running in Windows. Exit the File Manager and press Ctrl-Esc. From the list of programs displayed, double-click on WordPerfect. Then use the Shift-F10 command in WordPerfect to retrieve the document the old-fashioned way.

- ✔ If you created a PIF file for WordPerfect, you can type **WP.PIF** rather than the longer C:\WP51\WP.EXE pathname in Step 4 of these steps.

Chapter 19
Using WordPerfect for Windows

• •

In This Chapter
▶ Why on earth would you want to use WordPerfect for Windows?
▶ Making WordPerfect for Windows compatible with WordPerfect for DOS

• •

I am not a big WordPerfect 5.1 for Windows fan. This book covers it because the Windows version is kinda similar to the DOS version; you may, against your will, be forced to use WordPerfect 5.1 for Windows at some point. The problem is that WordPerfect 5.1 for Windows, when compared with other Windows word processors, has a rough and uncomfortable edge to it. Personally, I recommend using WordPerfect for DOS in Windows instead; refer to Chapter 18, please.

OK. These are all the nasty things I'm going to say about WordPerfect 5.1 for Windows — at least in the chapter opening. (They made me delete the chapter "Ten Reasons Not To Buy WordPerfect for Windows.") This chapter grinds away at a few key WordPerfect for Windows issues. If you don't have WordPerfect 5.1 for Windows, you don't need to read this chapter. If you do have the program, this chapter tells you how to get more out of WordPerfect for Windows as a former WordPerfect for DOS user.

Why on Earth Would You Want To Use WordPerfect for Windows?

WordPerfect is a great word processor. They just can't seem to bolt a good graphical interface to it. I experienced this shortcoming firsthand on the Macintosh. I bought WordPerfect for the Mac. I did it to be compatible with all the WordPerfect for DOS machines around the office. Big mistake. WordPerfect for the Mac was a terrible product: klutzy and buggy. WordPerfect 5.1 for Windows continues this fine tradition . . . ah, but I promised not to be too hard on it; I digress.

Here are a few reasons why you may want to become a WordPerfect 5.1 for Windows user (hold your nose):

1. You use Windows.

Obviously, WordPerfect for Windows is a Windows product, which justifies your investment in Windows as the DOS of the future. Or *is* WordPerfect for Windows really a Windows product? The debate continues.

2. You need to share files with other computers that use WordPerfect.

WordPerfect for Windows reads WordPerfect for DOS's files and vice versa. It also reads other WordPerfect formats, which makes WordPerfect for Windows nice to have as a common ground.

3. You like to see text on the screen the way it is.

This is perhaps one of the greatest advantages of WordPerfect for Windows. You see text on the screen the same way it looks when printed. You see boldface, underline, italics — even some of the more esoteric text appearances and sizes — on the screen as they print.

4. You want to work with multiple documents.

WordPerfect limits you to working on only two documents at once. You can work on a number of documents in WordPerfect for Windows, keeping several of them in memory at once.

5. WordPerfect for Windows has a better help system.

WordPerfect for Windows has a great help system — much better than plain ol' WordPerfect's — and it's much more detailed.

6. Someone else made you.

No explanation is necessary here.

7. You like pain.

OK. If you're just starting out, WordPerfect for Windows is a nice word processor. It's certainly better than anything Windows had a few years back. But, if you're used to real Windows word processors, you're in for a letdown. This program just isn't up to snuff in my opinion.

Maybe they'll come out with a book called *WordPerfect For Windows For Dummies*. Nope, too many *for*s in the title. It'll never fly.

Making WordPerfect for Windows Compatible with WordPerfect for DOS

If you're a veteran WordPerfect user, you can get along just fine in WordPerfect 5.1 for Windows. Many of the key commands you're used to are the same. For example, F10 is Save, F8 is Underline, F2 is Search Down, Shift-F7 is Print, and so on. And, if you're used to using the menu thing and love the mouse, you'll be comfortable at once.

To make WordPerfect for Windows more compatible with the DOS version of the program, select the Preferences item from the File menu and then select the Keyboard item. Select the desired WordPerfect for DOS keyboard filename to use the same key commands in WordPerfect for Windows as you're used to in WordPerfect for DOS. That's a lot of selecting and clicking with the mouse, but it gives you the old, WordPerfect for DOS comfortable key commands as a reward.

This works great, but be aware of one difference: The F1 and F3 keys are reversed. In WordPerfect for Windows, F1 is the Help key. Pressing it displays the help system, which isn't bad. But, when you want to cancel something, press F3. Sometimes only the Esc key works. Hmmm. Has your brain turned to fruit salad yet?

- ✔ Not all the keyboard commands are compatible, but most are close.

- ✔ WPDOS51.WWK is the specific keyboard file most compatible with the keyboard commands used in this book.

- ✔ WordPerfect's menu thing is covered in Chapter 17. It's very similar to the menu layout in WordPerfect for Windows.

Some hints to help ease the pain

Here is a list of helpful hints for the WordPerfect for DOS user who's forced — against his or her will, no less — to use WordPerfect 5.1 for Windows. Try these hints before visiting a gun store:

- ✔ Shortcut attribute keys are available: Press Ctrl-B for boldface and Ctrl-I for italics. Using these shortcut keys really speeds things up when you change the attributes of blocks and text on the screen.

- ✔ If you're more used to Windows key commands, select the Windows keyboard from the File Preferences Keyboard menu/item/thing. Click on the Default CUA or whatever button to use Windows key commands.

- ✔ Use Windows printing techniques: Select the Printer item from the File menu and then click on the Windows radio button. Using this technique avoids some printing hassles — especially the long delay when Windows first starts or loads documents.

- ✔ If the text is too tiny on the screen, use the Zoom command. Select the Zoom item from the View menu and pick a magnification factor from the submenu. I like 125 percent because I have a relatively small monitor.

- ✔ I wrote this chapter in WordPerfect for Windows. I am now in a terrible mood.

Part V
Help Me, Mr. Wizard!

The 5th Wave   By Rich Tennant

"GUESS WHAT DAD - THOSE CHOCOLATE DISKETTES FIT RIGHT INTO YOUR COMPUTER, NO PROBLEM."

In this part...

WordPerfect is not the sole cause of your woes. When you use a computer, you have several things to contend with: the computer, DOS, the printer, phases of the moon . . . . It's like starring in a bad French farce with too many villains. Fortunately, some humans — yes, humans — really *like* computers. When you're in dire straights, you can call on their expertise. Call them wizards. Call them gurus. Call them when you need help. And, when you can't call on them, refer to the chapters in this part of the book to help you through your troubles.

Chapter 20
Dealing with DOS

• •

In This Chapter

▶ Organizing files

▶ Creating a new directory

▶ Putting WordPerfect on the path

▶ Making a WordPerfect batch file

▶ Formatting disks

▶ Backing up

• •

*I*f WordPerfect is set up just so, you never have to mess with DOS, the computer's disk operating system. Yeah, right. And the check is in the mail, your kid really doesn't know who broke the lamp, and I'm from the government and I'm here to help you. Fortunately, it's possible to avoid DOS *most* of the time you're using WordPerfect. For those few times DOS and WordPerfect do clash, however, turn to this chapter for the help you need.

This chapter is seriously optional reading for the typical WordPerfect beginner. Only peer into these pages if you're stuck and have nowhere else to turn.

Organizing Files

DOS's main job is to put files on disk. It gobbles up the WordPerfect documents in memory and spits them out on the hard drive for later retrieval, editing, and printing. This is immensely handy, and I recommend that you save all your documents to disk; refer to Chapter 13 for the details.

The drawback to using the hard drive is that it can get cluttered quickly. To help you avoid the clutter, DOS enables you to organize files on the hard drive into separate storage places call *directories*. Each directory contains its own, separate set of files, and yet all the files are stored on the hard drive. The directories keep you organized.

I recommend that you use directories to organize various projects. You can even have directories within directories for two and three levels of organization. It can be fun, but it's not without its cryptic aspect.

- ✔ The subject of naming files and storing them on disk is covered in Chapter 14.

- ✔ If your guru has organized the hard drive, refer to the section on finding a place for your work in Chapter 14. Use the table there to write down the names of the various subdirectories your guru may have set up for you.

Creating a New Directory

Creating a new directory is like making a new garage or closet. Suddenly, you have all the storage space you dreamed of. Think of your power tools neatly organized and no more boxes piled waist high. And, for you men out there, think of all the shoes you could put into that closet. Too bad real life isn't as handy as a computer. When you need new space for organizing the documents, or you want to start a new project, you can create a new directory on disk.

To create a new directory for storing the documents and files — but no shoes — follow these steps in WordPerfect:

1. Press the List Files key, F5.

You see the following at the bottom of the screen:

```
Dir pathname
```

The pathname you see is WordPerfect's current directory. On the other side of the screen is the message `Type = to change default dir.`

2. Press = (the equal key).

You see the following prompt:

```
New directory = pathname
```

3. To create a new directory, type its full pathname.

For example, suppose that you want to create a directory named WORK on drive C. Type **C:\WORK** at the prompt.

4. Press Enter.

You see the following at the bottom of the screen:

```
Create C:\WORK? No (Yes)
```

5. Press Y (Yes).

The directory is created, but you're not yet using it. To use the directory, repeat steps 1 through 3, typing the same directory name. This action logs you to the new directory, where you can start using it at once.

✔ More information on using a directory can be found in the section about using a new directory in Chapter 14.

✔ Directories are named just like files: You can use from one to eight characters — letters and numbers only.

✔ You can use these steps to create subdirectories as well as directories. Just type the complete pathname for the subdirectory you want to create. For example, to create a subdirectory named POEMS in the WORK directory, type the following at Step 3:

C:\WORK\POEMS

Putting WordPerfect on the Path

The word *path* in the title of this section does not refer to that rose-lined walkway that extends from your front door to the mailbox. Nope. This is DOS, and nothing is charming. A *path* is an involved list of subdirectories that DOS searches for files. It's like a list of places DOS searches in the garage for missing garden tools. But, in this case, the tools are programs.

The advantage to putting WordPerfect on the path is that you can type **WP** at any DOS prompt, anywhere in the computer system, and WordPerfect immediately runs. DOS can always find the WP tool in its garage full o' stuff. This setup helps you avoid those odious Bad command or file name error messages.

If you're a total DOS beginner, and you want to put WordPerfect on the path, you need to know a few things. First, you need to know where the WordPerfect program files are located. For most of us, that's in the following directory:

C:\WP51

If your copy of WordPerfect is in a different directory, you need to specify its pathname in the PATH command. The path is how DOS finds the WordPerfect program when you type **WP.**

To put WordPerfect on the path, follow these steps:

1. Start with a new document in WordPerfect.

Save your stuff if you need to and then start over with a clean slate. Refer to the section on saving and starting over with a clean slate in Chapter 13.

2. Load the file AUTOEXEC.BAT for editing.

This is a special file DOS uses each time you start the computer. Press Shift-F10; at the prompt, type the following:

C:\AUTOEXEC.BAT

If the AUTOEXEC.BAT file appears on the screen, go to Step 3.

If nothing appears on the screen, your PC lacks an AUTOEXEC.BAT file. Gasp! How could you do such a thing? Never mind; type the following before anyone else notices:

PATH=C:\WP51

That is, type **PATH,** an equal sign (=), the letter **C,** a colon (:), a backslash (\), and **WP51.** This is the location of WordPerfect on the system. If WordPerfect is in a different directory, type that pathname rather than C:\WP51. Then press Enter and skip to Step 5.

3. Look for a line in the AUTOEXEC.BAT file that starts with the word *PATH.*

For example, you may see the following:

```
PATH=C:\DOS
```

If you already see WordPerfect listed on the path — a directory similar to C:\WP51, hidden somewhere on that line — there's nothing else to do here. Skip to Step 6.

If you don't see C:\WP51 or anything similar after the word *PATH,* move the cursor to the end of the PATH line by pressing the End key.

4. Type a semicolon (;) and the pathname for WordPerfect.

For example, type the following at the end of the PATH line:

;C:\WP51

That is, type a semicolon (;), the letter **C** and a colon (:) for drive C, a backslash (\), and **WP51.** If your copy of the program is in a different directory, type its pathname rather than WP51.

5. Save AUTOEXEC.BAT back to disk.

But AUTOEXEC.BAT must be saved as a DOS text file. Carefully press the following keys to save the file as a text file:

Ctrl-F5, T, S

Type **C:\AUTOEXEC.BAT** at the prompt for a filename and press Enter.

You are asked whether you want to overwrite the original file. Press Y (Yes).

6. **Exit the document and start over again with a clean slate.**

Press F7, N, N to exit and start over again.

✔ These steps put everything into place, but they don't turn the ignition switch. You have to quit WordPerfect and reset the computer for the magic to happen. ***Remember:*** Reset the PC *only* when you see a DOS prompt on the screen.

✔ Boy! This is sure complex. If you agree, have your guru do it all for you. But the advantage is that these steps enable the computer to always find WordPerfect when you type **WP** and press Enter at a DOS prompt.

✔ If you made a mistake, or something doesn't work right after you follow these steps, contact your guru for assistance. Explain that you tried your best on your own before calling him or her. Your guru will appreciate hearing that.

✔ If you put the WordPerfect directory on the path, there's no need for you to create a WordPerfect batch file, as described in the following section.

Making a WordPerfect Batch File

Batch files are — stand back! — *programs* you can create for DOS. Yes, this is programming. So what is the topic of programming doing in a . . . *For Dummies* book? Well, you asked: Chapter 1 probably directed you here, suggesting that you take a peek to see what a batch file can do to help you run WordPerfect.

Before reading any further, you should know that if you followed the steps for putting WordPerfect on the path in the preceding section, there's no need for you to create a WordPerfect batch file. Therefore, what remains of this section is for the stout hearted and for true batch-file believers.

A batch file can help you run WordPerfect in a painless and quick manner, just as a toaster in the bathtub can kill you in a painless and quick manner. This stuff requires some guts you may not be willing to forsake here. I mean, if you've already swallowed bright yellow text as italics, how much farther can we push it?

Here are the as-painless-as-possible steps for creating a WordPerfect batch file. Follow these steps to the letter:

1. **Start over with a clean slate in WordPerfect.**

Refer to the section on saving and starting over with a clean slate in Chapter 13 for details.

2. Type the following text, pressing Enter at the end of each line:

@ECHO OFF

C:\WP51\WP %1

There are only two lines to type: The first line starts with @ (an at sign), the word **ECHO,** a space, and the word **OFF.** There is no space between the @ and ECHO.

The second line is a pathname, indicating the location of WordPerfect on the hard drive. For this example, type the letter **C,** a colon (:), a backslash (\), **WP51,** another backslash (\), **WP,** a space, a percent sign (%), and the number **1.** (Reads like a secret code, no? Better go get the Captain Marvel decoder ring.)

If you have WordPerfect in a different location (on a different drive or in a different directory), specify that pathname as the first part of line 2. The second half of the line — the space and %1 — stays the same.

3. Save the batch-file creation to disk.

The file must be saved as a DOS text file. You do this procedure by pressing the following WordPerfect keys:

Ctrl-F5, T, S

At the prompt for a filename, type **C:\WP.BAT.** That's the letter **C** and a colon (:) for drive C, a backslash (\), and **WP.BAT,** the name of the file. Then press Enter.

✔ Here's a suggestion: Direct your DOS guru to do this stuff for you. Show him or her this book and point to the following paragraph, which is directed right at your guru:

Hello, Guru! I want you to create a WordPerfect batch file for my computer. Stick it in a directory on the path. Make sure that you specify the proper location for WordPerfect on my system. Refer to the preceding example for what I want. Don't get too fancy; I'm a WordPerfect beginner. Thank you. Your pizza is in the mail.

✔ If you're adept at these types of things, put the WP.BAT file in the DOS directory. Or put it in a special batch-file subdirectory if you've created one.

Formatting Disks

Formatting disks is something we all have to do. Disks begin life naked. All the disks in a new box are blank, like blank audio cassettes and video tapes. But unlike when recording music or a TV program, you must *format* a computer disk before you can use it. Here's how to do that in WordPerfect:

1. **Press Ctrl-F1.**

   This action activates the Shell command, which normally displays a lovely seafood and pasta platter. But, because you probably have an older version of WordPerfect, you see the following instead:

   ```
   1 Go to DOS; 2 DOS Command: 0
   ```

2. **Carefully press 2 (DOS Command).**

   You want to select the second item, the DOS command.

   If you accidentally press 1, ignore what you see on the screen. Type the word **EXIT** and press Enter to return to WordPerfect. Go back to Step 1.

   The following is displayed at the bottom of the screen:

   ```
   DOS Command:
   ```

3. **Type the following:**

   FORMAT A:

   That is, type the word **FORMAT,** a space, the letter **A,** and a colon (:).

4. **Press the Enter key.**

   This action directs DOS to run its FORMAT command, which prepares a floppy disk for use. The screen clears, and you see something like the following displayed:

   ```
   Insert new diskette for drive A:
   and press ENTER when ready...
   ```

5. **Stick a new floppy disk into drive A.**

   For the larger, 5¼-inch disk, close the drive's door latch.

6. **Press the Enter key.**

   DOS usually displays something mildly interesting while formatting takes place. Think of it like that annoying band of stock-market quotes that crawls along the bottom of the screen on *CNN Headline News* during the weekdays.

After formatting is complete, you see the following:

```
Format complete.
Volume label (11 characters, ENTER for none)?
```

The second line is DOS asking you to enter a volume label for the disk.

7. Press Enter.

You may see some interesting yet entirely meaningless statistics displayed.

DOS finally asks whether you want to format another disk:

```
Format another (Y/N)?
```

8. Press N.

At the bottom of the screen is a press any key to continue prompt.

9. Press Enter and you're back in WordPerfect.

✔ There are two disk sizes used by DOS: The small and compact 3½-inch disks and the larger and floppier 5¼-inch disks. Buy the right size for your computer. Compare sizes by measuring the floppy disk drive's gaping maw.

✔ There are also two disk capacities. Always buy the largest capacity the system can handle. For most of us, that's high capacity or high density. As long as you use these disks, formatting won't be a problem.

✔ Sometimes you can buy preformatted disks. They're a tad more expensive than the other disks, but they save you time and the hassle of repeating these steps every time you want to use a floppy disk.

✔ Chapter 10 in *DOS For Dummies,* published by IDG Books Worldwide, goes into great detail on buying, formatting, and using disks.

Backing Up

Backing up your stuff is as important as saving a document to disk. When you back up, you create duplicate documents on a second disk, usually a floppy disk. That way, if anything ever happens to the computer or its hard drive, you can recover quickly by using the backup copy.

You can back up in one of two ways. The first is to run a special backup program, such as DOS's BACKUP command — definitely something your guru needs to set up for you. Your guru should also give you a list of instructions on how and when to back up.

The second way you can back up is to use WordPerfect's File Copy command in the List Files window. In the List Files window, you mark the files you want copies of and then copy them all to a floppy disk in drive A. Follow the steps outlined in the section on copying files in Chapter 14 for more information.

- ✔ You should back up your files every day. If you use the List Files key, F5, to mark and copy files, check the file dates and copy everything that has today's date on it (all the files you worked on today). When WordPerfect asks whether you want to replace files already on the backup disk, press Y; you always want newer files to replace older ones.

- ✔ To use a floppy disk, you must first format it. Refer to "Formatting Disks," earlier in this chapter, for additional information.

- ✔ If you accidentally delete a file, you may be able to undelete it without having to resort to a backup copy of the file. Refer to Chapter 22 — the section entitled "Oops! I Deleted My Document!"

Chapter 21
Thinking of the Printer as Your Friend

. . . .

In This Chapter

▶ Feeding it paper

▶ Unjamming the printer

▶ Getting rid of incessant double spacing

▶ Replacing ribbons and toner

▶ Getting rid of weird characters

▶ Setting up a new printer

▶ Changing printers

▶ Selecting a network printer

. . . .

*I*s the printer your friend? Perhaps. Unfortunately, friend or foe, the printer is just as stupid as the computer. This means you must beat it with a stick a few times to get it to behave, or else you'll wind up hitting yourself in the head with the same stick. But give yourself a second to repose; consider leafing through this chapter before causing yourself or your printer any physical harm. (The subject of printing in WordPerfect is covered in Chapter 12 of this book.)

Feeding It Paper

The way the paper feeds into the printer depends on the printer you have. Some printers eat paper a page at a time. Other printers may suck up continuous sheets of fan-fold paper directly from the box (the spaghetti approach). And laser printers delicately lift one sheet of paper at a time from their paper trays and weld the image to the page by using dusty toner and inferno-like temperatures. Printing can be quite dramatic.

Whichever way the printer eats paper, make sure that you have a lot of it on hand. The end result of a word processor's labors is the printed document. So buy a box or two of paper at a time. I'm serious: You save money and trips to the store in the long run. As a suggestion, look for a huge paper store or supplier and buy printer paper from it rather than from an office supply or computer store. The prices are better.

- Try to get 20-pound paper. The 18-pound paper is too thin. I like 25-pound paper, which is thicker and holds up very well, but it's more expensive. Paper that's too thick, such as card stock, may not go through the printer.

- Colored paper and fancy stuff are OK.

- Do not print on erasable bond paper. This paper is awful. After all, the point behind erasable bond is that you can erase on it, which doesn't happen much with paper run through a computer printer.

- Avoid using fancy, dusted paper in a laser printer. Some expensive papers are coated with a powder. This powder comes off in a laser printer and gums up the works.

- Only buy two-part or three-part fan-fold paper if you need it. This kind of paper contains carbon paper and is commonly used for printing invoices and orders. Also, the old green-bar paper makes for lousy correspondence. It has *nerd* written all over it.

- If you need to print labels in the laser printer, get special laser-printer labels. I recommend Avery labels.

- Laser printers can print on clear transparencies but only those specially designed for use in a laser printer. Anything less than that melts inside the printer, and you're forced to clean out the gunk.

Unjamming the Printer

Next time you're in San Francisco, there's a little psychic you can visit on The Haight. She'll do a chart for your printer, to explain why it jams on some days and not on others. This is the best solution I can offer to the question "Why can't the paper always go through the printer like it's supposed to?"

If you have a dot-matrix printer and the paper jams, cancel printing in WordPerfect. (Refer to the section in Chapter 12 on canceling a print job.) Then turn the printer off. Rewind the knob to reverse-feed the paper back out of the printer. Don't pull on the paper or it will tear, and you'll have to take apart the printer to get the paper out. (If that happens, call someone else for help.)

If the paper jams in a laser printer, you have to pop open the lid, find the errant piece of paper, remove it, and then slam the lid shut. Watch out for various hot things inside the printer; be careful of what you touch. There's no need for you to cancel printing here because laser printers have more brain cells than their dot-matrix cousins. However, you may need to reprint the page jammed in the printer. Refer to the section on printing a specific page in Chapter 12.

If the jam was caused by using thick paper, retrying the operation probably won't work. Use thinner paper.

Getting Rid of Incessant Double Spacing

Nothing is quite as disenchanting as a printer that constantly produces double-spaced documents whether you want them double-spaced or not. This is a terribly annoying problem; fortunately, it has a handy one-time solution — provided that you kept the printer manual when you bought the printer.

Somewhere on the printer is a tiny switch. That switch controls whether the printer double-spaces all the time or only single-spaces. If the printer is double-spacing all the time, the switch is set to double-space no matter what. You need to find that switch and turn it off.

- ✔ Sometimes, the little switch is on the back or side of the printer; sometimes it's actually *inside* the printer.

- ✔ Turn the printer off before you flip the switch. This rule of thumb is especially important if the switch is inside the printer. Turning off the printer also prevents people from printing while your fingers are in the way of the printer's buzz-saw-like gears.

- ✔ The switch may be referred to as *LF after CR* or *line feed after carriage return* or *Add LF* or *stop double-spacing!* or something along these lines.

Replacing Ribbons and Toner

Always have a good ribbon or toner cartridge in the printer. *Always!* Most printers use ribbons; laser printers use toner cartridges. Never skimp on ribbons or toner cartridges lest the printer pixies come to you in your dreams and smear ink on your fingers.

- ✔ Keep a supply of two or three extra ribbons or toner cartridges on hand. This supply holds you in case you need a new one over a working weekend.

- ✔ When the ribbon gets old and faded, replace it. Some places may offer reinking services for ribbons. This approach works, provided that the ribbon fabric can hold the new ink. If the ribbon is threadbare, buy a new one.

- ✔ You can revitalize an old ribbon by carefully opening up its cartridge and spraying some WD-40 on it. Reassemble the cartridge and put the ribbon on some paper towels. Let it sit for a day before reusing it. This approach should give the ribbon some extra life, but you can do it only once.

- ✔ Ink printers use ink cartridges. Replace them when they run low on ink just as you replace a ribbon or toner cartridge.

- ✔ When a laser printer's toner cartridge gets low, you see a flashing toner light or the message Toner low displayed on the printer's control panel. Take the toner cartridge out and rock it a bit, which makes it last about a week longer. When you see the message again, replace the toner cartridge immediately.

- ✔ There are services that offer toner recharging. For a nominal fee, they refill old toner cartridges with new toner. Then you can use the toner cartridge again and squeeze some more money out of it. Nothing is wrong with this approach, and I recommend it as a good cost-saving measure. But never recharge a toner cartridge more than once, nor should you do business with anyone who says doing so is OK.

Getting Rid of Weird Characters

If strange characters appear on your output — almost like the printer burped — it's a sign that WordPerfect may not be set up to use the printer properly. Those stray @ and # characters that appear on the paper but not on the screen indicate that the printer driver may be improperly installed.

Refer to "Changing Printers" later in this chapter. Check the current printer (the one with the asterisk by it) and make sure that it has the same name as the printer hooked up to the PC. If not, select the proper printer from the list. And, if the printer isn't on the list, refer to the next section, "Setting Up a New Printer," for information on getting the printer to work properly with WordPerfect.

Setting Up a New Printer

Setting up the printer is both a physical and a mental activity. The physical part involves connecting a cable to both the PC and the printer. The part that makes you mental is the software part, where you gracefully grab WordPerfect by the throat and scream, "Look, bud, this is my printer! And I paid lots of money for it! Use those special fonts I paid for!"

Hopefully, someone else has set up the printer for you. This procedure is done when you first install WordPerfect. One of the many questions the installation process asks is "Which printer do you have?" Of the thousands of possibilities, WordPerfect knows about 800. This isn't something to poke fun at; of all PC software available, WordPerfect supports more printers than any other product. Chances are, you'll get to use all the printer power you paid for.

If WordPerfect isn't set up to use your printer, or if you've changed printers and need to reset everything for the new printer, follow these steps:

1. **Run the INSTALL program that came with WordPerfect.**

   This program is located in the same directory as WordPerfect. Chances are, you can type **INSTALL** at the DOS prompt, press Enter, and run the WordPerfect Installation program. If this approach doesn't work, scream out loud right now for help.

2. **Follow the directions on the INSTALL program's screen.**

   Read everything. Eventually, you see a menu where one of the items is `Setup Printer` or `Update Printer`. Select that item and continue to follow the instructions on the screen.

   You may have to insert one of the original Printer disks that came with WordPerfect. Check the software box or your disk caddy for those disks. You need them to install the new printer.

3. **Continue to follow the directions on the screen for setting up the printer.**

4. **After the printer setup is complete, quit the INSTALL program by pressing the Exit key, F7.**

You now can run WordPerfect again and enjoy the benefits of the new printer.

- ✔ When setting up printers for WordPerfect, install every possible printer you think you'll ever use. For example, I set up WordPerfect for every printer in the office, even though my PC has always used the same printer. I even added a few printers I'd like to buy but can't afford. That way, if I ever switch printers in the future, I won't need to go through these steps; I can go to the steps in the next section, "Changing Printers."

- ✔ If you can't find a disk for the printer you want to set up, call WordPerfect's printer support line. The number can be found in the manual. Of course, I've never found it there. If you can't either, dial 1-800-555-1212 and ask for WordPerfect printer support or just WordPerfect technical support. The 800 operator will give you the number. Write it down.

- ✔ Some manufacturers provide additional printer drivers for WordPerfect. Your printer may have come with disks that contain WordPerfect drivers. Scour the piles of junk around your desk for those disks.

Changing Printers

The multiple-choice printer game is necessary because a single PC can be connected to or have the potential of using several different printers. For example, you may change printers in the future or one day walk into your office and find that someone else has changed the printer for you. (How nice.) When that happens, you need to tell WordPerfect that you're using another printer.

To select another printer for WordPerfect, follow these steps:

1. Press Shift-F7, the Print command, to display the Print menu.

2. Press S to select a new printer.

The screen clears, and you see a list of printers WordPerfect knows about. (These printers were selected when WordPerfect was initially installed.)

The printers are listed by name and model number. For example, the Hewlett Packard LaserJet IIIP is listed on the screen as HP LaserJet IIIP.

The printer currently selected is highlighted and has an asterisk next to its name.

3. Locate the printer you want to switch to in the list.

Press the ↑ or ↓ key to highlight that printer and press Enter.

4. Press the F7 key to exit the Print menu.

You're done. WordPerfect is now set up to use the new printer.

✔ Selecting the proper printer in WordPerfect is a requirement. It means that WordPerfect will talk to the printer in a language they both understand, and if the entrails are favorable that day, things print as beautifully as you intended.

✔ There's no point in changing printers unless you have the new printer hooked up and ready to use with the computer. If that's not the case, don't mess with things.

✔ If the printer you want to change to is not listed, refer to the preceding section, "Setting Up a New Printer."

Selecting a Network Printer

If your computer is shackled to a network, the odds are pretty good that you use a network printer. This is the type of occasion worth wearing black for. When you use a network printer, it usually means the printer isn't tied directly to your computer by the printer umbilical cord. Instead, the printer is elsewhere, somewhere *out there,* in the network ether.

Printing to a network printer works just like printing to a regular printer. You still press Shift-F7 to bring up the Print menu, and all WordPerfect's printer commands and whatnot work the same. The difference is that the printer may not be in the room with you. You have to walk over to the printer room or to the boss's office to pick up your stuff from the printer.

✔ Follow the instructions in the preceding section, "Changing Printers," for information on selecting a specific network printer. You may also need to contact your network human to see which printer is in which office (although it may say so right on the screen; you never know).

✔ Why is it that only bosses (or the biggest PC crybabies — often both the same) always get the printer in their offices? Why can't we people who really use the printer have it in our offices? Revolt! Revolt!

Chapter 22
Help Me — I'm Stuck!

- -

In This Chapter

▶ I can't find WordPerfect!

▶ Are other copies of WordPerfect running?

▶ How do I find lost files?

▶ Where did my document go?

▶ Where am I now?

▶ It's not printing!

▶ Oops! I deleted my document!

▶ Oops! I just reformatted my disk!

▶ What's a nonhyphenating hyphen?

▶ The screen looks weird!

▶ The darn thing's run amok!

▶ The rest of my document is in italics/boldface/big text!

- -

*T*here I was, minding my own business, when all of a sudden — for no apparent reason — WordPerfect *fill in the blank*. Where's my baseball bat?

It happens all too often. And it happens to everyone. "It worked just great when I did this yesterday. Why doesn't it work today?" Who knows? Retrace your steps. Check the ground for signs of gypsies. But, in the end, turn to this chapter for some quick solutions.

I Can't Find WordPerfect!

Nothing induces that sensation that you've just stepped through a door marked *Twilight Zone* better than typing **WP** at the DOS prompt and seeing Bad command or file name. Uh-oh. Looks like WordPerfect found the car keys and is gone, gone, gone. But where did it go?

Type the following at the DOS prompt and press Enter:

C:

Typing **C:** and pressing Enter logs you to drive C, the main hard drive. You may have tried to run WordPerfect from an alien hard drive. Try typing **WP** at the DOS prompt now.

If the C: trick doesn't work, try typing this command and pressing Enter:

**CD **

That is, type **CD,** a space, and then the backslash character (not the forward slash you find under the question mark). Press Enter. Now try typing **WP** to start WordPerfect.

If this approach still doesn't help, reset the computer: Press Ctrl-Alt-Delete. That is, press and hold the Ctrl and Alt keys and then press the Delete key. Release all three keys. The computer will reset. When it's done, start over.

- ✔ You may also look for the file WP.EXE. Refer to "How Do I Find Lost Files?" later in this chapter for details.

- ✔ If this is a consistent problem, contact your guru and tell him or her what's going on. Also, refer to Chapter 20's sections about putting WordPerfect on the path and making a WordPerfect batch file.

Are Other Copies of WordPerfect Running?

Here's a dandy: You start up WordPerfect and you see the following message:

```
Are other copies of WordPerfect currently running?
```

Well, are they? Chances are that they may be if you use Microsoft Windows or a program like the DOS Shell, Software Carousel, or DESQview. In those computer environments, it's entirely possible to have more than one copy of WordPerfect running at the same time. So the answer appears to be yes — *but don't press Y or N yet!*

Press F7 to quit WordPerfect at once. Return to a menu and check to see whether WordPerfect is already running in a window, job, or task somewhere. If so, use that copy of WordPerfect and don't start another one.

If you can't find other copies of WordPerfect, type **EXIT** at the DOS prompt. You're magically returned to WordPerfect.

But wait! There is another circumstance where you can see that message and everything is 100 percent OK. Suppose that the computer just crashed. The last thing you remember before the lights went out is working on WordPerfect. If that just happened to you, press N when you're asked whether other copies of WordPerfect are running. Then WordPerfect starts as it normally does.

> ✔ If you see the message `Old backup file exists?` select the item that says `Rename`. Rename the backup file to OLD1. When you're back in WordPerfect, find and load the file named OLD1. This is how you recover a file after a crash but only if you've activated the autosave feature, described in Chapter 24.

> ✔ Refer to Chapter 18 for information on using WordPerfect in Windows.

How Do I Find Lost Files?

Sometimes DOS has a hard time bolting files down on a disk. Because the disk is constantly spinning, I assume that centrifugal force flings the files outward, plastering them to the inside walls of the disk drive like gum under a school desk. That's the mental picture I get. Whatever the case, you can find a lost file quite easily. It just takes time. A putty knife is optional.

If you're in WordPerfect, press the List Files key, F5. This command is covered in detail in Chapter 14. You may need to use the down-arrow key to view extra files not displayed on the screen. This is a common oversight. Just press the plus key on the numeric keypad to see the next screenful of files.

Another trick to use in the List Files window/thing is the N command. Press N to see the following at the bottom of the screen:

```
(Name search; Enter or arrows to exit)
```

Type the first letter of the filename you want to look for. Type the second letter. As you type, WordPerfect highlights a file in the list that starts with those letters. If you see the file you're looking for on the screen, use the arrow keys to highlight it.

If the F5 key doesn't help you locate the file, you have to use DOS. Exit WordPerfect. (Refer to the section on saving a document to disk and quitting in Chapter 13.) At the DOS prompt, type the following command:

```
C:\> DIR \LOSTFILE /S
```

That is, type **DIR,** a space, the backslash character, and the name of the file you're looking for. In this example, I'm looking for a file named LOSTFILE. You should type the complete filename you're looking for, including any file extensions. Be exact. Follow the filename with a space, the forward slash character, and an **S.**

Confirm that everything is typed properly. Then press Enter. If the file is found, you see something like the following on the screen:

```
Directory of C:\BERMUDA\TRIANGLE
LOSTFILE        1313  11-13-92 13:13p
  1 file(s)        1313 bytes
```

In this example, DOS has located the lost file in the subdirectory named C:\BERMUDA\TRIANGLE. Look on the screen for the line that starts `Directory of`. This text is followed by the directory in which the lost file was found. Use that directory name with DOS's CD command so that you can pinpoint the file. For example, type the following at a DOS prompt:

```
C:\> CD \BERMUDA\TRIANGLE
```

Follow the CD command with the directory name and press Enter. You are then in the same subdirectory as the lost file. From there, start WordPerfect and load the document or, better still, use DOS's COPY command to copy the file to where it belongs.

- ✔ If more than one matching filename appears, you may have to check several directories to see which file contains the document you're looking for.

- ✔ If the file isn't found, it may be on another disk drive. Type the drive letter and a colon and press Enter to log to another disk drive. Then use the DIR command to hunt for the file as described in this section.

- ✔ Consider that you may have saved the file under a different name.

- ✔ You can find additional information on the DIR and CD commands, and DOS in general, in the book *DOS For Dummies,* published by IDG Books Worldwide. (Buy it now. My kid needs braces.)

Where Did My Document Go?

Ever get the sensation that the computer is making faces at you when you turn away? Sometimes, when you look back, the computer won't even have the document on the screen. In the rush to hide its sneering grin, the computer may have put up DOS on the screen. You may not see the document at all.

The first thing you should try when this situation happens is pressing the Shift-F3 key combination, which is the Switch command; it switches from WordPerfect's Document 1 to Document 2 and back again. You may have accidentally pressed Shift-F3 when trying to type another key combination. If so, pressing Shift-F3 again gets you back to the first document. (Refer to the section in Chapter 13 on working on two documents at once for more information on the Switch command, Shift-F3.)

If you see a DOS prompt, try the EXIT command. For example, suppose that the
screen looks something like this:

```
Enter 'EXIT' to return to WordPerfect
C:\STUFF>
```

Type **EXIT** at the DOS prompt and press Enter. This action gets you back into
WordPerfect instantly with the document intact. (This trick also deserves a
major _whew!_)

Try moving the cursor up and down a few pages: Press PgUp or PgDn. What
may have happened is that the next page in the document is blank, and you're
only seeing the blank part on the screen. Fiddling with the cursor-control keys
should get you reoriented.

If you're running Windows, refer to Chapter 18. The section on temporarily getting out of WordPerfect explains how to return to WordPerfect if it vanished entirely from the screen.

Where Am I Now?

If the keys on your keyboard are too close together, or your fingers suddenly
swell, you may find yourself accidentally pressing the wrong cursor-control
keys, and, lo, you're somewhere else in the document. But where?

Rather than use your brain to figure things out, press Ctrl-Home twice.
Ctrl-Home is the Go To command; pressing Ctrl-Home, Ctrl-Home moves you to
the previous cursor position and resets the document as you remember it.
(Also refer to Chapter 2.)

It's Not Printing!

Golly, the printer can be a dopey device. You tell WordPerfect to print, and the
printer just sits there — deaf as a post. "Doe, dee, doe," it says. "Aren't you glad
you paid twice as much money for a laser printer? Yuck! Yuck! Yuck!"

Believe it or not, the printer is not stupid. In fact, you should check to make
sure that the printer is turned on and working. Then check to make sure that
there is paper to print on. Then confirm that the printer cable is still connected.
Only then can you slap the printer.

But wait! Before slapping it, press the following keys:

Shift-F7, C

This action displays the Print: Control Printer menu. Read any text next to the Message prompt on the screen to see whether WordPerfect knows what's wrong. Then read the text next to the Action prompt to see what to do about it.

- ✔ Do not try printing again; don't try pressing harder on the keys. When the printer doesn't work, it doesn't work. This problem requires more attention then telepathy.

- ✔ Refer to Chapter 12 for additional information about printing.

- ✔ Make sure that both the computer and printer are turned off before you plug in a printer cable.

Oops! I Deleted My Document!

Deleting files is necessary, just like stepping on cockroaches. But what if you found out that a dead cockroach was really a reincarnation of your Aunt Shirley? Wouldn't you want her back? The same thing holds true with files. Sometimes you may accidentally delete a file. If you do, follow these steps to reincarnate the file in WordPerfect:

1. Panic. Hate yourself. Say a dirty word.

2. Press F1 to exit the List Files window.

I'm assuming that you deleted the file in the List Files window. If not and you're at the DOS prompt, skip to Step 4.

3. Press Ctrl-F1, 2.

You see the DOS command prompt.

4. Type UNDELETE and press Enter.

You see a bunch of interesting stuff on the screen. Eventually, at the bottom, you see a line that starts with a question mark and ends with the prompt

```
Undelete (Y/N)?
```

The question mark replaces the deleted filename's first character.

If you see the message Bad command or file name on the screen, you don't have the UNDELETE command in your version of DOS.

5. **Is the filename that starts with the question mark the file you want to undelete? If so, press Y.**

   If not, press N and repeat the preceding step until the file you want to undelete is displayed.

6. **After pressing Y, you are asked to type the first letter of the filename; do so.**

   You know what the first letter of the file is better than I do.

   You see the message `File successfully undeleted`. It lives! It lives!

7. **Return to WordPerfect.**

   If you got to the DOS prompt from WordPerfect, just press Enter to return to WordPerfect. If you deleted the file from the DOS prompt in the first place, start up WordPerfect as you usually do: Type **WP** and press Enter.

✔ *Don't save anything to disk after deleting a file.* Pressing Ctrl-F1 in WordPerfect is the next thing you do after unintentionally deleting a file. This action improves your chances for recovering the file.

✔ If the file cannot be recovered — and it happens — you see the message `No entries found` or `File cannot be recovered`. Oh, well. Be more careful when you delete next time.

✔ You cannot use the UNDELETE command on a network drive. Contact your network guru and explain the problem. Try not to refer to anything as *dumb* or *asinine*.

Oops! I Just Reformatted My Disk!

This is why we label disks, so we don't accidentally format something that contains important files and other information. If you do pull this boo-boo, follow these steps *immediately* to recover:

1. **Press Ctrl-F1, 2.**

   You see the DOS command prompt.

2. **Type UNFORMAT A: and press Enter.**

   That is, type **UNFORMAT**, a space, the letter **A,** and a colon (:). Then press Enter.

3. **Follow the directions on the screen.**

   Insert the disk you just reformatted when you're told to. This operation takes some time to complete, so sit back and be patient.

- ✔ If you see the message `Bad command or file name` on the screen, you don't have the UNFORMAT command in your version of DOS.

- ✔ Unformatting a disk works best if you use the UNFORMAT command before putting any new files on the disk.

- ✔ After the disk is recovered, the documents may not have their original names. The UNFORMAT command may give them mechanical-sounding filenames. That's OK; the files' contents are unchanged. You can use the List Files key, F5, in WordPerfect to view the files and rename them. Refer to Chapter 14.

- ✔ Formatting disks is covered in Chapter 20.

What's a Nonhyphenating Hyphen?

The hyphen key works to hyphenate a long word at the end of a line. But sometimes you may not want the hyphen to split a word. For example, you may not want a phone number split over two lines. Yet, when you press the hyphen key, that's exactly what happens.

To create a nonhyphenating hyphen, press the Home key before you press the hyphen. This action inserts a *hard hyphen* into the document — one that won't split a phone number, part number, figure number, or mathematical problem over two lines.

The Screen Looks Weird!

Let me qualify the title of this section: the screen looks *more weird* than it usually does. For example, you may see a row of hyphens marking the end of a page where no page exists. Or after using the Thesaurus, you see several rows of hyphens that mark pages that aren't there. This stuff can really put fear into you if you don't know what's going on.

What *is* going on? I haven't a clue. But I do know that if you press the following keys, the nonsense goes away:

Ctrl-F3, R

This is the Rewrite command. This command redraws WordPerfect's screen. It eliminates any excess hyphens, lines up paragraphs properly, and puts the screen in order.

The Darn Thing's Run Amok!

Ah, the eternal and mysterious * Please wait * prompt. I've seen it many times. After about one minute, you begin to start looking around for Godot. Will you ever get to stop waiting?

Press the Cancel key, F1. This action wrestles WordPerfect to the ground, knocking some sense into it. Who knows what happened? Pressing F1 (Cancel) makes the message go away and gives you control again.

The Rest of My Document Is in Italics/Boldface/Big Text!

This practical joke may not be apparent to you until you print, but some astute WordPerfect users immediately notice that orange-on-chartreuse text running to the end of the document. Apparently, the best of your efforts have failed, and your character formatting is now applied not only to one word but to the rest of the document as well.

To switch off the endless character formatting, move the cursor to the place in the document where you want normal text to start. Then press Ctrl-F8, N. This action turns off all character formatting at that point and restores text to normal.

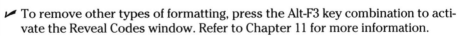 What happened was that you forgot to turn the character formatting off. Either that or WordPerfect is being difficult. (Most people suspect the latter.)

✔ To remove other types of formatting, press the Alt-F3 key combination to activate the Reveal Codes window. Refer to Chapter 11 for more information.

Part VI
The Part of Tens

In this part...

Don't you just love trivia? And what's the best type of trivia? Lists! "Ten ways to ease stress" or "ten snappy comebacks for when your kids ask imponderable questions" or "ten good explanations why you won't crawl into bed and find hundreds of cockroaches under the sheets" or "five hundred million senseless things the government buys with your tax dollars."

This book deals with WordPerfect, so this part of the book is devoted to interesting lists about WordPerfect.

Each chapter in this part contains ten items. You may think that some chapters should contain more items. But, if I was as thorough as I could be in Chapter 25, "Ten Features You Don't Use but Paid for Anyway," this book would be as fat as those other books about WordPerfect.

Chapter 23
The Ten Commandments
of WordPerfect

● ●

In This Chapter

▶ Thou shalt not use spaces.

▶ Thou shalt not press Enter at the end of each line.

▶ Thou shalt not press Enter to start a search.

▶ Thou shalt not reset or turn off thy PC until thou quittest WordPerfect.

▶ Thou shalt not manually number thy pages.

▶ Thou shalt not use the Enter key to start a new page.

▶ Thou shalt not quit without saving first.

▶ Thou shalt not press Y too quickly.

▶ Thou shalt not forget to turn on thy printer.

▶ Thou shalt not forget to back up thy work.

● ●

*J*ust imagine Charlton Heston as Moses. He looks like a 36-year-old guy in a white wig with a ridiculous white beard. But he has the glow of the Lord on his face. Either that or it's a 1K leko light with an amber gel. And he's walking down the mountain with the Ten Commandments of WordPerfect carved in stone. Yes, God's printer can print on any surface.

And, lo, it came to pass that the tablet was transcribed. And over the course of time, it found its way to this book. *Ahem!* It's very hard for me to write stiffly, like the narrator in a Cecil B. DeMille movie. Rather than drag this thing out, I'll just say that this chapter contains a bunch of dos and don'ts for working in WordPerfect. Most of these items were covered earlier in this book — particularly in Part I.

I: Thou Shalt Not Use Spaces

Generally speaking, you should never find more than two spaces in a row in any WordPerfect document. If you do, consider using the Tab key instead. Use the spacebar to separate words and sentences. If you're lining up lists of information or creating tables, use the Tab key.

II: Thou Shalt Not Press Enter at the End of Each Line

WordPerfect automatically wraps text down to the next line as you approach the right margin. There is no need for you to press Enter, except when you want to start a new paragraph. (Of course, if your paragraph is only a line long, pressing Enter at the end of that line is OK as well.)

III: Thou Shalt Not Press Enter To Start a Search

Press F2 to start a search or a search-and-replace operation. If you press Enter, you tell WordPerfect to look for the Enter character. And you still need to press F2 to start the search.

IV: Thou Shalt Not Reset or Turn Off Thy PC Until Thou Quittest WordPerfect

Always exit properly from WordPerfect. Refer to the section on saving a document to disk and quitting in Chapter 13. Only shut off or reset the computer when you see the DOS prompt on the screen — never when you're running WordPerfect.

V: Thou Shalt Not Manually Number Thy Pages

WordPerfect has an automatic page-numbering command. Refer to the section on where to stick the page number in Chapter 10.

VI: Thou Shalt Not Use the Enter Key To Start a New Page

Sure, it works: Press Enter a couple dozen times, and you're on a new page. But that's not the proper way, and you can mess up the new page if you go back and edit text. Instead, create a new page instantly by pressing Ctrl-Enter. This command inserts a hard-page break into the document. Refer to the description of starting a new page in Chapter 10.

VII: Thou Shalt Not Quit without Saving First

Save documents to disk before you quit. Refer to the section on saving a document to disk and quitting in Chapter 13.

VIII: Thou Shalt Not Press Y Too Quickly

WordPerfect has many Yes/No prompts. If you press Y without thinking about it, you may delete text, delete files, or perform a bad replace operation without knowing it. Always read the screen before you press Y.

IX: Thou Shalt Not Forget To Turn On Thy Printer

The biggest printing problem anyone has is pressing Shift-F7, 1 when the printer isn't turned on. Ensure that the printer is turned on, healthy, and ready to print before you tell WordPerfect to print something.

X: Thou Shalt Not Forget To Back Up Thy Work

Keeping emergency copies of important documents is vital. Computers are shaky houses of cards that can collapse at any sneeze or hiccup. Always make a safety copy of your files at the end of the day or as you work. Refer to the discussion of backing up files in Chapter 20.

Chapter 24
Ten Cool Tricks

I'm an old WordPerfect warrior. I have my receipt from 1985 when I first bought WordPerfect. Back then, in those rustic days, only real men could use WordPerfect. It was a cold and lonely life. Fortunately, so many long years of writing with the same software offers me some insight I'd be more than happy to share. After all, I wouldn't want anyone else to have to use this product for so long without knowing the ten cool tricks in this chapter.

Using the Autosave Feature

WordPerfect has an autosave feature. When it's active, the document is periodically saved to disk. Using the autosave feature isn't the same as pressing F10 to save the document. Instead, WordPerfect makes a secret backup copy every so often. In the event of a crash, you can recover your work from the backup copy — even if you've never saved the document to disk.

To turn on the autosave feature, press Shift-F1, E, B. This command brings up the Setup: Backup menu. Press T and then press Y to activate the autosave feature. Then type the backup interval in minutes. For example, I press 5 to have WordPerfect back up my documents every five minutes. If the power is unstable at your home or office, press 5, 3, 2, or even 1 minute as the backup interval. Press Enter and then F7 to return to the document.

To specify a location for WordPerfect to put the autosave files, press Shift-F1, L, B. Type the name of the directory where you want the backup files to be kept. If this instruction catches you with a blank stare on your face, type the following:

C:

Press Enter and then press F7 to return to the document.

- ✔ With the autosave feature activated, you won't recover all of a document in case of a mishap, but you do get most of it back.

- ✔ I recommend that you back up files to a temporary directory or to the main root directory on the hard drive. Never back up files to a RAM drive because the RAM drive is cleaned out in the event of a power outage or reset.

- ✔ When you restart WordPerfect after a power outage or crash, you see the message Are other copies of WordPerfect currently running? Press N. You may then be informed that old backup files exist. Select the option that renames them; rename the backup file OLD1. Then, when you start WordPerfect, use the Retrieve command to load OLD1 into memory: Press Shift-F10 and type **C:\OLD1** at the prompt. This action recovers the document.

Using Ctrl-Delete To Cut and Paste Blocks

The fastest way to cut and paste a block is to mark it first and then press Ctrl-Delete. Doing so cuts the block from the screen, just as if you pressed the more involved Ctrl-F4, B, M keys. Ctrl-Delete saves you three keystrokes.

After the block disappears, move the cursor to where you want to paste the block. Press Enter, and the block reappears.

- ✔ Refer to Chapter 6 for more information on blocks.

- ✔ This trick is only available on computers that have 101-key Enhanced Keyboards.

Using Ctrl-F4 To Copy and Paste Blocks

The quickest way to mark, move or copy, and then paste a block is to use the Ctrl-F4 key combination. You don't have to go through the pains of using the cursor-control keys or Alt-F4 to mark the block.

Start by positioning the cursor on the sentence, paragraph, or page you want to cut or copy. Press Ctrl-F4 and then press S for sentence, P for paragraph, or A for page. Then press M for move or C for copy. Move the cursor to where you want the block pasted and press Enter.

Using Ctrl-Home, Ctrl-Home To Return to Where You Were

Press Ctrl-Home, Ctrl-Home to restore the screen and the cursor to its previous position. You can use Ctrl-Home, Ctrl-Home after you issue the Search or Replace command, after a spell check, or just when you get lost.

Pressing Ctrl-Home activates the Go To command, which is also a handy way for you to zip right to a specific page in the document: Press Ctrl-Home, type the page number, press the Enter key, and you're there.

Using the Esc (Repeat) Key

You can use the Esc key to repeat a WordPerfect command a specific number of times. Pressing Esc, ↑ moves the cursor up eight lines; pressing Esc, ← moves the cursor left eight characters. This feature can be a handy way for you to speed up your on-screen editing.

Inserting Cool Characters

Use the Ctrl-V key combination to stick odd and wonderful characters into a document. A few of the character codes are listed in Appendix A. Simply press Ctrl-V, type the two numbers (making sure that they are separated by a comma), and press Enter; the character is inserted into the document. (The character may show up on the screen as a block, but the character should print properly.)

Refer to the section about inserting oddball characters in Chapter 8 for more information.

Inserting the Date

WordPerfect's Date command is Shift-F5, T. This command inserts the current date into a document just as if you typed it yourself.

If you press Shift-F5, C, a date *code* is inserted into the document. The date code always displays (or prints) the current date.

Seeing Italics and Underlines on the Screen

To see italicized or underlined text on the screen, you need to change WordPerfect's screen driver. To see italicized text, press Shift-F1, D, C, I and then press the F7 key to return to the document. To see underlined text, press Shift-F1, D, C, U and then press F7 to return to the document.

- ✔ Refer to the section about seeing real underlines in Chapter 16 for more information.
- ✔ This trick may not work on all PCs.

Sorting

To sort a group of lines on the screen, first mark them as a block. Refer to Chapter 6 for details about marking a block. To sort the lines of text in the block, press Ctrl-F9, 1.

Using the Unbreakable Hyphen

To insert a nonbreaking hyphen into a document, press the Home key and then press the hyphen. This feature prevents a phone number or word from being broken in two at the end of a line.

Chapter 25
Ten Features You Don't Use but Paid for Anyway

. . . .

In This Chapter

▶ Columns
▶ Graphics
▶ Hyphenation
▶ Line drawing
▶ Lists
▶ Math
▶ Outlines
▶ Tables
▶ Text boxes
▶ Macros

. . . .

*W*ordPerfect comes with many more features than you'll ever use. There are definitely more than ten and probably several dozen I've never heard of. Some people writing those massive, complete WordPerfect tomes have been known to disappear into a room and not emerge for months — or years. Indeed, I seriously doubt that anyone who knows everything WordPerfect can do has kept his or her sanity.

This chapter lists ten of the more interesting features you bought when you paid for WordPerfect. (I'm not even bothering to mention the extra utility programs that come with WordPerfect.) You probably didn't know that these goodies existed. That's OK; they're a bit technical to work with. This chapter covers each one briefly; don't expect to learn how to use any of these paid-for-but-forgotten features.

Columns

Columns are an interesting and complex aspect of WordPerfect. You can format a document to have two or more columns of text and actually see the different columns on the screen. But editing the columns is weird — especially when you try to use the arrow keys to move the cursor around.

The Columns command is Alt-F7, C. You need to define the columns before you turn them on. Then you need to turn the columns off when you want to return to regular text.

Columns work OK in WordPerfect. I've used them a few times but not often. The reason is that page-layout software works much better for arranging and organizing columns of text. If you really want columns, use something like PageMaker to make them. Compose the raw text in WordPerfect and then import that text into PageMaker.

Graphics

WordPerfect itself doesn't produce graphics, but you can include graphics in WordPerfect documents. The trick is to get the graphics into the WordPerfect graphic-file format. After it's there, you can use the Graphics command, Alt-F9, to put the graphics into the document. This works kind of like arranging a photo album in the dark.

The good side to the graphics issue is that WordPerfect comes with several interesting graphics pictures you can use right out of the box. The graphics files can be found in the WordPerfect directory; all their filenames end in WPG. The bad side to the graphics issue is that you can't see the graphics on the regular text screen. (You *can* see them in Page Preview mode and in the graphics editor.)

You can create WordPerfect graphics files by using a program called DrawPerfect. Yes, it's from the same crowd in Utah. You also can convert other graphics formats into the WordPerfect graphics format. A program named GRAPHCNV is included with WordPerfect. It converts PCX and other graphics files into the WPG format, no sweat. From there you can use the Alt-F9 key combination in WordPerfect to stick a graphics image on the page. But you're on your own from there.

Hyphenation

Hyphenation is an automatic feature that splits long words at the end of a line, making the text fit better on the page. Most people leave this option turned off because hyphenated words tend to slow down the pace at which people read. If you want to activate hyphenation for a document — and see it work as you type — press Shift-F8, L, 1.

Line Drawing

WordPerfect enables you to draw arrows and boxes in the text. Press Ctrl-F3, L to activate the Line Drawing command. First select a line style from the menu at the bottom of the page. Then use the cursor-control keys to draw lines and boxes on the screen. Press F1 when you're done.

Lists

The list feature is interesting, but it is cumbersome to use. You use the Alt-F5 key combination to mark the text. For example, you can press Alt-F5 to mark a word and tag it for inclusion in an index, a table of contents, or some other reference. Then, using other commands too complicated to mention here, you can have WordPerfect generate an automatic index or other page-reference list — and the list includes page numbers — based on the text you marked. This is a handy thing to have, but it takes time to learn, and you often don't need a full index for a five-page letter to Mom.

Math

Did it ever dawn on the WordPerfect people that math and English are two separate subjects for a reason? The math and English parts of the SAT scores are separate. Math and English are always taught as separate courses. So who needs a math function in a word processor? I don't know. Even if *you* do, I think it's easier to calculate numbers by using a desk calculator and then type them into a document manually.

Complaining aside, the Math command in WordPerfect is Alt-F7, 3. But, before issuing that command, you have to set up tabs to line up the rows and columns of numbers. Then you can press any of several keys that manipulate the numbers and calculate the results on the screen. Yech!

Outlines

Outlining in WordPerfect is ugly. The outline feature is not like a traditional outlining program where you can easily promote and demote topics, rearranging text at the touch of a few keys. Instead, the outline feature is more like a paragraph-numbering tool. And Outline mode can be annoying to work in if you're used to a real outlining program, like Symantec's GrandView (which I used to create the outline for this book).

To switch on WordPerfect's outline feature — and really begin a long process of head pains — press Shift-F5, 4. This command activates Outline mode, where the remaining paragraphs in the document are numbered according to standard outline format. (My advice? Don't use this feature unless you have some serious time to kill.)

Tables

The table feature is actually a handy feature, but few people know about it. Pressing Alt-F7, T enables you to create a table. You tell WordPerfect the number of rows and columns, and it puts up a grid on the screen. You can fill in the squares with all sorts of information, edit the table, resize it, and so on.

Text Boxes

A *text box* is a patch of text separate from the main document. In a way, it's like a graphics picture: You need to use a special command to edit the text in the box, and you can't see the box unless you edit its contents, use Print Preview, or print the document.

The neat thing about text boxes is that they provide a handy way for you to insert a sidebar or other interesting text right into the document. Because the box can be shaded or outlined, some people use the text box as a header for a document, which really does add some style. The text box command is Alt-F9, B.

Macros

Macros are automated processes — like little programs — that run in WordPerfect. For example, I have a Quick Save macro that saves a document to disk. To activate the macro, I press Alt-S. My document is then saved to disk and updated. That saves me a few keystrokes, and it saves me from having to remember that the F10 key is the Save command. For me, Alt-S makes much more sense.

Although macros can be really handy, they're a big hurdle to clear in the learning process. WordPerfect has a complete macro programming language, which can get very complex but is very powerful. Heck, entire books are written just on using WordPerfect's macros. I hear Berkeley even offers a graduate program in them.

If you're curious about creating a few handy macros, refer to Chapter 26.

Chapter 26
Ten Macros with Novocaine

● ●

In This Chapter

▶ Alt-B, Mark Block

▶ Alt-C, Copy Block

▶ Alt-I, Italics

▶ Alt-L, Mark Line

▶ Alt-P, Print Document

▶ Alt-R, Refresh Screen

▶ Alt-S, Quick Save

▶ Alt-T, Transpose

▶ Alt-V, Paste Block

▶ Alt-X, Cut Block

● ●

*T*he best way to make life easier in WordPerfect is to create some sensible commands to counter the hideous claw patterns. For example, wouldn't pressing Alt-S to save a document work better than pressing F10, Enter, Y? Or how about some handy Mark, Copy, Cut, and Paste commands for working with blocks? You can make all this possible by using WordPerfect's macro commands.

Now don't let your eyes go wide and freeze with fear. This book does not cover macros or how to program them. That subject is too esoteric for a book like this. Instead, this chapter tells you how to create ten highly useful macros — things you can start using in WordPerfect right now — without teaching you a thing. Just follow the directions, and you'll be living the easy life in a just a few pages.

These macros are available only with your copy of WordPerfect. If you use another computer with WordPerfect on it, you won't have access to these quick keys (unless you go through the steps outlined here to create the macros on that computer as well).

Alt-B, Mark Block

I would die without this macro. Use the Alt-B macro to instantly mark a block of text. It's the same as pressing Alt-F4 and then the Enter key to mark a paragraph. The difference? Alt-B is a one-key command and *B* logically stands for *Block*.

To create this macro, follow these steps:

1. Press Ctrl-F10, Alt-B.

2. At the Description prompt, type **Mark block** and press Enter.

3. Press Alt-F4, Enter.

4. Press Ctrl-F10.

You can press F1 to cancel the flashing Block on message at this point. The Alt-B (Mark Block) macro has been created. Use the Alt-B command to instantly mark a paragraph of text.

It helps if you have some text on the screen when you create this macro — at least a paragraph or two. If you don't, the computer beeps when you press Enter. That's OK. The macro is still created just fine.

Alt-C, Copy Block

You can use the Alt-C macro to copy a marked block on the screen. There are some advantages to using this macro: It saves you keystrokes (Alt-C is easier to remember than Ctrl-F4, B, C), and you can paste the block later by using the Alt-V macro, described later in this chapter. This means you can copy a block, edit a block a bit, and then paste in a block of text.

To create the Alt-C macro, follow these steps:

1. Press Ctrl-F10, Alt-C.

2. At the Description prompt, type **Copy block** and press Enter.

3. Press Ctrl-F4, B, C, F1.

4. Press Ctrl-F10.

Press the F1 key to remove any message that may be displayed on the screen.

> ✔ This macro only works if you first mark a block on the screen. If a block isn't marked, you may see * Please wait * displayed for a long time; press F1 to cancel this message.

> ✔ Paste the copied text with the Alt-V macro, described later in this chapter.

Alt-I, Italics

The Alt-I macro switches on the italics character format. Use this macro to turn on the italics attribute as you type. To turn it off, press Alt-I again. If you mark a block and press Alt-I, the text in that block appears in italics.

To create this macro, follow these steps:

    1. Press Ctrl-F10, Alt-I.

    2. At the `Description` prompt, type **Italic text format** and press Enter.

    3. Press Ctrl-F8, A, I.

    4. Press Ctrl-F10.

Alt-L, Mark Line

This macro works like the Alt-B macro, which marks a block of text. The difference is that the Alt-L macro marks text from the cursor's position to the end of the line. (Alt-B marks to the end of the paragraph.)

To create the Alt-L macro, follow these steps:

    1. Press Ctrl-F10, Alt-L.

    2. At the `Description` prompt, type **Mark line** and press Enter.

    3. Press Alt-F4, End.

    4. Press Ctrl-F10.

Press the F1 key to cancel the flashing `Block on` message.

Alt-L is handy for marking short parts of text. Use Alt-B for marking paragraphs.

Alt-P, Print Document

The Alt-P macro is a quick-print macro. Press Alt-P when you want to print a document instead of bothering your brain with Shift-F7 key combinations.

To create the Alt-P quick-print macro, follow these steps:

    1. Press Ctrl-F10, Alt-P.

    2. At the `Description` prompt, type **Quick print** and press Enter.

    3. Press Shift-F7, 1.

    4. Press Ctrl-F10.

In the process of creating this macro, WordPerfect prints the document currently on the screen. If your printer isn't turned on, press Shift-F7, C, C, Enter, G to cancel the most recent print job. (Also refer to the section on canceling a print job in Chapter 12.)

Have the printer on-line and ready to print before you start the Alt-P (Quick-Print) macro.

Alt-R, Refresh Screen

The reasons for using this macro aren't always apparent. Alt-R activates WordPerfect's Rewrite Screen command. This command tells WordPerfect to redraw the screen and straighten out paragraphs. If the screen looks weird, or at least weirder than it usually does, press Alt-R to straighten things up.

To create the Alt-R macro, follow these steps:

1. Press Ctrl-F10, Alt-R.

2. At the Description prompt, type **Refresh screen** and press Enter.

3. Press Ctrl-F3, R.

4. Press Ctrl-F10.

Alt-S, Quick Save

You can use the quick-save macro to save to disk the document you're working on. You can press Alt-S rather than the multikey and hard-to-remember Save command.

To create the Alt-S macro, follow these steps:

1. Press Ctrl-F10, Alt-S.

2. At the Description prompt, type **Quick save** and press Enter.

3. Press F10, Enter, Y.

4. Press Ctrl-F10.

If you haven't yet saved the current document to disk, press the F1 key after creating this macro.

The Alt-S macro only saves a document to disk if the document has already been saved to disk. If you haven't previously saved the document, the Alt-S macro displays an error message and then prompts you to enter a filename. (This is only a minor inconvenience.)

Alt-T, Transpose

Use the Transpose macro to quickly switch two letters. You place the cursor on the first letter, press Alt-T, and watch as the first letter and the one after it switch positions. This macro comes in really handy because the majority of spelling errors and typos are of the transposed-character variety.

To create the Alt-T macro, follow these steps:

1. Press Ctrl-F10, Alt-T.

2. At the Description prompt, type **Transpose** and press Enter.

3. Press Delete, ←, F1, 1.

4. Press Ctrl-F10.

Alt-V, Paste Block

When you've copied or cut a block of text with the Alt-C or Alt-X macro, use the Alt-V macro to paste the block back into text. Create the following macros to have easy ways to do the common actions of copying, cutting, and pasting text:

Alt-C = Copy

Alt-X = Cut

Alt-V = Paste

Although these keys aren't entirely mnemonic, they are all three together on the keyboard. (And they are the commonly used keys in Windows.)

To create the Alt-V macro, follow these steps:

1. Press Ctrl-F10, Alt-V.

2. At the Description prompt, type **Paste block** and press Enter.

3. Press Ctrl-F4, R, B.

4. Press Ctrl-F10.

You can quickly mark a block with Alt-B or Alt-L, copy or cut it with Alt-C or Alt-X, and then take your time and finally paste the block with Alt-V.

Alt-X, Cut Block

You can use Alt-X to cut a marked block of text on the screen. As with the Alt-C macro, this macro saves you time, is (almost) mnemonic, and gives you the ability to lazily paste the block with Alt-V instead of having to immediately use the cursor-control keys and the Enter key.

To create the Alt-X macro, follow these steps:

1. Press Ctrl-F10, Alt-X.

2. At the Description prompt, type **Cut block** and press Enter.

3. Press Ctrl-F4, B, M, F1.

4. Press Ctrl-F10.

Press the F1 key to remove any message that may be displayed on the screen.

✔ This macro works only if a block of text is marked on the screen. If a block is not marked, press F1 to cancel whatever may appear on the screen if you accidentally press Alt-X.

✔ Paste the cut text by using the Alt-V macro.

Chapter 27
Ten Unpopular Error Messages and How To Fix Them

● ●

In This Chapter

▶ Access denied

▶ Are other copies of WordPerfect currently running?

▶ Device not ready

▶ Invalid drive/path specification

▶ Invalid file name

▶ Not found

▶ Please wait

▶ Replace filename?

▶ WP disk full

▶ Write-protect error

● ●

*W*hen the cat finally succeeds at capturing and eating little Molly's hamster, someone has to sit down and explain things to her. And, in spite of Molly's insistence, you just can't cut off kitty's head as punishment. There is the same kind of happy, friendly logic behind a WordPerfect error message.

Error messages are a rude but necessary part of explaining that something unexpected has happened. The error message indicates a situation — like puffs of hamster fur all over the bedroom — that requires more attention than normal to get things corrected. This chapter contains ten such messages you are most likely to see when you use WordPerfect.

Access denied

Don't plug your ears. Klaxons do not sound, and government agents don't sweep in to arrest you for illegally accessing a file. Instead, this message indicates that one of the following has occurred:

- ✔ You've tried to save to disk a document that won't fit on the disk.
- ✔ You've tried to save to disk a document that already exists and is protected against being overwritten.
- ✔ You've used the name of a directory already on disk.

The solution is to try to save again with a different filename. If the error persists, save the file in a subdirectory work area. Contact a WordPerfect guru to help you set up a subdirectory work area.

Are other copies of WordPerfect currently running?

This error message may occur after the computer crashes in the middle of running WordPerfect or if you're running WordPerfect in an environment such as Microsoft Windows, the DOS Shell, or DESQview. Refer to Chapter 22's discussion about this message.

Device not ready

If you see this message, odds are pretty good that you tried to save a file to a floppy disk and the disk isn't in the drive or the drive's door latch is open. Stick the disk into the drive; if it's already in there, close the latch. Try the WordPerfect command again.

Invalid drive/path specification

The disk drive or subdirectory you mentioned doesn't exist. Check your typing and try again.

Invalid file name

You used an illegal, forbidden, and terribly naughty letter in a filename. Try again, this time typing a proper filename. Remember that you can name a file by using only letters and numbers. Refer to Chapter 14.

Not found

The text you searched for was not found in the document. If you were using the Search Down command, F2, try using the Search Up command, Shift-F2, instead. Alternatively, press Home, Home, Home, ↑ and try the Search command again.

To search for text in headers, footers, and note boxes, press the Home key before you press F2 to start the search.

Please wait

WordPerfect is busy. Sit and wait.

If this message hangs on the screen longer than, say, two minutes, press the F1 key to regain control. Sometimes, during some complex maneuvers or macros, WordPerfect may say * Please wait * for long periods of time. Have patience.

Replace filename?

You tried to save a document to disk with the name of a file that already exists. If you're updating a file on disk, press Y to replace the older version with the new copy. But, if this message appears as a surprise, press N to keep the old file on disk. Think up a new name for the file you're saving.

WP disk full

WordPerfect has been stuffed to the gills. You see this message for every character you type because everything is full and WordPerfect just can't swallow another byte. (Ha, ha! Computer humor.)

The solution is to save the document to disk immediately. Then quit WordPerfect and start over.

If this problem persists, have your WordPerfect guru check the /D option WordPerfect uses when it starts. The drive specified by /D is becoming full too quickly, and another drive should be used.

Write-protect error

You tried to save a document to a floppy disk, and WordPerfect won't let you. It's not being stubborn; WordPerfect is telling you that the disk you want to use has been *write-protected*, which means that it has been modified so that no information can be changed or added. Write-protecting is usually done for a reason, so my first suggestion is to try using another disk.

To unwrite-protect a disk, remove the sticky tape from the left edge of a 5¼-inch disk (the left edge as the disk is facing you, label up). Doing so uncovers a notch in the side of the disk, makes your fingers sticky, and enables you to write information to the disk (or change information on the disk).

For a 3½-inch disk, flip the disk over and slide the little tile doohickey over the little square hole. (If the disk has two holes, only one of them has the sliding-tile thing.)

A disk is write-protected on purpose and for a reason. Be careful when you write new information to it and think twice about it — especially if you want to alter information already on the disk.

Chapter 28
The Ten Most Common Claw Patterns

Only a very twisted WordPerfect user would sit down and memorize all 40 function-key commands. Truly, this type of dementia requires years of laborious psychiatric care. With a keyboard template, especially one as friendly as the one included with this book, there's no need for you to memorize Word-Perfect commands. But, if you feel compelled to do it, there are only a few common claw patterns worth remembering. I've listed ten of them here for your convenience — or obsessions, depending on how deep you're into this subject.

Block, Alt-F4

Move the cursor to where you want to start the block and press Alt-F4. This action turns on block-marking mode and the blink, blink, blinking Block on indicator in the lower left corner of the screen. Use the cursor-control keys to highlight text to be included in the block. (Refer to Chapter 6 for more information on blocks.)

Cut/Copy, Ctrl-F4

You can use Ctrl-F4 to cut or copy a block. If the block has already been highlighted, Ctrl-F4 enables you to cut or copy the highlighted block. If no block has been highlighted, Ctrl-F4 enables you to select a sentence, paragraph, or page to cut or copy.

Files, F5

Press F5 and Enter to bring up the List Files window/menu/thing. This window/thing enables you to manipulate, copy, rename, or delete files, and peer into their contents. Using the F5 key is definitely more fun than using the DOS prompt for these same operations. (Refer to Chapter 14 for additional information.)

Format, Shift-F8 and Ctrl-F8

Pressing Shift-F8 displays the main line/page/document formatting menu. Pressing Ctrl-F8 displays the character/font formatting menu.

Print, Shift-F7

Next to saving a document, the most common WordPerfect action is printing. Pressing Shift-F7 brings up the Print menu; pressing Shift-F7, 1 prints the entire document you're working on.

Replace, Alt-F2

You can activate WordPerfect's Replace (or search-and-replace) command by pressing Alt-F2.

Retrieve, Shift-F10

To load a document from disk into WordPerfect, press Shift-F10. WordPerfect prompts you to name a document file on disk; when you type its name and press Enter, that file is visible on the screen. (Also refer to Chapter 13.)

Save, F10

The key you should be using most often in WordPerfect is the Save key, F10. In fact, you should program yourself to press F10, Enter, Y every so often as you work on a document. This action updates the document file on disk and gives you a safety copy if anything nasty happens to the one on the screen. (Refer to Chapter 13.)

Search, F2

Activate the basic Search command by pressing F2. Type the text you want WordPerfect to find in the document and press F2; WordPerfect goes looking for it. (Refer to Chapter 5.)

Spell Check, Ctrl-F2

Most people don't do a spell check because it takes too long. Yet a neatly spelled document — even if you have the grammar of a 10-year-old — is better than a poorly spelled document (with the grammar of a 10-year-old). Press Ctrl-F2, 3 to spell-check all the words in a document. (Refer to Chapter 7.)

Chapter 29
Ten Things Worth Remembering

● ●

In This Chapter

▶ Don't be afraid of the keyboard.

▶ Have a supply of disks ready.

▶ Keep printer paper, toner, and supplies handy.

▶ Keep references handy.

▶ Keep your files organized.

▶ Remember the F1 key.

▶ Save the document before a search and replace.

▶ Save the document often.

▶ Start WordPerfect with a document name.

▶ Use clever, memorable filenames.

● ●

*T*here's nothing like finishing a book with a few heartening words of good advice. As a WordPerfect beginner, you need this kind of encouragement and motivation. WordPerfect can be unforgiving, but it's not necessarily an evil thing to work with. This book has shown you that it's possible to have a lot of fun with WordPerfect and still get your work done. To help send you on your way, I want to discuss a few things worth remembering.

Don't Be Afraid of the Keyboard

Try to avoid repeatedly pressing Enter to start a new page, using the spacebar when the Tab key works better, or manually numbering pages. There's a handy WordPerfect command to do just about anything. You'll never know that if you're afraid to try the commands.

Have a Supply of Disks Ready

You need disks to use a computer — even if you have a hard drive. You need disks for backup purposes and for exchanging files with other PCs running WordPerfect, such as between home and the office.

Keep one or two boxes of disks available. Always buy the proper size disk for your PC: 5 ¼-inch or 3 ½-inch disks. And make sure that you buy the highest capacity as well — usually the high-capacity or high-density disks. And format those disks! Refer to Chapter 20 for details.

Keep Printer Paper, Toner, and Supplies Handy

When you buy paper, buy a box. When you buy a toner cartridge or printer ribbon, buy two or three. Also keep a good stock of pens, paper, staples, paper clips, and all the other necessary office supplies (including disks) handy.

Keep References Handy

WordPerfect is a writing tool. Therefore, you need to be familiar with and obey the grammatical rules of your language. If that language happens to be English, you have a big job ahead of you. Even though a dictionary and a thesaurus are an electronic part of WordPerfect, I recommend that you keep a paper dictionary and thesaurus handy. Strunk and White's *The Elements of Style* is a great book for finding out where the apostrophes and commas go. If you lack these books, visit the reference section of your local bookstore and plan on paying about $50 to stock up on quality references.

Keep Your Files Organized

Use subdirectories on the hard drive for storing document files. Keep related documents together in the same subdirectory. You may need someone else's help to set up subdirectories. Refer to Chapters 13, 14, and 20 for additional information.

Remember the F1 Key

The F1 key is the Undo key. If you're typing and editing away in WordPerfect, press F1 to undelete any text you may have mistakenly deleted. This feature works for individual letters, sentences, paragraphs, pages, and large chunks of deleted text. But be quick because the Undelete command only remembers the last three chunks of text you deleted.

The F1 key is also the Cancel key. Press F1 to cancel a menu selection or back out of a series of menus. F1 also stops a Search command, a spell check, or any other WordPerfect command that takes awhile to run.

Save the Document before a Search and Replace

About the only nasty thing that's not undo-able in WordPerfect is the search-and-replace operation. I once had an assistant who carefully searched for all the spaces in a document and replaced them with . . . nothing. The end result was a document with three long words rather than three paragraphs of many words. The only way to undo such a mistake is to retrieve an original version of the document. And the only way you can do that is if you save the document before you press Alt-F2 to search and replace.

Save the Document Often

Save the document to disk as soon as you get a few meaningful words down on the screen. Then save every so often after that. Even if you use the autosave feature (discussed in Chapter 24), continue to manually save the document to disk: Press F10, Enter, Y.

Start WordPerfect with a Document Name

To quickly start WordPerfect and load a document on the screen for editing, type **WP** at the DOS prompt and follow it with a space and the name of a document file you want to edit. For example, type the following at the DOS prompt:

WP CHAP29.WP

This command starts WordPerfect and loads a file called CHAP29.WP (Chapter 29) from disk for editing.

Use Clever, Memorable Filenames

A file named LETTER is certainly descriptive, but what does it tell you? A file named LTR2MOM is even more descriptive but still lacking some information. A file MOM0023 may indicate the 23rd letter you've written to Mom. Even better is LTR2MOM.23. You get the idea here: Use creative and informative filenames.

DOS only gives you eight characters to name a file. You can use letters and numbers in the filename, and you can add a period and up to three characters as an extension. This setup doesn't leave much room for being descriptive, but it opens wide the door to being creative.

Sadly, short filenames also make for extremely cryptic filenames. To help hunt down a file, press the List Files key, F5. Refer to Chapter 14 for additional information.

Appendix A
WordPerfect's
Oddball Characters

• •

*F*ollowing is a list of the weird characters you can insert into WordPerfect with the Ctrl-V command. First, look in the second column to find the character you want to insert. Press Ctrl-V and, at the Key= prompt, type the two numbers in the first column, making sure that they are separated by a comma. Press Enter. This action inserts the weird character into the document. (Also refer to the section on oddball characters in Chapter 8.)

Code	Character	Description
4,0	●	Dot
4,1	○	Hollow dot
4,2	▪	Square
4,5	¶	Paragraph symbol
4,6	§	Section symbol
4,7	¡	Upside-down exclamation point
4,8	¿	Upside-down question mark
4,11	£	English Pound symbol
4,12	¥	Japanese Yen symbol
4,17	½	One-half
4,18	¼	One-quarter
4,19	¢	Cents
4,20	^{2}	Squared
4,22	®	Registered symbol
4,23	©	Copyright symbol
4,25	¾	Three-quarters

Code	Character	Description
4,26	^{3}	Cubed
4,30	"	Start quotation mark
4,31	"	End quotation mark
4,32	"	Inverted start quotation mark
4,33	–	En dash
4,34	—	Em dash
4,41	™	Trademark symbol
4,51	ff	FF ligature
4,54	fi	FI ligature
4,55	fl	FL ligature
4,64	⅓	One-third
4,65	⅔	Two-thirds
4,66	⅛	One-eighth
4,67	⅜	Three-eighths
4,68	⅝	Five-eighths
4,69	⅞	Seven-eighths

Code	Character	Description
5,0	♥	Heart
5,1	◆	Diamond
5,2	♣	Club
5,3	♠	Spade
5,4	♂	Male
5,5	♀	Female
5,7	☺	Hollow happy face
5,8	☻	Happy face
5,9	♪	Eighth note
5,10	♫	Double eighth note
5,21	☞	Right-pointing hand
5,22	☜	Left-pointing hand
5,23	✓	Check mark
5,26	☹	Mr. Grumpy
5,30	☎	Phone
5,31	☺	Watch

Code	Character	Description
6,19	∞	Infinity (the concept, not the car)
6,21	→	Right arrow
6,22	←	Left arrow
6,23	↑	Up arrow
6,24	↓	Down arrow
6,36	°	Degree symbol (temperatures)
6,184	★	Star

You may be able to find the complete list of oddball WordPerfect characters somewhere in the WordPerfect manual.

Index

REMEMBER

DOS Commands I Should (Not!) Remember

What It Is	What It Does

The Fun & Easy Way™ to learn about computers and more!

10/31/95

Windows® 3.11 For Dummies,® 3rd Edition
by Andy Rathbone
ISBN: 1-56884-370-4
$16.95 USA/
$22.95 Canada

Mutual Funds For Dummies™
by Eric Tyson
ISBN: 1-56884-226-0
$16.99 USA/
$22.99 Canada

DOS For Dummies,® 2nd Edition
by Dan Gookin
ISBN: 1-878058-75-4
$16.95 USA/
$22.95 Canada

The Internet For Dummies,® 2nd Edition
by John Levine & Carol Baroudi
ISBN: 1-56884-222-8
$19.99 USA/
$26.99 Canada

Personal Finance For Dummies™
by Eric Tyson
ISBN: 1-56884-150-7
$16.95 USA/
$22.95 Canada

PCs For Dummies,® 3rd Edition
by Dan Gookin & Andy Rathbone
ISBN: 1-56884-904-4
$16.99 USA/
$22.99 Canada

Macs® For Dummies,® 3rd Edition
by David Pogue
ISBN: 1-56884-239-2
$19.99 USA/
$26.99 Canada

The SAT® I For Dummies™
by Suzee Vlk
ISBN: 1-56884-213-9
$14.99 USA/
$20.99 Canada

Here's a complete listing of IDG Books' ...For Dummies® titles

Title	Author	ISBN	Price
DATABASE			
Access 2 For Dummies®	by Scott Palmer	ISBN: 1-56884-090-X	$19.95 USA/$26.95 Canada
Access Programming For Dummies®	by Rob Krumm	ISBN: 1-56884-091-8	$19.95 USA/$26.95 Canada
Approach 3 For Windows® For Dummies®	by Doug Lowe	ISBN: 1-56884-233-3	$19.99 USA/$26.99 Canada
dBASE For DOS For Dummies®	by Scott Palmer & Michael Stabler	ISBN: 1-56884-188-4	$19.95 USA/$26.95 Canada
dBASE For Windows® For Dummies®	by Scott Palmer	ISBN: 1-56884-179-5	$19.95 USA/$26.95 Canada
dBASE 5 For Windows® Programming For Dummies®	by Ted Coombs & Jason Coombs	ISBN: 1-56884-215-5	$19.99 USA/$26.99 Canada
FoxPro 2.6 For Windows® For Dummies®	by John Kaufeld	ISBN: 1-56884-187-6	$19.95 USA/$26.95 Canada
Paradox 5 For Windows® For Dummies®	by John Kaufeld	ISBN: 1-56884-185-X	$19.95 USA/$26.95 Canada
DESKTOP PUBLISHING/ILLUSTRATION/GRAPHICS			
CorelDRAW! 5 For Dummies®	by Deke McClelland	ISBN: 1-56884-157-4	$19.95 USA/$26.95 Canada
CorelDRAW! For Dummies®	by Deke McClelland	ISBN: 1-56884-042-X	$19.95 USA/$26.95 Canada
Desktop Publishing & Design For Dummies®	by Roger C. Parker	ISBN: 1-56884-234-1	$19.99 USA/$26.99 Canada
Harvard Graphics 2 For Windows® For Dummies®	by Roger C. Parker	ISBN: 1-56884-092-6	$19.95 USA/$26.95 Canada
PageMaker 5 For Macs® For Dummies®	by Galen Gruman & Deke McClelland	ISBN: 1-56884-178-7	$19.95 USA/$26.95 Canada
PageMaker 5 For Windows® For Dummies®	by Deke McClelland & Galen Gruman	ISBN: 1-56884-160-4	$19.95 USA/$26.95 Canada
Photoshop 3 For Macs® For Dummies®	by Deke McClelland	ISBN: 1-56884-208-2	$19.99 USA/$26.99 Canada
QuarkXPress 3.3 For Dummies®	by Galen Gruman & Barbara Assadi	ISBN: 1-56884-217-1	$19.99 USA/$26.99 Canada
FINANCE/PERSONAL FINANCE/TEST TAKING REFERENCE			
Everyday Math For Dummies™	by Charles Seiter	ISBN: 1-56884-248-1	$14.99 USA/$22.99 Canada
Personal Finance For Dummies™ For Canadians	by Eric Tyson & Tony Martin	ISBN: 1-56884-378-X	$18.99 USA/$24.99 Canada
QuickBooks 3 For Dummies®	by Stephen L. Nelson	ISBN: 1-56884-227-9	$19.99 USA/$26.99 Canada
Quicken 8 For DOS For Dummies,® 2nd Edition	by Stephen L. Nelson	ISBN: 1-56884-210-4	$19.95 USA/$26.95 Canada
Quicken 5 For Macs® For Dummies®	by Stephen L. Nelson	ISBN: 1-56884-211-2	$19.95 USA/$26.95 Canada
Quicken 4 For Windows® For Dummies,® 2nd Edition	by Stephen L. Nelson	ISBN: 1-56884-209-0	$19.95 USA/$26.95 Canada
Taxes For Dummies,™ 1995 Edition	by Eric Tyson & David J. Silverman	ISBN: 1-56884-220-1	$14.99 USA/$20.99 Canada
The GMAT® For Dummies™	by Suzee Vlk, Series Editor	ISBN: 1-56884-376-3	$14.99 USA/$20.99 Canada
The GRE® For Dummies™	by Suzee Vlk, Series Editor	ISBN: 1-56884-375-5	$14.99 USA/$20.99 Canada
Time Management For Dummies™	by Jeffrey J. Mayer	ISBN: 1-56884-360-7	$16.99 USA/$22.99 Canada
TurboTax For Windows® For Dummies®	by Gail A. Helsel, CPA	ISBN: 1-56884-228-7	$19.99 USA/$26.99 Canada
GROUPWARE/INTEGRATED			
ClarisWorks For Macs® For Dummies®	by Frank Higgins	ISBN: 1-56884-363-1	$19.99 USA/$26.99 Canada
Lotus Notes For Dummies®	by Pat Freeland & Stephen Londergan	ISBN: 1-56884-212-0	$19.95 USA/$26.95 Canada
Microsoft® Office 4 For Windows® For Dummies®	by Roger C. Parker	ISBN: 1-56884-183-3	$19.95 USA/$26.95 Canada
Microsoft® Works 3 For Windows® For Dummies®	by David C. Kay	ISBN: 1-56884-214-7	$19.99 USA/$26.99 Canada
SmartSuite 3 For Dummies®	by Jan Weingarten & John Weingarten	ISBN: 1-56884-367-4	$19.99 USA/$26.99 Canada
INTERNET/COMMUNICATIONS/NETWORKING			
America Online® For Dummies,® 2nd Edition	by John Kaufeld	ISBN: 1-56884-933-8	$19.99 USA/$26.99 Canada
CompuServe For Dummies,® 2nd Edition	by Wallace Wang	ISBN: 1-56884-937-0	$19.99 USA/$26.99 Canada
Modems For Dummies,® 2nd Edition	by Tina Rathbone	ISBN: 1-56884-223-6	$19.99 USA/$26.99 Canada
MORE Internet For Dummies®	by John R. Levine & Margaret Levine Young	ISBN: 1-56884-164-7	$19.95 USA/$26.95 Canada
MORE Modems & On-line Services For Dummies®	by Tina Rathbone	ISBN: 1-56884-365-8	$19.99 USA/$26.99 Canada
Mosaic For Dummies,® Windows Edition	by David Angell & Brent Heslop	ISBN: 1-56884-242-2	$19.99 USA/$26.99 Canada
NetWare For Dummies,® 2nd Edition	by Ed Tittel, Deni Connor & Earl Follis	ISBN: 1-56884-369-0	$19.99 USA/$26.99 Canada
Networking For Dummies®	by Doug Lowe	ISBN: 1-56884-079-9	$19.95 USA/$26.95 Canada
PROCOMM PLUS 2 For Windows® For Dummies®	by Wallace Wang	ISBN: 1-56884-219-8	$19.99 USA/$26.99 Canada
TCP/IP For Dummies®	by Marshall Wilensky & Candace Leiden	ISBN: 1-56884-241-4	$19.99 USA/$26.99 Canada

For scholastic requests & educational orders please call Educational Sales at 1. 800. 434. 2086

FOR MORE INFO OR TO ORDER, PLEASE CALL ▶ 800 762 2974

For volume discounts & special orders please call Tony Real, Special Sales, at 415. 655. 3048

The Internet For Macs® For Dummies® 2nd Edition	by Charles Seiter	ISBN: 1-56884-371-2	$19.99 USA/$26.99 Canada
The Internet For Macs® For Dummies® Starter Kit	by Charles Seiter	ISBN: 1-56884-244-9	$29.99 USA/$39.99 Canada
The Internet For Macs® For Dummies® Starter Kit Bestseller Edition	by Charles Seiter	ISBN: 1-56884-245-7	$39.99 USA/$54.99 Canada
The Internet For Windows® For Dummies® Starter Kit	by John R. Levine & Margaret Levine Young	ISBN: 1-56884-237-6	$34.99 USA/$44.99 Canada
The Internet For Windows® For Dummies® Starter Kit, Bestseller Edition	by John R. Levine & Margaret Levine Young	ISBN: 1-56884-246-5	$39.99 USA/$54.99 Canada

MACINTOSH

Mac® Programming For Dummies®	by Dan Parks Sydow	ISBN: 1-56884-173-6	$19.95 USA/$26.95 Canada
Macintosh® System 7.5 For Dummies®	by Bob LeVitus	ISBN: 1-56884-197-3	$19.95 USA/$26.95 Canada
MORE Macs® For Dummies®	by David Pogue	ISBN: 1-56884-087-X	$19.95 USA/$26.95 Canada
PageMaker 5 For Macs® For Dummies®	by Galen Gruman & Deke McClelland	ISBN: 1-56884-178-7	$19.95 USA/$26.95 Canada
QuarkXPress 3.3 For Dummies®	by Galen Gruman & Barbara Assadi	ISBN: 1-56884-217-1	$19.99 USA/$26.99 Canada
Upgrading and Fixing Macs® For Dummies®	by Kearney Rietmann & Frank Higgins	ISBN: 1-56884-189-2	$19.95 USA/$26.95 Canada

MULTIMEDIA

Multimedia & CD-ROMs For Dummies® 2nd Edition	by Andy Rathbone	ISBN: 1-56884-907-9	$19.99 USA/$26.99 Canada
Multimedia & CD-ROMs For Dummies® Interactive Multimedia Value Pack, 2nd Edition	by Andy Rathbone	ISBN: 1-56884-909-5	$29.99 USA/$39.99 Canada

OPERATING SYSTEMS:

DOS

MORE DOS For Dummies®	by Dan Gookin	ISBN: 1-56884-046-2	$19.95 USA/$26.95 Canada
OS/2® Warp For Dummies® 2nd Edition	by Andy Rathbone	ISBN: 1-56884-205-8	$19.99 USA/$26.99 Canada

UNIX

MORE UNIX® For Dummies®	by John R. Levine & Margaret Levine Young	ISBN: 1-56884-361-5	$19.99 USA/$26.99 Canada
UNIX® For Dummies®	by John R. Levine & Margaret Levine Young	ISBN: 1-878058-58-4	$19.95 USA/$26.95 Canada

WINDOWS

MORE Windows® For Dummies® 2nd Edition	by Andy Rathbone	ISBN: 1-56884-048-9	$19.95 USA/$26.95 Canada
Windows® 95 For Dummies®	by Andy Rathbone	ISBN: 1-56884-240-6	$19.99 USA/$26.99 Canada

PCS/HARDWARE

Illustrated Computer Dictionary For Dummies® 2nd Edition	by Dan Gookin & Wallace Wang	ISBN: 1-56884-218-X	$12.95 USA/$16.95 Canada
Upgrading and Fixing PCs For Dummies® 2nd Edition	by Andy Rathbone	ISBN: 1-56884-903-6	$19.99 USA/$26.99 Canada

PRESENTATION/AUTOCAD

AutoCAD For Dummies®	by Bud Smith	ISBN: 1-56884-191-4	$19.95 USA/$26.95 Canada
PowerPoint 4 For Windows® For Dummies®	by Doug Lowe	ISBN: 1-56884-161-2	$16.99 USA/$22.99 Canada

PROGRAMMING

Borland C++ For Dummies®	by Michael Hyman	ISBN: 1-56884-162-0	$19.95 USA/$26.95 Canada
C For Dummies® Volume 1	by Dan Gookin	ISBN: 1-878058-78-9	$19.95 USA/$26.95 Canada
C++ For Dummies®	by Stephen R. Davis	ISBN: 1-56884-163-9	$19.95 USA/$26.95 Canada
Delphi Programming For Dummies®	by Neil Rubenking	ISBN: 1-56884-200-7	$19.99 USA/$26.99 Canada
Mac® Programming For Dummies®	by Dan Parks Sydow	ISBN: 1-56884-173-6	$19.95 USA/$26.95 Canada
PowerBuilder 4 Programming For Dummies®	by Ted Coombs & Jason Coombs	ISBN: 1-56884-325-9	$19.99 USA/$26.99 Canada
QBasic Programming For Dummies®	by Douglas Hergert	ISBN: 1-56884-093-4	$19.95 USA/$26.95 Canada
Visual Basic 3 For Dummies®	by Wallace Wang	ISBN: 1-56884-076-4	$19.95 USA/$26.95 Canada
Visual Basic "X" For Dummies®	by Wallace Wang	ISBN: 1-56884-230-9	$19.99 USA/$26.99 Canada
Visual C++ 2 For Dummies®	by Michael Hyman & Bob Arnson	ISBN: 1-56884-328-3	$19.99 USA/$26.99 Canada
Windows® 95 Programming For Dummies®	by S. Randy Davis	ISBN: 1-56884-327-5	$19.99 USA/$26.99 Canada

SPREADSHEET

1-2-3 For Dummies®	by Greg Harvey	ISBN: 1-878058-60-6	$16.95 USA/$22.95 Canada
1-2-3 For Windows® 5 For Dummies® 2nd Edition	by John Walkenbach	ISBN: 1-56884-216-3	$16.95 USA/$22.95 Canada
Excel 5 For Macs® For Dummies®	by Greg Harvey	ISBN: 1-56884-186-8	$19.95 USA/$26.95 Canada
Excel For Dummies® 2nd Edition	by Greg Harvey	ISBN: 1-56884-050-0	$16.95 USA/$22.95 Canada
MORE 1-2-3 For DOS For Dummies®	by John Weingarten	ISBN: 1-56884-224-4	$19.99 USA/$26.99 Canada
MORE Excel 5 For Windows® For Dummies®	by Greg Harvey	ISBN: 1-56884-207-4	$19.95 USA/$26.95 Canada
Quattro Pro 6 For Windows® For Dummies®	by John Walkenbach	ISBN: 1-56884-174-4	$19.95 USA/$26.95 Canada
Quattro Pro For DOS For Dummies®	by John Walkenbach	ISBN: 1-56884-023-3	$16.95 USA/$22.95 Canada

UTILITIES

Norton Utilities 8 For Dummies®	by Beth Slick	ISBN: 1-56884-166-3	$19.95 USA/$26.95 Canada

VCRS/CAMCORDERS

VCRs & Camcorders For Dummies™	by Gordon McComb & Andy Rathbone	ISBN: 1-56884-229-5	$14.99 USA/$20.99 Canada

WORD PROCESSING

Ami Pro For Dummies®	by Jim Meade	ISBN: 1-56884-049-7	$19.95 USA/$26.95 Canada
MORE Word For Windows® 6 For Dummies®	by Doug Lowe	ISBN: 1-56884-165-5	$19.95 USA/$26.95 Canada
MORE WordPerfect® 6 For Windows® For Dummies®	by Margaret Levine Young & David C. Kay	ISBN: 1-56884-206-6	$19.95 USA/$26.95 Canada
MORE WordPerfect® 6 For DOS For Dummies®	by Wallace Wang, edited by Dan Gookin	ISBN: 1-56884-047-0	$19.95 USA/$26.95 Canada
Word 6 For Macs® For Dummies®	by Dan Gookin	ISBN: 1-56884-190-6	$19.95 USA/$26.95 Canada
Word For Windows® 6 For Dummies®	by Dan Gookin	ISBN: 1-56884-075-6	$16.95 USA/$22.95 Canada
Word For Windows® For Dummies®	by Dan Gookin & Ray Werner	ISBN: 1-878058-86-X	$16.95 USA/$22.95 Canada
WordPerfect® 6 For DOS For Dummies®	by Dan Gookin	ISBN: 1-878058-77-0	$16.95 USA/$22.95 Canada
WordPerfect® 6.1 For Windows® For Dummies® 2nd Edition	by Margaret Levine Young & David Kay	ISBN: 1-56884-243-0	$16.95 USA/$22.95 Canada
WordPerfect® For Dummies®	by Dan Gookin	ISBN: 1-878058-52-5	$16.95 USA/$22.95 Canada

Fun, Fast, & Cheap!™

The Internet For Macs® For Dummies® Quick Reference
by Charles Seiter

ISBN:1-56884-967-2
$9.99 USA/$12.99 Canada

Windows® 95 For Dummies® Quick Reference
by Greg Harvey

ISBN: 1-56884-964-8
$9.99 USA/$12.99 Canada

Photoshop 3 For Macs® For Dummies® Quick Reference
by Deke McClelland

ISBN: 1-56884-968-0
$9.99 USA/$12.99 Canada

WordPerfect® For DOS For Dummies® Quick Reference
by Greg Harvey

ISBN: 1-56884-009-8
$8.95 USA/$12.95 Canada

Title	Author	ISBN	Price
DATABASE			
Access 2 For Dummies® Quick Reference	by Stuart J. Stuple	ISBN: 1-56884-167-1	$8.95 USA/$11.95 Canada
dBASE 5 For DOS For Dummies® Quick Reference	by Barrie Sosinsky	ISBN: 1-56884-954-0	$9.99 USA/$12.99 Canada
dBASE 5 For Windows® For Dummies® Quick Reference	by Stuart J. Stuple	ISBN: 1-56884-953-2	$9.99 USA/$12.99 Canada
Paradox 5 For Windows® For Dummies® Quick Reference	by Scott Palmer	ISBN: 1-56884-960-5	$9.99 USA/$12.99 Canada
DESKTOP PUBLISHING/ILLUSTRATION/GRAPHICS			
CorelDRAW! 5 For Dummies® Quick Reference	by Raymond E. Werner	ISBN: 1-56884-952-4	$9.99 USA/$12.99 Canada
Harvard Graphics For Windows® For Dummies® Quick Reference	by Raymond E. Werner	ISBN: 1-56884-962-1	$9.99 USA/$12.99 Canada
Photoshop 3 For Macs® For Dummies® Quick Reference	by Deke McClelland	ISBN: 1-56884-968-0	$9.99 USA/$12.99 Canada
FINANCE/PERSONAL FINANCE			
Quicken 4 For Windows® For Dummies® Quick Reference	by Stephen L. Nelson	ISBN: 1-56884-950-8	$9.95 USA/$12.95 Canada
GROUPWARE/INTEGRATED			
Microsoft® Office 4 For Windows® For Dummies® Quick Reference	by Doug Lowe	ISBN: 1-56884-958-3	$9.99 USA/$12.99 Canada
Microsoft® Works 3 For Windows® For Dummies® Quick Reference	by Michael Partington	ISBN: 1-56884-959-1	$9.99 USA/$12.99 Canada
INTERNET/COMMUNICATIONS/NETWORKING			
The Internet For Dummies® Quick Reference	by John R. Levine & Margaret Levine Young	ISBN: 1-56884-168-X	$8.95 USA/$11.95 Canada
MACINTOSH			
Macintosh® System 7.5 For Dummies® Quick Reference	by Stuart J. Stuple	ISBN: 1-56884-956-7	$9.99 USA/$12.99 Canada
OPERATING SYSTEMS:			
DOS			
DOS For Dummies® Quick Reference	by Greg Harvey	ISBN: 1-56884-007-1	$8.95 USA/$11.95 Canada
UNIX			
UNIX® For Dummies® Quick Reference	by John R. Levine & Margaret Levine Young	ISBN: 1-56884-094-2	$8.95 USA/$11.95 Canada
WINDOWS			
Windows® 3.1 For Dummies® Quick Reference, 2nd Edition	by Greg Harvey	ISBN: 1-56884-951-6	$8.95 USA/$11.95 Canada
PCs/HARDWARE			
Memory Management For Dummies® Quick Reference	by Doug Lowe	ISBN: 1-56884-362-3	$9.99 USA/$12.99 Canada
PRESENTATION/AUTOCAD			
AutoCAD For Dummies® Quick Reference	by Ellen Finkelstein	ISBN: 1-56884-198-1	$9.99 USA/$12.95 Canada
SPREADSHEET			
1-2-3 For Dummies® Quick Reference	by John Walkenbach	ISBN: 1-56884-027-6	$8.95 USA/$11.95 Canada
1-2-3 For Windows® 5 For Dummies® Quick Reference	by John Walkenbach	ISBN: 1-56884-957-5	$9.95 USA/$12.95 Canada
Excel For Windows® For Dummies® Quick Reference, 2nd Edition	by John Walkenbach	ISBN: 1-56884-096-9	$8.95 USA/$11.95 Canada
Quattro Pro 6 For Windows® For Dummies® Quick Reference	by Stuart J. Stuple	ISBN: 1-56884-172-8	$9.95 USA/$12.95 Canada
WORD PROCESSING			
Word For Windows® 6 For Dummies® Quick Reference	by George Lynch	ISBN: 1-56884-095-0	$8.95 USA/$11.95 Canada
Word For Windows® For Dummies® Quick Reference	by George Lynch	ISBN: 1-56884-029-2	$8.95 USA/$11.95 Canada
WordPerfect® 6.1 For Windows® For Dummies® Quick Reference, 2nd Edition	by Greg Harvey	ISBN: 1-56884-966-4	$9.99 USA/$12.99/Canada

For scholastic requests & educational orders please call Educational Sales at 1. 800. 434. 2086

FOR MORE INFO OR TO ORDER, PLEASE CALL ▶ 800. 762. 2974

For volume discounts & special orders please call Tony Real, Special Sales, at 415. 655. 3048

10/31/95

Macworld® Mac® & Power Mac SECRETS,™ 2nd Edition

by David Pogue & Joseph Schorr

HOT!

This is the definitive Mac reference for those who want to become power users! Includes three disks with 9MB of software!

WINNERS 1994-95 TECHNICAL PUBLICATIONS AND ART COMPETITIONS OF THE SOCIETY FOR TECHNICAL COMMUNICATION

ISBN: 1-56884-175-2
$39.95 USA/$54.95 Canada

Includes 3 disks chock full of software!

NEWBRIDGE BOOK CLUB SELECTION

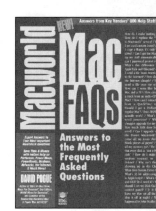

Macworld® Mac® FAQs™

by David Pogue

HOT!

Written by the hottest Macintosh author around, David Pogue, *Macworld Mac FAQs* gives users the ultimate Mac reference. Hundreds of Mac questions and answers side-by-side, right at your fingertips, and organized into six easy-to-reference sections with lots of sidebars and diagrams.

ISBN: 1-56884-480-8
$19.99 USA/$26.99 Canada

Macworld® System 7.5 Bible, 3rd Edition

by Lon Poole

ISBN: 1-56884-098-5
$29.95 USA/$39.95 Canada

NATIONAL BESTSELLER!

Macworld® ClarisWorks 3.0 Companion, 3rd Edition

by Steven A. Schwartz

ISBN: 1-56884-481-6
$24.99 USA/$34.99 Canada

NATIONAL BESTSELLER!

Macworld® Complete Mac® Handbook Plus Interactive CD, 3rd Edition

by Jim Heid

BMUG SPRING 1995 CHOICE PRODUCT

ISBN: 1-56884-192-2
$39.95 USA/$54.95 Canada

Includes an interactive CD-ROM.

NEWBRIDGE BOOK CLUB SELECTION

Macworld® Ultimate Mac® CD-ROM

by Jim Heid

ISBN: 1-56884-477-8
$19.99 USA/$26.99 Canada

CD-ROM includes version 2.0 of QuickTime, and over 65 MB of the best shareware, freeware, fonts, sounds, and more!

Macworld® Networking Bible, 2nd Edition

by Dave Kosiur & Joel M. Snyder

ISBN: 1-56884-194-9
$29.95 USA/$39.95 Canada

WINNER

Macworld® Photoshop 3 Bible, 2nd Edition

by Deke McClelland

ISBN: 1-56884-158-2
$39.95 USA/$54.95 Canada

Includes stunning CD-ROM with add-ons, digitized photos and more.

WINNERS 1994-95 TECHNICAL PUBLICATIONS AND ART COMPETITIONS OF THE SOCIETY FOR TECHNICAL COMMUNICATION

NEW!

Macworld® Photoshop 2.5 Bible

by Deke McClelland

ISBN: 1-56884-022-5
$29.95 USA/$39.95 Canada

NATIONAL BESTSELLER!

Macworld® FreeHand 4 Bible

by Deke McClelland

ISBN: 1-56884-170-1
$29.95 USA/$39.95 Canada

Macworld® Illustrator 5.0/5.5 Bible

by Ted Alspach

ISBN: 1-56884-097-7
$39.95 USA/$54.95 Canada

Includes CD-ROM with QuickTime tutorials.

"**Macworld Complete Mac Handbook Plus CD** covered everything I could think of and more!"

Peter Tsakiris, New York, NY

"**Very useful for PageMaker beginners and veterans alike— contains a wealth of tips and tricks to make you a faster, more powerful PageMaker user.**"

Paul Brainerd, President and founder, Aldus Corporation

"**Thanks for the best computer book I've ever read—*Photoshop 2.5 Bible*. Best $30 I ever spent. I *love* the detailed index....Yours blows them all out of the water. This is a great book. We must enlighten the masses!**"

Kevin Lisankie, Chicago, Illinois

"**Macworld Guide to ClarisWorks 2 is the easiest computer book to read that I have ever found!**"

Steven Hanson, Lutz, FL

"**...thanks to the *Macworld Excel 5 Companion*, 2nd Edition occupying a permanent position next to my computer, I'll be able to tap more of Excel's power.**"

Lauren Black, Lab Director, Macworld Magazine

Macworld® QuarkXPress 3.2/3.3 Bible
by Barbara Assadi & Galen Gruman
ISBN: 1-878058-85-1
$39.95 USA/$52.95 Canada
Includes disk with QuarkXPress XTensions and scripts.

Macworld® PageMaker 5 Bible
by Craig Danuloff
ISBN: 1-878058-84-3
$39.95 USA/$52.95 Canada
Includes 2 disks with PageMaker utilities, clip art, and more.

Macworld® FileMaker Pro 2.0/2.1 Bible
by Steven A. Schwartz
ISBN: 1-56884-201-5
$34.95 USA/$46.95 Canada
Includes disk with ready-to-run data bases.

Macworld® Word 6 Companion, 2nd Edition
by Jim Heid
ISBN: 1-56884-082-9
$24.95 USA/$34.95 Canada

Macworld® Guide To Microsoft® Word 5/5.1
by Jim Heid
ISBN: 1-878058-39-8
$22.95 USA/$29.95 Canada

Macworld® ClarisWorks 2.0/2.1 Companion, 2nd Edition
by Steven A. Schwartz
ISBN: 1-56884-180-9
$24.95 USA/$34.95 Canada

Macworld® Guide To Microsoft® Works 3
by Barrie Sosinsky
ISBN: 1-878058-42-8
$22.95 USA/$29.95 Canada

Macworld® Excel 5 Companion, 2nd Edition
by Chris Van Buren & David Maguiness
ISBN: 1-56884-081-0
$24.95 USA/$34.95 Canada

Macworld® Guide To Microsoft® Excel 4
by David Maguiness
ISBN: 1-878058-40-1
$22.95 USA/$29.95 Canada

Microsoft is a registered trademark of Microsoft Corporation. Macworld is a registered trademark of International Data Group, Inc.

For scholastic requests & educational orders please call Educational Sales, at 1. 800. 434. 2086

FOR MORE INFO OR TO ORDER, PLEASE CALL ▶ 800. 762. 2974

For volume discounts & special orders please call Tony Real, Special Sales, at 415. 655. 3048

10/31/95

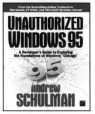

Unauthorized Windows® 95: A Developer's Guide to Exploring the Foundations of Windows "Chicago"
by Andrew Schulman

ISBN: 1-56884-169-8
$29.99 USA/$39.99 Canada

Unauthorized Windows® 95 Developer's Resource Kit
by Andrew Schulman

ISBN: 1-56884-305-4
$39.99 USA/$54.99 Canada

Best of the Net
by Seth Godin

ISBN: 1-56884-313-5
$22.99 USA/$32.99 Canada

Detour: The Truth About the Information Superhighway
by Michael Sullivan-Trainor

ISBN: 1-56884-307-0
$22.99 USA/$32.99 Canada

PowerPC Programming For Intel Programmers
by Kip McClanahan

ISBN: 1-56884-306-2
$49.99 USA/$64.99 Canada

Foundations™ of Visual C++ Programming For Windows® 95
by Paul Yao & Joseph Yao

ISBN: 1-56884-321-6
$39.99 USA/$54.99 Canada

Heavy Metal™ Visual C++ Programming
by Steve Holzner

ISBN: 1-56884-196-5
$39.95 USA/$54.95 Canada

Heavy Metal™ OLE 2.0 Programming
by Steve Holzner

ISBN: 1-56884-301-1
$39.95 USA/$54.95 Canada

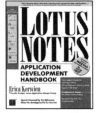

Lotus Notes Application Development Handbook
by Erica Kerwien

ISBN: 1-56884-308-9
$39.99 USA/$54.99 Canada

The Internet Direct Connect Kit
by Peter John Harrison

ISBN: 1-56884-135-3
$29.95 USA/$39.95 Canada

Macworld® Ultimate Mac® Programming
by Dave Mark

ISBN: 1-56884-195-7
$39.95 USA/$54.95 Canada

The UNIX®-Haters Handbook
by Simson Garfinkel, Daniel Weise, & Steven Strassmann

ISBN: 1-56884-203-1
$16.95 USA/$22.95 Canada

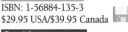

Learn C++ Today!
by Martin Rinehart

ISBN: 1-56884-310-0
34.99 USA/$44.99 Canada

Type & Learn™ C
by Tom Swan

ISBN: 1-56884-073-X
34.95 USA/$44.95 Canada

Type & Learn™ Windows® Programming
by Tom Swan

ISBN: 1-56884-071-3
34.95 USA/$44.95 Canada

ORDER FORM

IDG BOOKS WORLDWIDE

Order Center: **(800) 762-2974** *(8 a.m.–6 p.m., EST, weekdays)*

9/19/95

Quantity	ISBN	Title	Price	Total

Shipping & Handling Charges

	Description	First book	Each additional book	Total
Domestic	Normal	$4.50	$1.50	$
	Two Day Air	$8.50	$2.50	$
	Overnight	$18.00	$3.00	$
International	Surface	$8.00	$8.00	$
	Airmail	$16.00	$16.00	$
	DHL Air	$17.00	$17.00	$

*For large quantities call for shipping & handling charges.
**Prices are subject to change without notice.

Ship to:

Name _____

Company _____

Address _____

City/State/Zip _____

Daytime Phone _____

Payment: ☐ Check to IDG Books Worldwide (US Funds Only)

☐ VISA   ☐ MasterCard   ☐ American Express

Card # _____ Expires _____

Signature _____

Subtotal _____

CA residents add
applicable sales tax _____

IN, MA, and MD
residents add
5% sales tax _____

IL residents add
6.25% sales tax _____

RI residents add
7% sales tax _____

TX residents add
8.25% sales tax _____

Shipping _____

Total _____

Please send this order form to:

IDG Books Worldwide, Inc.
7260 Shadeland Station, Suite 100
Indianapolis, IN 46256

Allow up to 3 weeks for delivery.
Thank you!

IDG BOOKS WORLDWIDE REGISTRATION CARD

RETURN THIS REGISTRATION CARD FOR FREE CATALOG

Title of this book: **WordPerfect For Dummies**

My overall rating of this book: ❑ Very good [1] ❑ Good [2] ❑ Satisfactory [3] ❑ Fair [4] ❑ Poor [5]

How I first heard about this book:

❑ Found in bookstore; name: [6] _____ ❑ Book review: [7]

❑ Advertisement: [8] ❑ Catalog: [9]

❑ Word of mouth; heard about book from friend, co-worker, etc.: [10] ❑ Other: [11]

What I liked most about this book:
_____
_____

What I would change, add, delete, etc., in future editions of this book:
_____
_____

Other comments:
_____

Number of computer books I purchase in a year: ❑ 1 [12] ❑ 2-5 [13] ❑ 6-10 [14] ❑ More than 10 [15]

I would characterize my computer skills as: ❑ Beginner [16] ❑ Intermediate [17] ❑ Advanced [18] ❑ Professional [19]

I use ❑ DOS [20] ❑ Windows [21] ❑ OS/2 [22] ❑ Unix [23] ❑ Macintosh [24] ❑ Other: [25]_____
(please specify)

I would be interested in new books on the following subjects:
(please check all that apply, and use the spaces provided to identify specific software)

❑ Word processing: [26] ❑ Spreadsheets: [27]

❑ Data bases: [28] ❑ Desktop publishing: [29]

❑ File Utilities: [30] ❑ Money management: [31]

❑ Networking: [32] ❑ Programming languages: [33]

❑ Other: [34]

I use a PC at (please check all that apply): ❑ home [35] ❑ work [36] ❑ school [37] ❑ other: [38] _____

The disks I prefer to use are ❑ 5.25 [39] ❑ 3.5 [40] ❑ other: [41]_____

I have a CD ROM: ❑ yes [42] ❑ no [43]

I plan to buy or upgrade computer hardware this year: ❑ yes [44] ❑ no [45]

I plan to buy or upgrade computer software this year: ❑ yes [46] ❑ no [47]

Name: _____ Business title: [48] _____ Type of Business: [49] _____

Address (❑ home [50] ❑ work [51]/Company name: _____)

Street/Suite# _____

City [52]/State [53]/Zipcode [54]: _____ Country [55] _____

❑ **I liked this book!** You may quote me by name in future
IDG Books Worldwide promotional materials.

My daytime phone number is _____

IDG
BOOKS ®

THE WORLD OF
COMPUTER
KNOWLEDGE

❏ **YES!**

Please keep me informed about IDG's World of Computer Knowledge.
Send me the latest IDG Books catalog.